'A lot of what passes as "critical" in management circles tends to be pedestrian, pendantic or esoteric in terms of both the content and the form of engagement employed in the work. As a result, the inherent level of critique is often limited, lightweight and frequently begs the question: so what? By contrast, this text contains contributions which are substantive, polemic and grounded. In short, this volume showcases the benefits of embracing an approach to critique based upon the established tenets of practical criticism.'

Professor Cliff Oswick, Queen Mary University of London

'At a time when pretty much any subject benchmark statement feels obliged to insist upon a "critical perspective" or "critical evaluation", one would perhaps expect space for criticism and embrace of its virtues to be on the rise. But as many of the contributors to this volume make clear, the "critique" so encouraged might be a little less critical than some of us might hope. Not here. Substantive criticism leaps from the pages of this text. While it continues to do so, those of us who might hope can continue to do so. A vital book, exemplifying all that is best in a re-enlivened tradition of practical criticism. Critique worthy of the name and more necessary than ever.'

Professor Simon Lilley, University of Leicester

Today, at one and the same time, scholarly publishing is drawn in two directions. On the one hand, this is a time of the most exciting theoretical, political and artistic projects that respond to and seek to move beyond global administered society. On the other hand, the publishing industries are vying for total control of the ever-lucrative arena of scholarly publication, creating a situation in which the means of distribution of books grounded in research and in radical interrogation of the present are increasingly restricted. In this context, MayFlyBooks has been established as an independent publishing house, publishing political, theoretical and aesthetic works on the question of organization. MayFlyBooks publications are published under Creative Commons license free online and in paperback. MayFlyBooks is a not-for-profit operation that publishes books that matter, not because they reinforce or reassure any existing market.

1. Herbert Marcuse, *Negations: Essays in Critical Theory*
2. Dag Aasland, *Ethics and Economy: After Levinas*
3. Gerald Raunig and Gene Ray (eds), *Art and Contemporary Critical Practice: Reinventing Institutional Critique*
4. Steffen Böhm and Siddhartha Dabhi (eds), *Upsetting the Offset: The Political Economy of Carbon Markets*
5. Peter Armstrong and Geoff Lightfoot (eds), *'The Leading Journal in the Field': Destabilizing Authority in the Social Sciences of Management*

‘THE LEADING JOURNAL IN THE
FIELD’

'The Leading Journal in the Field': Destabilizing Authority in the Social Sciences of Management

Peter Armstrong and Geoff Lightfoot (eds)

www.mayflybooks.org

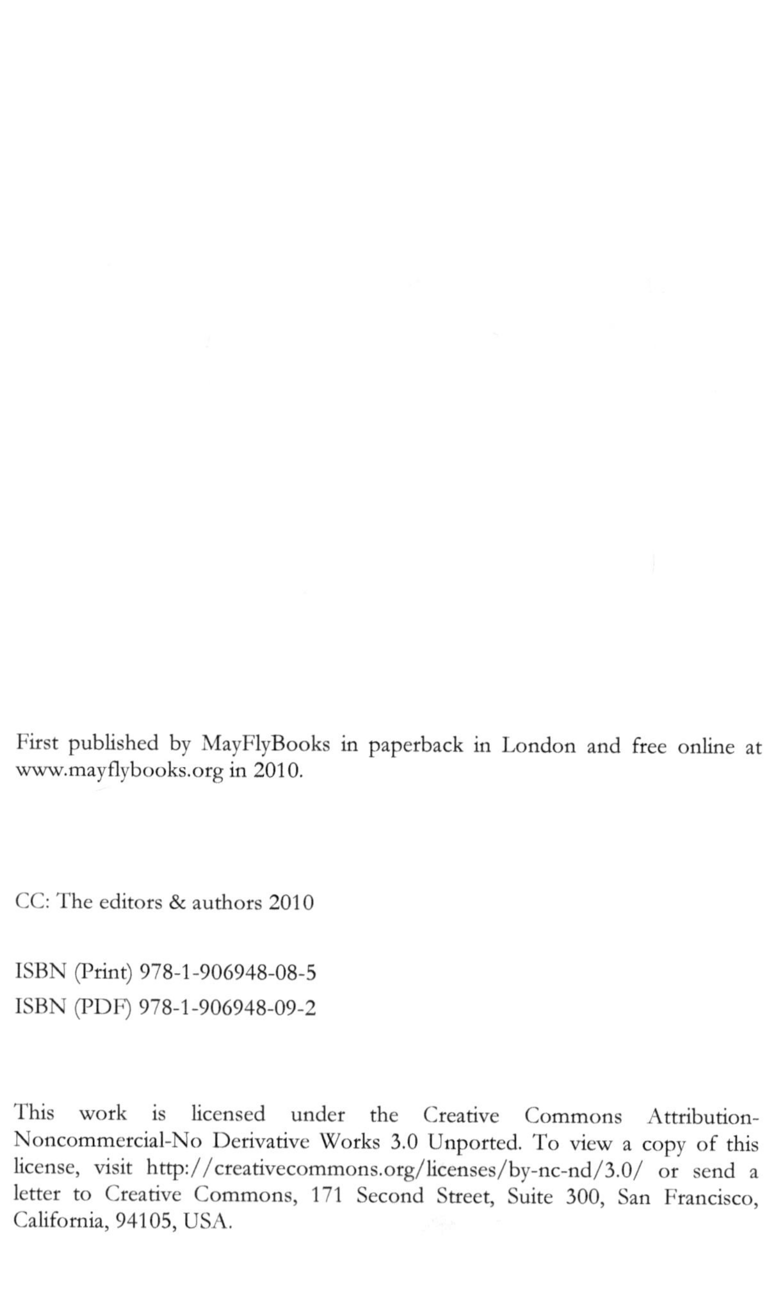

First published by MayFlyBooks in paperback in London and free online at www.mayflybooks.org in 2010.

ISBN (Print) 978-1-906948-08-5
ISBN (PDF) 978-1-906948-09-2

Contents

Contributors   vii

1   Introduction   1
    Peter Armstrong and Geoff Lightfoot

2   Towards a Clinical Study of Finance: The DeAngelos
    and the Redwoods   9
    Geoff Lightfoot

3   *Marienthal* At Work   35
    Norman Jackson and Pippa Carter

4   'Lessons for Managers and Consultants': A Reading of
    Edgar H. Schein's *Process Consultation*   61
    Nick Butler

5   Multiple Failures of Scholarship: Karl Weick and the
    Mann Gulch Disaster   85
    Thomas Basbøll

6   The 'Nature of Man' and the Science of Organization   103
    Jeroen Veldman

7   **Performativity: From J.L. Austin to Judith Butler**   119
    Alan McKinlay

8   **Four Close Readings on Introducing the Literary in
    Organizational Research**   143
    Christina Volkmann and Christian De Cock

9   **From Bourgeois Sociology to Managerial Apologetics:
    A Tale of Existential Struggle**   165
    Peter Armstrong

Contributors

Peter Armstrong is Emeritus Professor at Leicester University School of Management, having previously held chairs at the Universities of Sheffield and Keele. His first career was as a research and development engineer, mainly with the Central Electricity Generating Board. He then took a Masters degree in sociology of science at Bath University and subsequently worked with Theo Nichols and Huw Beynon on the well-known 'Chemco' studies in Industrial Sociology. He has published in a number of fields, including industrial relations, the sociology of the professions, product innovation, design studies and entrepreneurship, but is best-known for his work in critical accounting.

Thomas Basbøll is the resident writing consultant at the Department of Management, Politics and Philosophy of the Copenhagen Business School.

Nick Butler is a Lecturer in Organization Studies at the School of Management, University of St Andrews.

Having spent a long time working for a living, **Pippa Carter** decided to try living for a living instead, and finds that it 'works' very well. As part of this, she continues to research and publish on organization, inspired by Deleuze's 'active escape', following an unidentified Jackson, 'I don't stop running, but while running, I look for weapons'. She continues to hope to make a difference, while there is still time. She is further much comforted by her appointment as a Visiting Fellow at the School of Management, University of Leicester, UK.

Christian De Cock is Professor of Management at the Essex Business School, University of Essex. Christian has a long-standing interest in the role of the arts, literature and social theory in thinking about organization. His current research focuses on particular features and manifestations of capitalism with his most recent fieldwork, exploring various dimensions of finance capitalism.

Reassured by Deleuze and Guattari's confirmation that the 'capitalist machine does not run the risk of becoming mad, it is mad', **Norman Jackson** spends his time being cynical about organizations and organization studies. The contribution of management in hastening the arrival of **the** *'tipping point'* currently refreshes his fascination with contemporary organizations. After too many years serving the 'mad machine', he is experiencing respite care, as a Visiting Fellow at the School of Management, University of Leicester, UK, amongst other misfits.

Geoff Lightfoot is a senior lecturer in the School of Management and a member of the Centre for Philosophy and Political Economy at the University of Leicester, and a reader at the Univeriteit voor Humanistiek, Utrecht. He is currently working on a critical history of financial thought.

Alan McKinlay is a Professor at St Andrews University. He has published widely on business and labour history; contemporary industrial relations and work organization; and on the philosophy of Michel Foucault.

Jeroen Veldman is a PhD student at the School of Management, University of Leicester and an associate lecturer at the Utrecht School of Governance, University of Utrecht. Over the last four years, he has been writing on the construction of the separate legal entity in legal and economic scholarship and the influence of this concept on organization studies. The historical development of this concept and the way it drives the development of concepts of corporate governance is a central focus of this project.

Christina Volkmann is a Lecturer in Management at Essex Business School, University of Essex. Her background in literary criticism and philology informs her theoretical approach in terms of textual, interpretative and hermeneutic practice. Her current research focuses on concepts of space in the organizational context. She is particularly interested in the architectural spaces of organization(s) and the urban context in which we find them.

Introduction

Peter Armstrong and Geoff Lightfoot

The papers collected in this volume are from the Second Conference of Practical Criticism in the Managerial Social Sciences with the exception of Armstrong's which is a hold-over from the First Conference. The conferences were launched in 2007 out of a sense that the standards of scholarship prevailing in the social sciences of management were indicative of an atrophy of the critical function – ironically so in the case of those areas of study which claimed to *be* critical. This, it was observed, had resulted not in state of intellectual anomie, as might have been expected, but in a kind of tribalized authoritarianism, a dispersed oligarchy of the gatekeepers in which the congeniality of ideas and findings with their own had replaced judgments based on the quality of argument and evidence. At the same time it was recognised that to begin with a declaration of what standards might be appropriate, as has been attempted by Pfeffer (1993) in the USA and Hodgkinson, Herriot and Anderson (2001) in the UK, would itself be inappropriate in a discipline whose strength is precisely a plurality of approach and method. Accordingly inspiration was sought in the field of literary criticism, a field in which judgments of quality face broadly similar problems.

In 1919, Sir Arthur Quiller-Couch, head of Cambridge University's English Department, asked I. A. Richards to prepare a course with the brief that it should enable the students to turn out a passable book review. Richards' response was both logical and straightforward, at least in principle. His premise was that the students would best learn how to form interpretations and judgments of a text which were simultaneously their own and publicly justifiable, by first doing it and then submitting their efforts to the comments of the group. Accordingly they were asked to prepare critical assessments of anonymized excerpts which were then circulated for group discussion, the ground rules of which stipulated that all statement about a text had to be justifiable by reference to that text. The course was called 'Practical Criticism' and it proved both popular and immensely influential. The story of how it became the principle intellectual tool of 'Cambridge English' through the agency of Richards' student, F.R. Leavis, has been outlined in the introduction to the collection of papers from the First Conference (Armstrong and Lilley, 2008).

The interest of this approach (as distinct from certain aspects of the later practice of both Richards and Leavis) is that the interpolation of group discussion into a process of trial and error allowed for the emergence of group standards of criticism without attempting to legislate in advance what these should be and without, even, articulating them as a set of principles. In miniaturized form, the example of Richard's classes suggests a non-authoritarian model of how norms of scholarship might develop in other communities through a process analogous to Practical Criticism, namely group discussion of close readings of particular pieces of work, paying particular attention to their arguments and recourse to evidence. The model also clarifies the conditions needed for such norms to emerge: that it must be possible for criticism of scholarly outputs – particularly those of established authority-figures to be heard and debated. Whilst not entirely absent, such conditions are not presently widespread in the managerial social sciences and it was the intention that the Conferences of Practical Criticism should provide for them.

It was important to Richards' pedagogy that the texts distributed to the student were anonymized. That way, the students were prevented from recycling received judgments or, more insidiously, from projecting into a text those experiences which they were supposed to discover. In academic fields of study we are not so well served. Though the refereeing process is anonymous – in theory at least – all other readings of a text are exposed to the full battery of reputational effects: author, co-authors, institutional affiliation, and, as the title of this volume indicates, the standing of the journal in which it appears. Separable only in principle, these indices of status interact in a vicious circle of inclusion and exclusion. As MacDonald and Kam (2007) have pointed out, the status of 'leading journal' rests on a circularity: 'top' academics from 'top' institutions publish in 'top' journals, while those journals establish their 'top' ratings by having 'top' academics from 'top' institutions publish in them. Meanwhile the pressures on junior staff to produce some 'objective' indicator of their suitability for employment or promotion by publishing in prestigious journals leads them to pay particular attention to the work of their editorial boards, thereby adding to the citation counts which are the very essences of top-ness. A commonplace spectacle, particularly at US conference, is the post-session crowd of anxious young people dancing attendance on an important editor for all the world like flies around a cow-pat. One has only to encounter a few instances of this kind of low-level self-abasement to realize that the destabilization of academic authority is an urgent moral need as well as an intellectual one.

Geoff Lightfoot's contribution to this project of emancipation examines a paper which was published in the prestigious *Journal of Financial Economics* by one of its associate editors. DeAngelo and DeAngelo claim that their study of the media reportage of a takeover in the Californian lumber industry bears out a theory of the press developed by one of the founding editors of the journal in question. According to Michael Jensen, the popular press operates in a market for ideas which is defined by a widespread inability to tolerate ambiguity. It therefore reports financial affairs as a narrative of black-and-white confrontation between the 'good' of public interest and an 'evil' of financial markets. As Lightfoot reveals, the arguments which led Jensen to this philosophical anthropology of mass stupidity read like something a satirist would reject as lacking that indispensable element of believability. In real life, however – if one can use such a term of the *Journal of Financial Economics* – the endorsement of Jensen's thinking through the medium of an empirical study seems to be the only reasonable explanation of the publication of the De Angelos' paper, since this is able to achieve its forced marriage of hard science and soft theory only through a doubtful presentation of statistical data and a thoroughly one-sided account of the press reports in question.

Norman Jackson and Pippa Carter connect their contribution to I.A. Richards' observation that the antidote to the hegemony of received ideas is the habit of close and critical scrutiny of the knowledge-claims upon which they rest. The subject of their examination is one of the ur-texts of a belief which is now lodged deep in the disciplinary unconscious of managerial sociology: that people, or more precisely, workers, have fundamental psychological needs which can only be satisfied by labour. During the early 1930s, Marienthal, a small town in Austria, was experiencing widespread and semi-permanent unemployment. The influential sociologists Marie Jahoda, Paul Lazarsfeld and Hans Zeisel used this as a natural experiment in the social psychology of work deprivation. Jackson and Carter's detailed re-reading of their text reveals that this interpretation was partly the product of a middle-class incomprehension of a working-class way of life and partly the result of projecting into their observations a preconceived notion of how the workless *should* behave. The study could, perhaps, be read as an invitation to perform similar close reading analyses of other samples of managerial sociology.

Nick Butler's thoughtful examination of Edgar Schein's process consultation suggests yet another direction in which the practical criticism of managerial writings might develop – that of projecting forward the political and organizational implications of managerial thinking. Employing Armstrong's ideas on the connection between the 20th century ascendancy of managerial capitalism and the largely unexamined notion that management consists of a set of context-independent organizational and interpersonal skills, he argues that Edgar Schein's process consultation proposes a similar abstraction of consultancy from the knowledge of particular managerial or technical processes. Whilst the insistence that interpersonal process is fundamental to management succeeds in representing Schein's brand of consultancy as dealing with the core of management, and particularly so at the senior levels, Schein's notion that management itself is a species of consultancy simultaneously threatens to absorb consultancy back into management itself. One is left to wonder what the future holds for a corporate economy dominated by ideas of management and consultancy which are sublimated to this extent.

Doyen of the Academy of Management and consultant to some of the world's major corporations, Karl Weick holds that individuals are incapable of constructive and co-ordinated action in the face of crisis in the absence of the wisdom and sense-making which it is the mission and prerogative of managerial leadership to supply. A staple of leadership theory, Weick's best-known exposition of this view is his re-analysis of Maclean's account of the Mann Gulch disaster, a forest fire in which thirteen young fire-fighters lost their lives. Thomas Basbøll's careful forensic analysis of this celebrated exercise in armchair ethnography shows that Weick's reading of this disaster as a failure of leadership, and specifically of its sense-making role, is actually a projection of Weick's own presuppositions into Maclean's account. A necessary consequence of such a re-writing of the record is to throw the blame for the deaths of the firemen onto their team leader. Basbøll's tone never varies from that of the patient and meticulous scholar but his anger at this aspect of Weick's re-interpretation is palpable.

The Resourceful, Evaluative, Maximizing Model (REMM) of human behaviour originating in the Rochester School of Finance has been hugely influential amongst those inclined by temperament or institutional affiliation to ditch the socio-political crap in favour of a 'hard science' approach to management and organizations. Jeroen Veldman uses a close reading of Jensen and Meckling's would-be definitive account of *The Nature of Man* to explore its implications for the ontology and politics of organization. He finds the approach permeated by an intellectually threadbare yet dogmatic methodological individualism which can only depict organizations as 'purely conceptual artefacts', a convenient way of describing networks of freely-negotiated contracts between autonomous and initially equal individuals. This, as Veldman points out, creates difficulties for the REMM model in theorizing those contractual relationships in which organizations figure as separate legal entities. The difficulty is 'overcome' − to the satisfaction of REMM theorists at least - by abstracting the REMM model to a level which encompasses both the individual human being and the 'separate legal entity' of the firm, whilst simultaneously insisting that the latter is a 'purely conceptual' entity. This exercise in doublethink, Veldman concludes, enables Jensen and Meckling 's 'science of organizations' to suppress the contradiction involved in arguing against state regulation of the corporation on the ground of liberal individualism.

It has been said of the best literary criticism that it makes the reader want to return to its subject. The evident delight with which Alan McKinley explores speech act theory as it is expounded in the writings of J.L Austin and Judith Butler is a case in point. McKinley depicts speech act theory as a body of thought in motion. Where there is a certain stasis implicit in Austin's posit of a community of speech which understands certain utterances in a performative sense, Butler, approaching Austin through Derrida and being more concerned to explore the possibilities of subverting gender as performance, emphasizes the potential instabilities of performativity. Since management as a practice depends heavily on performative utterances, McKinley suggest that its critical study will need to make a serious engagement with speech act theory at some point. He does, however, caution against taking a recent intervention by Spicer, Alvesson and Kärreman (2009) as indicative of its potential.

In his discussion of the international circulation of ideas, Bourdieu (1999: 222) remarked that the importation of ideas from one culture into another frequently has the effect of stripping them of their context of debate. It is a remark which applies both directly and by analogy to the importations of literary theory into management and organizational studies (MOS) discussed by Christina Volkmann and Christian De Cock: directly inasmuch as the theories in question were first developed in languages other than English and by analogy inasmuch as literary theory is a subculture – perhaps many subcultures – differing in its ontology, epistemology and norms of scholarship from those of MOS. Most importantly, argue Volkmann and De Cock, literary theory to its practitioners is not a fixed entity in which there exist established truths but a conversation structured around a variety of approaches. Its importation into MOS however, has so far taken the form of summary statements of the key ideas of particular literary theorists as if these constituted expert testimony. The irony is that the rationale offered for the importation of literary theory into MOS in the first place was precisely to open up new perspectives.

Peter Armstrong's contribution, finally, presents us with the familiar and unedifying spectacle of an author complaining that he has been traduced. For those who can be bothered with this kind of thing, the occasion is Hugh Willmott's development of a theory of managerial agency which takes due account of the social relations of production (as he says 'bourgeois analysis' does not) whilst simultaneously avoiding the reduction of human agency to personifications of economic categories (as he thinks Armstrong does). Willmott's solution (so says Armstrong) is to allow social structures into his theory only as they are instantiated and, once instantiated, to influence the social action through which they are instantiated only through the subjectivities of the actors who are doing the instantiating. Specifically and notwithstanding the structural pressures to concentrate on the job in hand, Willmott thinks that most managers are more interested in their own subjectivities than they are in profit, that this makes a difference to what they do and hence, by changing the manner of their instantiation, to the capitalist social relations of production. He also believes that a number of the major industrial ethnographies of the 20th century demonstrate that this is the case – or rather, that they would have done so had their authors paid sufficient attention to subjectivities. Armstrong says that Willmott's re-readings are pure conjecture and that his alternative to bourgeois sociology is just as bourgeois as bourgeois sociology. That's what he thinks.

2

Towards a Clinical Study of Finance: The DeAngelos and the Redwoods

Geoff Lightfoot

Introduction

In this chapter, I want to explore an example of how 'theory' is established and promulgated within the academic discipline of finance. It takes the example of a paper published in a leading journal which builds on theory developed by Michael Jensen, one of the leading and most cited figures within the field.

A couple of years ago, a colleague mentioned that he had sent a paper to *The Journal of Financial Economics* – one of the top three ranked journals in the field of finance – for which he had paid a submission fee of $500. Luckily, however, his paper was returned by the editor within a quarter of an hour – deemed unsuitable – and he only had to pay $100 for this privilege. He was furious because his paper had won a prize at a prestigious conference and he didn't feel that it could have been properly read in the time twixt receipt and return. I was more curious about the idea of submission fees. When publishing in a journal, it's accepted that you do all the work and the publisher takes all the money (and copyright) for the uncertain status benefits that might accrue to you. Paying hard cash to be mugged in this way seemed a further affront.

Happily the journal is open about its submission details. Even proud, perhaps, for they publish a graph (see below) that sets fees against submissions.

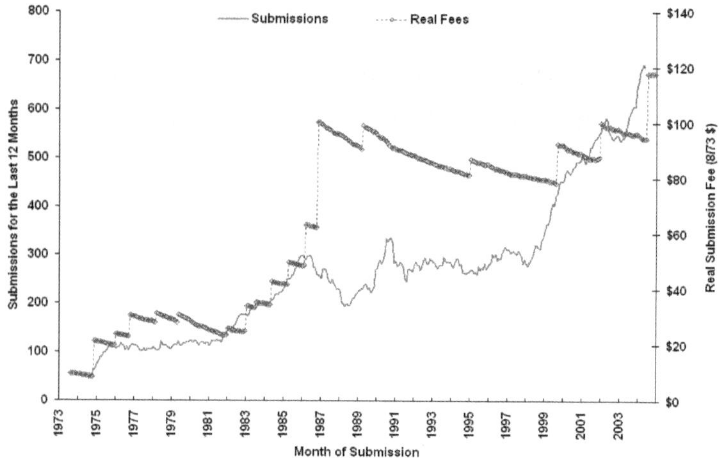

Figure 1: JFE Submissions & Real Submission Fees[1]

The editor of the journal suggests that this demonstrates the effective way in which increasing fees has acted to cap the number of submissions.[2] A cynic may well suggest that the graph indicates that the more you charge, the longer the queue. But it is not entirely clear what service you might expect for your payment - the editor, together with editors from two other leading finance journals, line up to castigate those whose behaviour they 'feel is counterproductive to the collegial process of producing high quality academic journals', 'undervalue[s] the services they receive' by 'submit[ting] papers to journals at a relatively early stage of production in the hope that "the referee will help me figure out how to revise it to make it publishable." In effect, by paying a submission fee the author is buying very cheap consulting advice on how to write the paper.' (Green, O'Hara and Schwert, undated).[3] If only it were so, as my colleague could attest.

Intrigued, I started to pay more attention to the journal. I had read the occasional article from it over the years but never subscribed, nor really considered who published what in it. Helpfully, the journal does publish a list of its most published authors. It also publishes a list of its advisory and associate editors, which for ease of reference, I have combined into one table.[4]

Rank	Author		Papers/CoAuthor[5]	Papers/Author	Editorial Connection
1	Fama	E.F.	12.00	18	Advisory
2	Stulz	R.M.	10.42	21	Advisory
3	Stambaugh	R.F.	8.33	12	Previous Associate
5	French	K.R.	7.33	13	Advisory
6	Schwert	G.W.	7.33	10	Editor
4	DeAngelo	H.	7.33	17	Associate
7	Roll	R.	7.00	10	Previous Associate
8	Smith	C.W.	6.50	11	Advisory
9	Ruback	R.S.	5.83	8	Previous Editor
10	Harvey	C.R.	5.75	11	Previous Associate

Table 1: JFE Most published authors and their editorial affiliation.[6]

To get more of a handle on how the journal worked, I needed to look at the work of one of these authors in more detail. But whose? Well, a quick skim through the home pages of the authors in this table revealed that out of his last 12 publications, Harry DeAngelo had 11 of them printed in *The Journal of Financial Economics*.[7] Such symbiosis surely deserves study and perhaps by examining his work I might get more of an understanding of what makes a paper worthy of a top-ranked finance journal.

In this chapter, I want to concentrate on the paper published in 1998 (with Linda DeAngelo), 'Ancient Redwoods and the Politics of Finance: The Hostile Takeover of the Pacific Lumber Company'.[8] Although my interest was piqued by the 'Politics of Finance' in the title, it is perhaps timely to revisit this article as Pacific Lumber, the focus of the DeAngelos' tale, filed for bankruptcy in January 2007. Pacific

Lumber, a northern Californian timber company, was taken over by MAXXAM Inc. in 1986, initially financed through junk-bonds via Drexel Burnham Lambert. Following the takeover, MAXXAM increased the rate at which timber was harvested, leading to heightened conflict with environmental groups and, apparently, stoking media interest. The DeAngelos look at media reporting of the case and they suggest that this was a fine example of how a hostile and misguided press was responsible for antipathy to Wall Street and takeovers at that time.

The Birth of the Clinic

The DeAngelos article is described as a 'clinical study', a slightly unusual terminology in the social sciences. The remit for what might be one of these rare beasts is first set out by the editorial board of *JFE* in Jensen *et al.* (1989: 3):

> The objective of this section is to provide a high-quality professional outlet for scholarly studies of specific cases, events, practices, and specialized applications. By supplying insights about the world, challenging accepted theory, and using unique sources of data, clinical studies stand on their own as an important medium of research. Like the medical literature from which the term 'clinical' is borrowed, these articles will frequently deal with individual situations or small numbers of cases of special interest.

Essentially, then, we are talking about case studies. Since case studies have a long history in the social sciences, with research methods and techniques vigorously discussed, how do the editors of *JFE* propose to make use of this expertise. Well, by ignoring it and starting from scratch, effectively:

> There is currently no standard or accepted model for clinical financial papers. We will, over time, uncover the principles that ensure the integrity and reliability of these efforts. (1989: 6)

Of course, such issues still trouble case study research beyond finance, but why should there be such antipathy towards learning from other disciplines. Partly, the answer comes from the wish of finance academics (and colleagues from economic faculties) to be seen as scientists – and case studies have no place in science as they conceive of it. This view still predominates through a slightly more realistic commentary from 12 years later, when Tufano (2001) looks back at the evolution of the clinical study: 'Throughout history, scientists and historians of science have debated about how 'science' should be and is carried out' (2001: 182). Rather alarmingly, he continues, '*JFE* readers perhaps have little patience for enduring long methodological debates', and thus unsurprisingly avoids directly addressing the ontological and epistemological issues that case study research might raise as part of a discipline devoutly eschewing inductive analysis. However, he does point out that such research does demand consideration of 'how we advance ideas' (2001: 182) and suggests that clinical studies may have four roles: developing theory; testing theory; applying 'useful' theory; and communicating theory. Which might best fit the DeAngelos' work? They introduce the paper by suggesting that:

> [Pacific Lumber...] is therefore an important case to study to understand the process through which the general public came to hold such negative views of Wall Street in the wake of the 1980s takeover wave (see e.g., Jensen, 1991, 1993). (1998: 5)

They conclude by suggesting that:

> The media treatment of the PL case closely fits the pattern predicted by Jensen (1979), who argues that market demand induces the media to publish entertaining stories that portray dramatic conflicts as confrontations of 'good' versus 'evil' personalities. (1998: 30).

In the absence of developing, testing or applying theory according to the rules outlined by Tufano, communicating theory seems to be the most likely. Tufano suggests that this might involve, 'communicat[ing] knowledge to theorists, empiricists, and educators, providing them with carefully documented descriptions of behaviors and innovations that will influence the way they write theory, construct tests, or teach classes' (Tufano, 2001: 183-4), and a brief trawl through Google shows that, although the paper may not be widely cited, it appears on the syllabi of courses at both UCLA and DuPaul universities. But this leads to a further question: what theory is being communicated?

Toward a Theory of the Press

It is to Jensen's paper that we turn, specifically the 1979 paper cited, 'Toward a Theory of the Press'. There are early indications that we may be in for a wild ride as we press toward this elusive theory. Jensen warms up to his theme with a dictionary quotation:

> Webster's defines romantic as
>
> 1: consisting of or resembling a romance 2: having no basis in fact: imaginary 3: impractical in conception or plan: visionary 4: marked by the imagination or emotional appeal of the heroic, adventurous, remote, mysterious or idealized...
>
> Surely no better word can be found to describe the content of the press. (Jensen, 1979: 1)

I imagine Jensen is alluding to definitions 2 and 4, here, although this might have no basis in fact. He certainly seems very sceptical of the press but we must hope such an influential author and scientist rises above such simple prejudice to provide solid evidence. Unfortunately, it doesn't seem that it is going to be that straightforward as Jensen instead includes, approvingly, substantial chunks from articles by H. L. Mencken – a newspaperman (*sic*) and author. In these pieces Mencken does not seem enamoured of his trade:

> The average American newspaper, especially of the so-called better sort, has the intelligence of a Baptist evangelist, the courage of a rat, the fairness of a Prohibitionist boob-bumper, the information of a high-school janitor, the taste of a designer of celluloid valentines, and the honor of a police-station lawyer. (Mencken, 1920 in Jensen, 1979: 1)

Well, Mencken does have an interestingly cynical take, for sure. And I've no complaints with polemical attacks on the press in general but there seems to be an odd move in that all the work by other journalists is imaginary, whereas somehow Mencken's account is factual. Jensen is surprisingly quiet on the rationale for this distinction. But this is mere scene setting for the key question for Jensen: 'Why is it that the public at large and the press that reflects its views are so basically antagonistic toward markets in general?' (1979: 10) Again, perhaps unsurprisingly, there is no evidence presented that this is so and lesser mortals might believe that, indeed, the press is generally extremely sympathetic to markets and business – especially compared to, say, command economies and trade unions. Still, no matter the implausibility of the premise and the lack of evidence, Jensen is keen to run with it as incontrovertible and therefore seeks roots for this supposed bias. He finds it within the family:

> [P]eople seem to carry over their training from the home, supported and formalized in most religious traditions, and the Golden Rule, to the outside world. They apparently find it difficult to see that the informal, long-run, non-quid pro quo exchange mechanism appropriate to the family environment is simply an inefficient mechanism for organizing exchanges when the frequency of contact is much lower and where the opportunity for symmetric provision of favors is nonexistent. (Jensen, 1979: 13)

Oikos, nomos and the economic? Let us see what is this exchange mechanism in the family that is so inappropriate. Jensen helps by detailing some of the calculus of his patrician home life:

> I consent to the wishes of my wife (for instance, by accompanying her to a movie or concert she wishes to attend) to make her happy and to maintain good relations – goodwill that I can draw upon the next time I unexpectedly bring home a colleague for dinner (or, worse yet, forget to come home for dinner). If I ignore her preferences too flagrantly, or she mine, the "exploited party" can retaliate in this game of life by voluntarily withholding future services or favors in many dimensions of the relationship. (Jensen, 1979: 11)

Withholding future services and favours? Have we arrived at a theory of the press from Jensen being denied his Friday night rumpy-pumpy because he came home late from work? But that would be too facile: inappropriate service in the office also casts a long shadow:

> [T]hese considerations of exchange extend to the employer-employee relationship in the business world – for example, the executive and his secretary. (Jensen, 1979: 12)

This non-*quid pro quo* long-run exchange relationship provides a refreshing antidote to the visions of the workplace one might encounter in *Human Relations*. But we need to make a couple more steps to draw to a complete theory: the first takes us from the family to the individual. We are confronted with the 'fact' that 'people (especially those who are not members of the scientific community) have an enormous *intolerance of ambiguity*' (Jensen, 1979: 6). At the same time, drawing upon Jensen and Meckling's REMM (Resourceful, Evaluative, Maximizing Model of human behaviour) in 'The Nature of Man' (see Veldman's analysis in this volume) Jensen suggests that it is not in individuals' interests to pay attention to politics and other matters of import. Instead, he suggests that his 'study (*sic*) of the history of mankind – its religions, drama, literature, operas, and fairy tales' demonstrate 'that people like to have stories told and problems explained in the context of Good versus Evil' (Jensen, 1979: 8). This plays out in financial reportage as a series of easily digestible stories of heroes and villains for the ambiguity-hating non-scientific public. Wall Street vs Main Street, with the financiers as the bad guys, obviously. And this still seems to be happening – even now people are blaming bankers for the recent financial mayhem.

Now, it may simply be that I have missed a cunning joke (and not for the first time), for Jensen's own tale seems rather thin on shades of grey. But if we bite our cheeks and assume that Jensen is playing it straight, what are we left with? We start with an odd perception as to how the world is, filter it through prejudice, leaven it with strange theoretical constructs and season with cod-scientism and sexism. Low on evidence, long on assertion, flitting weirdly between deductivist and inductivist arguments, it is a theory, albeit one so ludicrous that it seems incredible that any academic would take seriously.[9] Why, then, have the DeAngelos? One clue is perhaps in the acknowledgements.

> We are also grateful to … especially Michael Jensen (the editor) for useful comments. (DeAngelo and DeAngelo, 1998: 31)

The knot tying editors and contributors gets tighter – and we shall return to some of the implications of this later. But for now, let's return to the DeAngelos' paper now that we realised what 'theory' is being communicated and explore some of the inherent problems with case study research when the researcher enters the site with the theoretical frame already fixed.

Getting Wood

The DeAngelos contend that:

> The media *universally* blame MAXXAM's junk bond-financed takeover for the threat to Headwaters Forest [a hitherto apparently unthreatened and untouched tract of Californian Redwood trees, some up to 2000 years old], and the sheer number of seemingly independent stories offering essentially the same interpretation lends credence to this view.

The media tell a gripping tale of Wall Street greed versus the environment that pits an evil corporate raider against environmentalists and a paternalistic former management. The broad readership appeal of this story gave environmentalists a powerful case to mobilize public opinion in favor of preserving Headwaters Forest. Its apparent evidence of the destructive environmental impact of Wall Street greed prompted politicians to hold hearings that appealed to the environmentally conscious voter of the 1990s. (DeAngelo and DeAngelo, 1998: 4, emphasis added).

Effectively, the argument rests upon media widely disseminating their 'misreading of economic facts' (ibid.: 29) to the general public who, demanding simplistic morality tales, end up with 'erroneous perceptions' (ibid.). Thus, for the purposes of the argument here, we need to look both at the supposedly misread facts and the way in which the media supposedly promulgates them.

The key mistakes made in the reporting are claimed to be that:

- MAXXAM's takeover didn't cause the trees to be felled because;
- There are economic reasons to harvest old-growth timber; and
- They would have been felled anyway, just as they have been historically
- Pacific Lumber before the takeover wasn't;
- A family firm; or
- Well run
- Raising profits, not paying off debt, was the reason for increasing production.

That there are economic reasons to harvest old-growth timber would seem unremarkable, perhaps. After all, a single one of these Californian Redwoods was at the time valued at up to $100,000. But the DeAngelos seek to make a different point when investigating 'the real economic threat' (DeAngelo and DeAngelo, 1998: 13): 'that profit-oriented owners have incentives to harvest old-growth redwoods and replace them with young trees that will generate a greater volume of salable wood product' (ibid.: 19). They also provide a table, illustrating the difference in growth between old and young growth – reproduced below.

Tree age	Average growth
20-30	10.8 %
30-40	6.5 %
40-50	4.1 %
50-60	3.0%
60-70	2.4 %
70-80	1.9 %
80-90	1.6 %
90-100	1.3 %
Old growth	Nil or negative

Table 2: Average annual growth rate (%) of redwood tree volume at various ages. Reproduced from DeAngelo and DeAngelo (1998: 19).

It is always useful to be suspicious when price, normally the means by which arguments in finance are settled, disappears in place of volume and long-term planning enters at the expense of short-term profit maximization. For not only is percentage added to existing volume misleading in itself, because of the size of existing trees (or existing volume per acre), but it is not just volume that counts, but quality of timber. And old growth timber is less knotty, finer-grained, more sought after and therefore substantially more expensive. And thus the obvious economic imperative – that there are always incentives to harvest old-growth timber, whether or not the site is replanted with what will become younger, faster-growing trees (as deforestation worldwide has historically shown) – slips away.

The second point is related. The DeAngelos contend that all the virgin old-growth timber would have been felled at some point. Unrestricted and unregulated, I have little doubt that this would have happened, given the economic incentives. But such unmitigated freedom does not exist for logging in California, and the DeAngelos provide some rather murky illustrations to help them argue otherwise. The paper presents a table, part of which is reproduced below.

	Maintain Pacific Lumber's pre-takeover virgin forest harvest rate (1)	Maintain long-run harvest rate from the formation of Pacific Lumber (2)	Maintain long-run harvest rate from the inception of logging in Northern California (3)
Historical annual reduction in virgin forest inventory	1200.0 acres per year	1654.3 acres per year	1225.4 acres per year
Years until all virgin forests are logged if harvesting continues at given pre-takeover rate	13.4 years	9.7 years	13.1 years

Table 3: Estimated time until all of Pacific Lumber's holdings of virgin forest are logged (from 1 January 1986). Reproduced from DeAngelo and DeAngelo (1998: 15).

Column (1) is taken from a single line taken from an internal memo from October 1985, presented at the Congressional Hearing on the takeover which said, 'Presently we are cutting about 1,200 acres of virgin old-growth each year to meet the mill requirements' (DeAngelo and DeAngelo, 1998: 15). Given the limited possibilities of assessing the context and accuracy of that memo, we shall let it stand. But the other two columns are more interesting, and a graphical representation of this might help. The DeAngelos provide one.

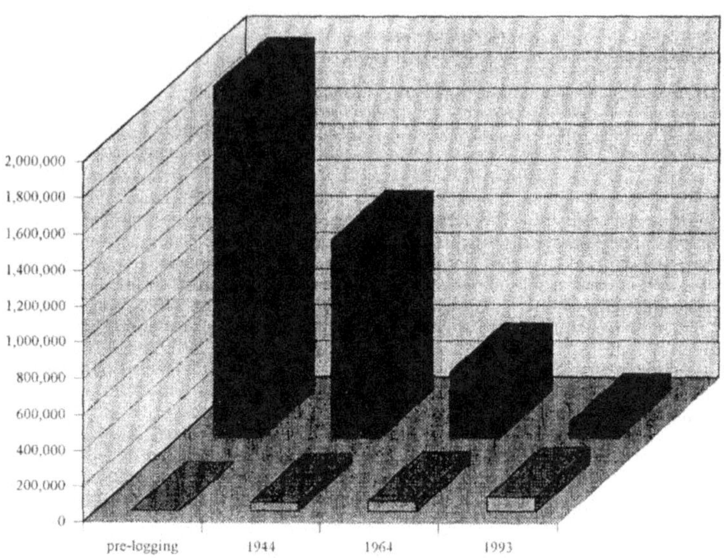

Figure 2: Total acres of old-growth redwoods (rear) and acres of old growth protected in parks (front) at various dates from the pre-logging period through 1993. From DeAngelo and DeAngelo (1998: 18).

Now, this chart has dates at irregular intervals, which can be a mite confusing (as well as generally being considered bad practice). But when we also have the DeAngelos discussing the long-run logging rates as a linear progression it becomes even more misleading. By way of demonstration, I have taken (approximate) data values of non-park old-growth redwood from the DeAngelos chart and plotted them against date, then let Excel draw a graph with these data points. This produces Figure 3, which shows massive deforestation post-war, and a reduction in felling rates since 1964. With the benefit of hindsight, we can add a further data point to illustrate this – the roughly 50,000 acres of old-growth redwood currently remaining in private hands[10] which produces Figure 5.

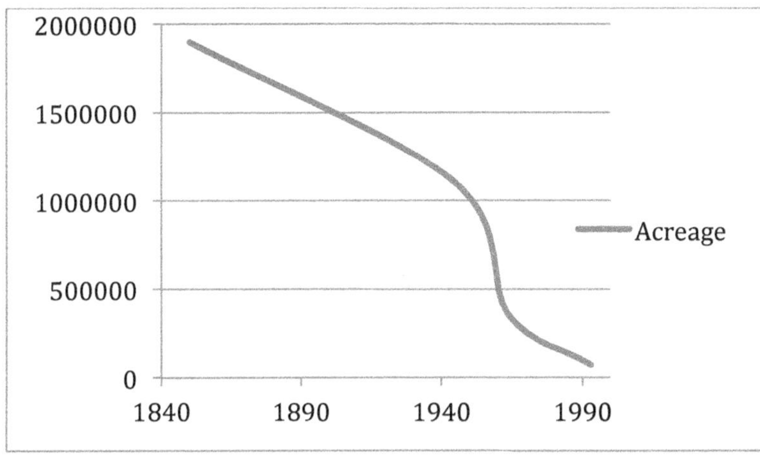

Figure 3: Total acres of remaining old-growth redwoods, 1845-1993. Estimated from DeAngelo and DeAngelo (1998: 18).

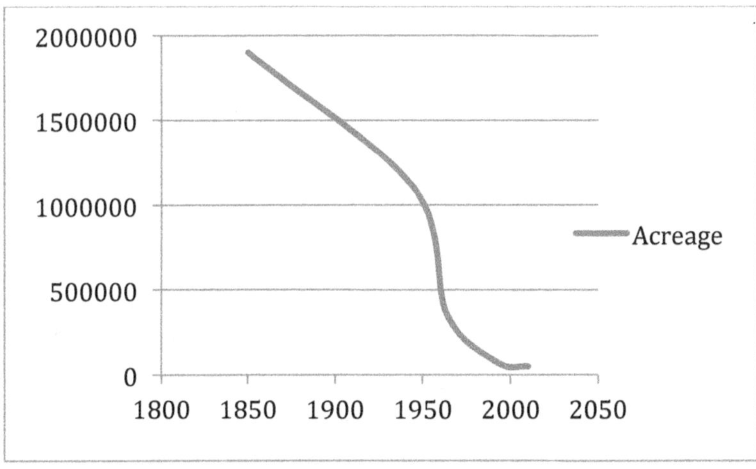

Figure 4: Total acres of remaining old-growth redwoods, 1845-2007. Estimated from DeAngelo and DeAngelo (1998: 18) and Redwood National Park.[11]

This representation is crude, but it illustrates just how markedly harvesting rates have changed, particularly since the war. Figures 4 and

5 cover all old-growth in private hands, not just Pacific Lumber, but especially given the weight of Pacific Lumber's holdings in the total, it is probably not too dissimilar to the pattern of their acreage. Table 6 illustrates how the DeAngelos' linear projection based on the long-run harvesting rate differs from the pattern derived from the data. But we shouldn't be too unkind – if they'd merely extrapolated the trend from 1944 to 1963, they could have pointed out that such a linear projection would show all old-growth had indeed *already* been felled by 1972.

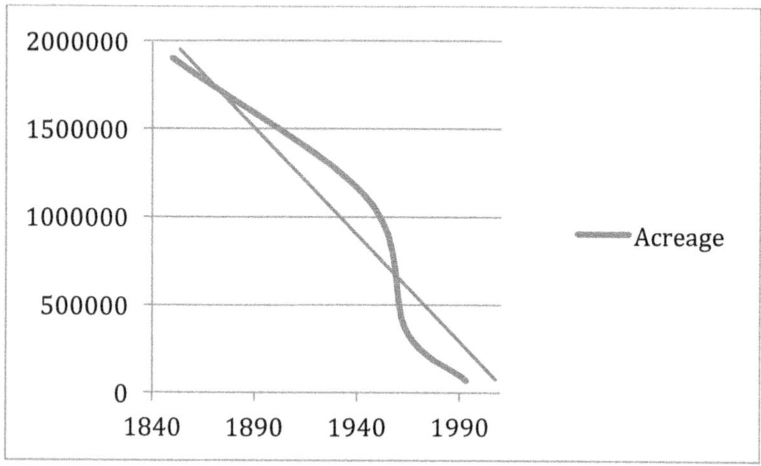

Figure 5: Total acres of remaining old-growth redwoods, 1845-1993, with 'long-run trend' superimposed. Estimated from DeAngelo and DeAngelo (1998: 18)

Their third point is undoubtedly correct: Pacific Lumber was not a 'family firm' by any normal definition, but many media reports did consistently label it as such. The fourth: the question of whether it was 'well-run' is more complex. For some, pointing out that the company failed to go bankrupt in the first 100 years of its life but did under the ownership of MAXXAM would be enough to suggest it was at least better run before. But that ignores the 'advances' made in modern finance theory which argues both that debt is a significant incentive and that bankruptcies offer opportunities. Given the difference between everyday perceptions of business that would see bankruptcy as evidence of mismanagement, we should not expect consensus on what defines the well-run enterprise.

Certainly, some of the DeAngelos material seems to suggest a somewhat lackadaisical approach by managers: that MAXXAM became interested in a deal because shareholders more than readily subscribed to a share buyback offer and that Pacific Lumber's own estimates of its assets were woefully inadequate, for example. Others are less convincing – that the share price that reached a high of $33-34 in 1981 was in the low $20s in 1984 can at least partially be explained by the recession in 1981/2 during which timber prices first fell dramatically and then failed to recover. And others just reflect the hopeless divide between the perceptions of finance theorists and other commentators. Thus, although the DeAngelos are undoubtedly right when they say that increasing debt in exchange for equity will have significant tax benefits (the proceeds of which can be passed to shareholders) the alternative position – that this produces unnecessary risk – is not part of their discourse and thereby ignored. The surplus in the pension fund is treated as evidence of poor management rather than prudence while the paternal aspects of the firm, such as the company-owned town and all the amenities provided, are granted little purchase as they do not conform to the accepted wisdom within the discipline of finance that, following Friedman's (1965; 1970) contentious claims, the only responsibility of company directors is to maximise returns to shareholders. I do not wish to claim here that one perception is right and the other wrong, but merely to point out that evidence of what constitutes a 'well-run' firm will differ considerably and cannot, as the DeAngelos attempt, be settled from a single paradigm.

Similar differences arise when considering the environmental credentials of Pacific Lumber. The different media reports suggest that the company did avoid confrontation with environmental groups. That this was more about seeking a quiet life rather than any deep commitment to environmental principles seems a reasonable supposition and the DeAngelos do provide enough evidence to show that Pacific Lumber did what it thought it could easily get away with. Yet, when discussing this issue, the DeAngelos are not afraid to identify the villains of the piece. Thus, the environmentalists Earth First!'s 'methods include dramatic civil disobedience... neo-Luddite tactics such as sabotage of logging equipment and threats to spike trees with metal rods that seriously endanger timber workers. Earth First! activists illegally 'explored' PL's property...' (DeAngelo and DeAngelo, 1998: 4) I am not sure how 'threats' stack up, against, say, the bomb that was attached to one environmentalists car or the death of another (which remain unmentioned in the DeAngelos' account), but it is pleasing to see them trying to prove Jensen right by supplying a simplistic morality tale of 'good' (that untrammelled property rights are a universal good scarcely needs mentioning) and 'evil' for the environmental activists. Yet it is this selectivity that lies at the heart of the DeAngelos' tale.

Partly, this is reflected in the treatment of the fifth point above – that the increased cutting rate was caused by the need to pay off debt, rather than from the desire to increase profit. As the DeAngelos acknowledge, this partly arises from claims that MAXXAM themselves made – 'likely they did so because the need to generate cash to meet debt obligation is an excusable motive to most people whereas the desire for greater profit is not' (DeAngelo and DeAngelo, 1998: 23). Leaving aside that this suggests that the media *didn't* demonise financiers wherever possible – all they would have had to do was merely report what the DeAngelos believe to be true – this scarcely seems to have been universally reported. Some accounts merely state that the junk bonds financed the takeover by the profit-oriented MAXXAM, others quote company officers' rebuttals of such claims by 'critics'. But discovering such alternate positions requires unpicking much of the DeAngelos' presentation of their analysis and returning to the underlying sources.

Unlikely Stories, Mostly

The DeAngelos deploy an unusual approach to their presentation of data:

> To give readers a reasonably comprehensive yet parsimonious picture of the media version of the PL case, we next present it using direct quotations from the articles in the Appendix, i.e., using journalists' own words. For simplicity of presentation, we omit quotation marks, although all passages are quoted verbatim. The number in brackets following the quote gives the Appendix location of the more complete abstract. We do not claim that the dramatization we next present characterizes the media treatment in every case, as one finds an occasional even-handed discussion of the necessity to trade off the interests of commercial timber firms and those of the public. Moreover, we quote the more colorful phrases from each article. (DeAngelo and DeAngelo, 1998: 10-11)

It's an interesting approach (and I don't mean that in an entirely negative way). Forming a collage out of quotes from different sources is, in my view, a legitimate way of coherently presenting qualitative data and does provide the possibility (as in this case) of stitching together a readable story. However, the obvious danger is that each quote is ripped from its original context and applied in a different one. Possibly not a problem in some instances but one that should set off all kinds of alarms when you are attempting to illustrate widespread misreading. The let-out that the DeAngelos attempt 'not… every case… occasional even-handed' is rather inadequate, especially given their quantification elsewhere. And the selection can be eye-catching. Let's have a close look at one of the sources cited from *Time*, 8th April 1991;[12] since it is fairly short, I've reproduced it here in full.

'Debt-for-nature' swaps are the method of the moment for well-heeled environmentalists wishing to put parts of the Third World off limits to development. If it works with debt-straitened countries, why not with similarly strapped companies? That's the reasoning behind the latest swap plan, intended to protect a 2,900-acre redwood forest in Northern California's Humboldt County.

The main player is Maxxam, a Houston conglomerate that issued junk bonds in order to purchase the lumber firm that formerly owned the forest. Among the bond buyers: the infamous Columbia Savings & Loan of Beverly Hills, which was seized by the government in January. The seizure has left Uncle Sam holding Columbia's share of the Maxxam bonds. Maxxam, left short of cash by the takeover, has increased the cutting and selling of the redwood timber, thus infuriating local conservationists.

In an effort to protect the forest, California wants to buy from the Federal Government some $60 million of Maxxam bonds, hopefully at a discount. The state would then hand the bonds back to Maxxam, freeing the company from ever having to repay that debt. In return for the bonds and an undetermined additional payment, Maxxam would give the forest to the state.

Happy ending: the Federal Government unloads some bonds, Maxxam gets rid of some debt, Californians get to keep some 1,700-year-old redwoods and Governor Pete Wilson upgrades his image with environmentalists, who opposed his election.

I quite like this story – slyly mocking throughout (and especially of Governor Pete Wilson). How might this fit into the DeAngelos' tale? Well, none of it appears in their collage and the extract reproduced in their appendix is simply, 'Buy a junk bond, save a redwood (picture caption)' (DeAngelo and DeAngelo, 1998: 36). So, one of the DeAngelos' occasional 'even-handed' articles, then.

It's just that there do seem to be an awful lot of these occasional articles. Another example, this time from the *Christian Science Monitor*.[13] The DeAngelos extract

> THE 3,000-acre Headwaters Forest in northern California harbors trees taller than Norman Schwarzkopf and older than the Crusades. ... "It is like the last great buffalo herd," says John Amodio, environmental adviser to California Gov. Pete Wilson. (DeAngelo and DeAngelo, 1998: 36)

Their extract was taken from the introduction – I've included the rest of the first 4 paragraphs to get more of a sense of how this story unfolds:

> THE 3,000-acre Headwaters Forest in northern California harbors trees taller than Norman Schwarzkopf and older than the Crusades. It is the largest privately owned grove of redwoods in the world. Until recently, it seemed many of these ancient sentinels would end up as someone's deck or hot tub. Now, under a novel 'debt-for-nature' swap being put together, they could become the crown jewel of a decades-long quest to preserve what remains of the world's tallest trees.
>
> "It is like the last great buffalo herd," says John Amodio, environmental adviser to California Gov. Pete Wilson, one of the parties trying to broker the deal.
>
> The talks between the state and federal governments and Pacific Lumber Company, owner of Headwaters, is one of two major thrusts in California that could affect the cutting of redwoods and perhaps affect forestry practices nationwide.
>
> The second effort, less amicable and far more encompassing, is an attempt by environmental groups to reduce overall timber harvesting in the state and limit the controversial practice of clear-cutting.

Already, we can see that, if anything, this article is shaping up with a degree of hostility to environmental protestors – and so it continues.

Also, worryingly, this article is not part of the media 'universally' blaming junk-bonds for the threat to the forest – the link is never made despite discussion of the bonds.

Another, this time from the *New York Times*.[14] The DeAngelos take:

> "This was the crown jewel of the North American timber industry," he (Mr Bertain) said. "I was just stunned for four months after the takeover…"

> For many residents of this community (Eureka), the Pacific Lumber takeover has come to epitomize the social and environmental costs of the junk bond era of the 1980's.

> Environmentalists have used Pacific Lumber's logging practices as the rallying point in their battle to save the remaining stands of California's old-growth redwood forests. "This is in-your-face forestry," said Joshua Kaufman, a Humboldt County paleontologist who helped form an environmental coalition after he saw Pacific Lumber trucks rolling up and down the road on which he lives. (DeAngelo and DeAngelo, 1998: 37)

The original article is much more nuanced – largely a tragic tale of a misguided campaigner. But the companies contrasting opinion is spelt out and Hurwitz, boss of MAXXAM, is portrayed as 'vilified' and 'daring' as well as having pulled off 'a business coup'. A larger extract follows:

> In a cluttered office overflowing with filing boxes and legal briefs, William H. Bertain is standing fast in his quixotic campaign to wrest back control of the Pacific Lumber Company, which was acquired in 1986 by Charles E. Hurwitz, a Houston financier.

> A child of the lush redwood forests in this fog-shrouded country, Mr. Bertain has dedicated the last seven years to a legal fight that few believe can be won, returning the company to the Murphy family that had managed it since the turn of the century.

> Mr. Hurwitz's Maxxam Inc. bought Pacific Lumber for about $900 million in a buyout financed largely with junk bonds handled by Drexel Burnham Lambert, and three members of the Murphy family have retained Mr. Bertain to have the buyout undone, asserting that shareholders were defrauded. Maxxam also faces a barrage of lawsuits

from employees, shareholders and environmentalists seeking to halt the harvesting of old-growth timber.

Despite demoralizing odds, Mr. Bertain says he carries on the crusade because outside investors – whom he calls 'corporados' – are threatening to destroy a way of life.

"This was the crown jewel of the North American timber industry," he said. "I was just stunned for four months after the takeover, but then I set out by committing to do everything that was legal and moral to stop this."

Mr. Bertain's campaign has set him at odds with John Campbell, the president of Pacific Lumber and a 24-year veteran of the company, the world's largest holder of virgin redwood forests. "He's barking up the wrong tree," Mr. Campbell said in a telephone interview. "He's a zealot and he has his emotions and his ego involved."

Pacific Lumber is not practicing cut-and-run forestry, the Australian-born lumberman insists. Countering critics who charge that Mr. Hurwitz had to increase the company's cutting rate to pay nearly $800 million of debt incurred when it was taken over, Mr. Campbell says the company has shown that it intends to be a positive long-term economic force here in Humboldt County, on the Northern California coast nearly 300 miles north of San Francisco. ...

For many residents of this community, the Pacific Lumber takeover has come to epitomize the social and environmental costs of the junk bond era of the 1980's. But beyond being vilified as a corporate raider, Mr. Hurwitz has never been charged with violating any laws, and in the short run at least, his company has increased employment in the region. Mr. Bertain's supporters include members of labor unions, community leaders and environmentalists. ...

Unfazed by the various lawsuits against his holdings, Mr. Hurwitz has forged ahead, moving to reduce the debt load of Pacific Lumber. He recently refinanced Pacific Lumber's $510 million debt and split the company into three concerns, leading many industry executives to say – and even some environmentalists to concede – that the Houston financier had pulled off a business coup.

"They got a phenomenal decrease in the cost of capital," said Craig Gilmore, a financial analyst at Gilmore & Company in Carlsbad, Calif.

> In a daring stroke, Mr. Hurwitz shifted Pacific Lumber's timber assets
> to two new companies, Scotia Pacific and Salmon Creek, cutting back
> on the company's short-term debt, financed by junk bonds, and
> replacing it with bonds backed by 179,000 acres of redwood and
> Douglas fir timberland.

These are not isolated examples of selective quoting which entirely changes the picture given, and even these few examples are taken mainly from journals that wouldn't necessarily be expected to be supportive of MAXXAM. Yet, in the DeAngelos' account any diversity is remorselessly trampled down: 'The Pacific Lumber case illustrates (1) how a misreading of economic facts can take on a life of its own when reported by enough credible and apparently independent media sources' (DeAngelo and DeAngelo, 1998: 29); 'By portraying the PL takeover as a case of 1980s Wall Street greed versus the environment, the media wove a fascinating morality tale with broad readership appeal' (ibid.: 29-30); 'the media, environmentalists, and politicians likely portrayed the Pacific Lumber takeover as a case of Wall Street greed destroying the environment' (ibid.: 30); 'Our circulation data establish that the PL parable was widely disseminated' (ibid.); 'The resource implications of the media treatment of PL are immense' (ibid.); 'The personalization of the PL case' (ibid.); 'The demonization of Charles Hurwitz and MAXXAM' (ibid.); 'the public portrayal of the PL case.' (ibid.: 31).

More Fun with Numbers

There is another aspect to the selectivity in the DeAngelos article: when looking through our library's electronic resources to check some of the material the DeAngelos cite, I found that in the *Nexis* database, the American newspaper with the most articles containing the search terms 'MAXXAM' and 'Pacific' was the *Houston Chronicle* – from the city where MAXXAM was headquartered. Many of these articles were overwhelmingly positive towards MAXXAM – perhaps because the only sources reported were MAXXAM employees or representatives – but this paper didn't fit the DeAngelos carefully constructed search criteria (National media such as the *New York Times*, business media such as the *Wall Street Journal* and Californian newspapers). And with the Californian press markedly more hostile to MAXXAM than the Texan media, perhaps it is to the differences between the two that we should turn.

Except we won't be finding such nuances within the DeAngelos' case. Despite the ironing out of contrary positions, they claim:

> Nonetheless, the sheer volume of articles – 76 in major periodicals – indicates that media dramatization of the PL case is a widespread phenomenon. (DeAngelo and DeAngelo, 1998: 11)

This quote illustrates the way in which widespread coverage has shifted to widespread 'media dramatisation' and how the (not-so) 'occasional' becomes obscured within a single 'dramatisation'. However, the idea of one 'dramatisation' assists considerably when it comes to defining what might be meant by 'widespread'. Take the DeAngelos approach (1998: 9, table 1):

> Pacific Lumber print media coverage: annual incidence of articles in major outlets and circulation of periodicals that published them over January 1986-December 1996.

> This table gives a yearly summary of the 76 articles abstracted in the Appendix that appeared in national newspapers or magazines, the national financial press, and in two major California newspapers. See the Appendix for a summary of the sampling algorithm used to identify these articles. The far right column gives the per issue (e.g., one day's average circulation for the Wall Street Journal, one week for Time magazine, etc.) total domestic circulation of the publication sources for the year that each article appeared. The circulation figures are obtained from various issues of Audit Bureau of Circulations (FAS-FAX Report), Gale Directory of Publications and Broadcast Media, and Working Press of the Nation.

Year	Number of articles	Total circulation
1986	1	706,577
1987	10	10,064,887
1988	8	5,553,529
1989	8	22,125,587
1990	5	6,367,160
1991	4	5,502,117
1992	2	2,365,812
1993	6	5,346,586

Year	Number of articles	Total circulation
1994	6	12,125,556
1995	3	1,656,024
1996	23	28,764,745
Total	76	100,578,580

This is a rather unusual way of grouping together very different publications. Circulation ranges from the tiny (the *Christian Science Monitor*, say) to the vast (*Reader's Digest*), different types of articles (short book reviews to extended investigations) and publications (local newspapers to international journals). Grouping them all together does give a satisfyingly large number – over 100 million – but completely obliterates potential differences. A pleasing irony in a paper that attempts to lambast the media, following Jensen (1979), for providing 'simplistic explanations rather than the carefully detailed analysis required to understand complex phenomena' (1979: 30).

Concluding Comments

That this article so vividly displays the faults of which it accuses the media would merely be an amusing anecdote had it been published in an inconsequential journal or on some vitriolic blog, say. But it is the status of the journal that makes this more important, for it tells us much about how knowledge is created and travels through the finance academy. Jensen's 'theory of the press', with its preference for prejudice over evidence, patrician values and absurd reductionism, would almost anywhere else be gleefully mocked and held up as glorious evidence of the intellectual failure of the modern university. It would normally be astonishing to find it as the lynchpin theory in the conclusions of an article, were it not that Jensen was at the time editor of the *Journal of Financial Economics*. I am not trying to imply malpractice here – rather it is that ideological sympathies apparently preclude critical scrutiny and it is the solipsistic world of academic finance that is my concern. For it is the refusal to engage with other social sciences, both in terms of theory and methodology, that seem to lie behind some of the worst excesses within and without the finance academy. Thus, although there is panoply of approaches to the media across the social sciences, because they are not established within the finance literature, they are disregarded and the only acceptable text becomes the bereft Jensen's. That this then becomes promulgated within a leading journal gives it a misleading authority and credibility; establishment within the canon of finance literature.

Also apparent in this tale of two papers is a haphazard approach to a 'scientific' ideal – that once scientific authority has been sufficiently asserted then anything goes – freeing authors from rigour in approaches to quantitative and qualitative data or, indeed, to testing theory. If the DeAngelos wanted to remain within a quasi-scientific paradigm, then there is more than enough material in the reports that they cite to easily disprove Jensen's theory – surely a more satisfying approach within scientific lore than taking empirical liberties in an attempt to justify it.

References

DeAngelo, H. and L. DeAngelo (1998) 'Ancient redwoods and the politics of finance: The hostile takeover of the Pacific Lumber Company', *Journal of Financial Economics*, 47(1): 3-53.

Friedman, M. (1962) *Capitalism and Freedom*, Chicago: University of Chicago Press.

Friedman, M. (1970) 'The social responsibility of business is to increase its profits', *The New York Times Magazine*, September 13.

Green, R., M. O'Hara and G. W. Schwert (undated) *Joint Editorial.* Available at http://jfe.rochester.edu/jointed.htm (accessed 30 January 2010).

Jensen, M. C. (1979) 'Toward a theory of the Press'. Available at http://papers.ssrn.com/sol3/papers.cfm?abstract_id=94038 (accessed 20 June 2009). Also available in Karl Brunner, (ed.), *Economics and Social Institutions*, Boston, MA: Martinus Nijhoff Publishing Company.

Jensen, M. C. (1991) 'Corporate control and the politics of finance', *Journal of Applied Corporate Finance*, 4(2): 13-33.

Jensen, M. C. (1993) 'The modern industrial revolution, exit, and the failure of internal control systems', *Journal of Finance* 48(3): 831-880.

Jensen, M. C., E. F. Fama, J. B. Long, R. S. Ruback, G. Schwert, C. W. Smith and J. Warner (1989) 'Clinical papers and their role in the development of financial economics', *Journal of Financial Economics*, 24(1): 3-6.

Mencken, H.L. (1920). 'On journalism' in T. J. Lippman (ed.) *A Gang of Pecksniffs*. New Rochelle, NY: Arlington House:

Tufano, P. (2001) 'HBS-JFE conference volume: complementary research methods', *Journal of Financial Economics*, 60(2-3): 179-185.

Notes

1 Source: http://jfe.rochester.edu/jfe_newfee.htm (accessed 30 January 2010).

2 See http://jfe.rochester.edu/jfe_newfee.htm (accessed 30 January 2010).

3 The editors '… hope these comments are taken in the spirit in which they are given. The opportunity to serve as an editor is a privilege. It provides each of us with the chance to observe the inner workings of a community of scholarship. It imparts a deep appreciation for the importance of the peer review process, and of the generosity of the hundreds of individuals who help us, and help their colleagues, by sharing their time, their expertise, and their creativity in serving as referees. We encourage authors to value these shared resources as well.'

4 Adapted from: http://jfe.rochester.edu/editor.htm and http://jfe.rochester.edu/authorpapers.htm (accessed 30 January 2010).

5 Papers/Author is the total number of papers submitted with the author's name on them. Papers/CoAuthor divides each paper by the number of authors.

6 Adapted from http://jfe.rochester.edu/editor.htm and http://jfe.rochester.edu/authorpapers.htm (accessed 30 January 2010).

7 See http://marshallinside.usc.edu/deangelo/pubs.htm (accessed 30 January 2010).

8 A slightly different version of this paper is freely available on SSRN: http://papers.ssrn.com/sol3/papers.cfm?abstract_id=1910.

9 It does seem unfair to single out the DeAngelos for this. Michael Jensen was awarded the 2010 Morgan Stanley-American Finance Association Award For Excellence In Finance, which is 'granted based on an individual's career achievements in outstanding thought leadership in the field of financial economics'. See: http://www.afajof.org/association/morganstanley.asp (accessed 12 February 2010).

10 Derived from data at: http://www.shannontech.com/ParkVision/Redwood/Redwood.html (accessed 30 January 2010).

11 Source: http://www.shannontech.com/ParkVision/Redwood/Redwood.html (accessed 30 January 2010).

12 Available at: http://www.time.com/time/magazine/article/0,9171,972663,00 .html.

13 Available at: http://www.csmonitor.com/1991/0401/01091.html.

14 Available at: http://query.nytimes.com/gst/fullpage.html?res=9F0CE0D 81F31F937A357 55C0A965958260&sec=&spon=&pagewanted=1.

3

Marienthal At Work

Norman Jackson and Pippa Carter

If we wish for a population easy to control by suggestion we shall decide what repertory of suggestions it shall be susceptible to and encourage this tendency except in the few. But if we wish for a high and diffused civilisation, with its attendant risks, we shall combat this form of mental inertia. (Richards, 1964 [1929]: 314)

Introduction

It would appear that students of managerial and organizational knowledge, whoever they may be, are particularly prone to an uncritical acceptance of knowledge claims, of the 'wisdom', in the field. Perhaps it is the very popularity of this field of knowledge amongst consumers that stimulates knowledge producers to provide a constant supply of easily digestible formulae revealing how to achieve the organizational nirvana, formulae which are then enthusiastically embraced, without thorough interrogation of their credentials, logic or implications. Richards proposed that, in the field of literature, the antidote to this kind of suggestibility is close textual examination, in order to proceed beyond the surface, the obvious, the received, to enable informed and critical judgement, "'to rouse the mind, to assist observation, to make people sociable, to excite indignation'" (Richards, 1964: 292, quoting Confucius). How much is this proactive and questioning engagement even more necessary in the Social Sciences, and especially in Management and Organization Studies, where research produces knowledge claims that inform and shape policy, strategy and practice at all levels of society.

A close textual reading, in our view, focuses primarily on the principles and quality of scholarship, as embodied in a text. It is an interrogatory process that should be undertaken *before* engagement with the findings or proposals of any particular piece of research, *before* any attempt to refute, replicate or apply such findings or proposals. If we miss out this, we would suggest, crucial evaluation, we are able only reactively to respond to findings, to approach issues only on the basis of an agenda pre-set by the researcher, rather than to address the issues themselves. In this view, critical textual readings are not especially concerned with 'findings' – although some such may inevitably be thrown into doubt by the practice itself – they are about matters of scholarship. The question that is being foregrounded here is: can good quality knowledge be produced from poor quality research?

In this chapter we propose a close textual reading of the book, *Marienthal: The Sociography of an Unemployed Community*, by Jahoda, Lazarsfeld and Zeisel (2002, first published in 1933, by the Leipzig-based publisher, Hirzel), a study that is still widely celebrated, and that is regarded by many as a 'landmark' examination of the effects of long-term unemployment (see, for example, Fleck, 2002). The eponymous Marienthal was a small village in 1930s Austria, not far from Vienna, which was largely dependent upon a single factory – a textile mill – for employment. During the Great Depression this factory closed, making most of the workers jobless with little prospect of finding alternative employment. *Marienthal* is a study of how the village coped with this dire situation. The study itself comprises eight chapters, occupying 98 pages (in the 2002 edition). These are accompanied by a contemporaneous *Afterword: towards a history of sociography*, written by one of the authors, Zeisel, reflecting on the history of such studies, in terms of both methodology and subject matter, a *Foreword*, written by another of the authors, Lazarsfeld, some forty years after the original publication of the study, on the occasion of its translation into English, and, in the 2002 edition, an *Introduction*, written by a contemporary commentator, Fleck. The chapter titles beyond the introductory chapters give a good indication of the concerns, and conclusions, of the study: *The Living Standard, Menus and Budgets, A Weary Community, Responses to Deprivation, The Meaning of Time, Fading Resilience*.

It might, of course, be asked whether a study of so long ago has any contemporary relevance. Perhaps, whatever its strengths and shortcomings were, these have been negated by time. However,

Marienthal, as a piece of research, is still regarded as important in, and beyond, its field, in terms of its findings, as an exemplary way of doing research and as an important case study in social science studies, (see, for example, Fleck, 2002, and Cole, 2007, who also offers a catalogue of references to the use of the study in sociology, psychology and social psychology).[1] *Marienthal* is also regarded as especially significant in the field of study of work organization(s), in terms of its 'implications' for 'the meaning of work'.

The association of the study with the field of research into 'work organization' was made explicit because the knowledge claims emanating from *Marienthal* foreshadowed what was later, and influentially, to be glossed by one of the authors as 'the latent functions of work' (Jahoda, 1979). The original study identified a number of characteristic features of daily existence experienced by the long-term unemployed – namely, lack of time structure, loss of social relations, loss of sense of social purpose, loss of social status and personal identity, and lack of regular activity. In other words, when workers experience an extended period of unemployment, not only do they lose their income, but they also suffer social and psychological problems associated with motivation, sense-making, interpersonal relations, their sense of self, and their sense of self-worth. *By inverting these observations, these problems became the very things that employed work, and work organizations, solved for the worker* (see, for example, Jahoda and Rush, 1980: 11). This, then, gives some indication of why *Marienthal* is regarded as such a seminal piece of work: if indeed the study did uncover certain eternal verities about the centrality of wage labour to psychological well-being and a stable social structure, then it has huge implications for both economic and social policy, and for our understanding of the labour process.

We do not share the general enthusiasm for *Marienthal*, as a study or in terms of the implications so neatly drawn from its findings. On first becoming acquainted with *Marienthal*, we experienced some unease with interpretations of the data and some scepticism about the coherence and integrity of these interpretations. A further close textual reading generated more questions about the whole project and the validity of its knowledge claims, to the extent that every aspect of it started to look more dubious.

There are two kinds of problem that it is relevant to identify in particular: problems of interpretation of the data, and problems related to the research process itself. However, the ubiquity of these issues in the study presents problems, in turn, for this analysis. For example, individual details of the research process, which taken singly may be relatively unimportant or innocuous, when aggregated appear to discredit the entire project. Secondly, to analyse every claim, illustration, association, practice, and so on, would be to produce a paper many times longer than the original book. Accordingly, we concentrate our critique on some specific examples of weakness in scholarship represented in the research. We should emphasise that our critical reading is almost exclusively internal to the text *Marienthal.* In other words, where we question, for example, interpretations of the data, or details of the research process, the basis for such questions is contained within the text itself, but has been, perhaps, overlooked, ignored or even repressed by the authors, in favour of their preferred understandings and attributed meanings. Thus, we have not sought to locate the study in terms of the wider body of research on cognate issues, nor have we sought to apply judgements about the quality of the scholarship and the probity of the findings from sources external to the text itself. *Marienthal* is unusual, in our experience, in containing within the text all the material that is needed to question its validity.

The Meanings of *Marienthal*

On examination of the text of *Marienthal,* a considerable range of issues almost immediately announces itself as potentially problematic to the process of data interpretation. There is, for example, quite clearly a 'cultural blindness' – the strangeness of the working class – imbuing the observations of the researchers. This cultural blindness leads them, despite their very best intentions, to regard the subjects of their study as objects, as other, as different in kind to themselves. This has implications for both the management of the research and the management of its findings. Cultural blindness is reinforced by the evidence within the text of judgemental attitudes informed by fundamentally middle class values and the uncomfortable confrontation of the metropolitan and the provincial.

The quality of the data is also affected by a certain naivety on the part of the researchers. For example, they seem to be unaware of the possibility that their respondents might manipulate the situation to serve their own interests, even though they have identified this tendency in other respects, such as attempts by the villagers to gain access to as many forms of relief as possible, regardless of strict eligibility. Access to the respondents was almost exclusively based on 'bribery', in the form of charitable works, welfare initiatives, even competitions with prizes. The researchers did not, apparently, consider that this might, in itself, affect how people responded to their surveys, that data might be 'bought' for potential reward, that they might even be told, therefore, what people thought they wanted to hear. There is, indeed, a pervasive lack of truthfulness in the study. The researchers did sometimes feel that people were being 'duplicitous' (Jahoda et al., 2002: 41) with others, especially with those in positions of authority or in control of resources (but not with them?), and were critical of this. However, they themselves were duplicitous in their dealings with the villagers – for example, claiming objectives other than a study – but did not regard such opportunism in the same light as that of the villagers. Perhaps they believed that it was somehow justifiable in their own case, because their desire was to do good?

Our initial disquiet with *Marienthal* arose from the posited causal relations determined from the data and the questionable interpretations of observed behaviour. One of the most significant examples of the former is an apparent conflation between unemployment and poverty. It might be argued that, for those whose only income derives from selling their labour to others, loss of job is the same as loss of income. However, we would argue that such conflation leads to different conclusions about the value of employment to those reached if the distinction is maintained – in other words, if the conditions experienced in the village are simply the consequence of unemployment, then, crudely put, the 'solution' is to provide employment; if, however, the conditions experienced are a consequence of the burden of unemployment on top of pre-existing poverty, then any 'solution' must involve a much wider range of strategies than merely providing work, such as social policy to mitigate poverty.

There is considerable attention paid in the study to the economic aspects of the situation in Marienthal, and much quantitative data provided from a variety of sources. For example, there is information, *inter alia*, on schoolchildren's packed lunches (Jahoda et al., 2002: 17), on the extent of relief payments (ibid.: 18), on the incidence of meat in the diet (ibid.: 26). There is no particular reason to doubt these data.

However, some of the conclusions drawn from such data are much more questionable. For example, the authors offer (ibid.: 39-40) some rather superficial statistics (in percentages rather than in actual sales figures) which purport to show a significant decline in the purchase of the newspaper, the *Arbeiter Zeitung*, the central organ of the Austrian Social Democratic Party, (by far the dominant political party in Marienthal), even though it is sold at a reduced rate to those who are unemployed. They declare, on this basis, the very significant conclusion that this demonstrates a dramatic decline in 'interest in politics' (ibid.: 40) among the villagers. However, this is not necessarily a justifiable correlation. Reduced sales does not necessarily signify reduced readership – people may have been sharing copies, for example, and a not inconsiderable proportion of the population of Marienthal had actually left the village entirely since the factory closure (ibid.: 40, 59). Equally, reduced sales, or even reduced readership, do not necessarily signify reduced interest.

Unemployment or Poverty?

This difficulty applies *a fortiori* to the qualitative data. These data are intended to illustrate issues that might be described as relevant to, in modern parlance, 'the quality of life'. The text 'illuminates' the poor clothing, the attenuated social life, the lack of motivation, the strained interpersonal relationships, among the villagers, and attributes all this to their unemployment. It is this ascription of causality that is one of the most obvious problems with *Marienthal*. We have already noted that it might be argued that, since the inhabitants of Marienthal derived their income from employment, loss of employment did indeed cause their problems. But it can be suggested that this is an overly simplistic interpretation. That the conditions found in the village were simply the direct effect of unemployment is an assumption of causality that actually warrants more demonstration before it can be accepted. For example, that people were going short came from a lack of resources to exchange for what they needed. Adequate welfare relief, for instance, would have offset some of these problems. Contrary to the assertion that '(t)he only real remedy, of course, is a return to work' (Jahoda et al., 2002: 24), return to work is neither a necessary nor a sufficient condition to ensure that people have enough disposable resources to alleviate want. Then, as now, there was no guarantee that full time employment precluded the experience of want. It is, indeed, noted in the text that wages in 'neighbouring factories' were 'at times lower than some of the unemployment relief rates' and so 'families working in the surrounding area differ little, in their standard of living, from the unemployed' (ibid.: 20).

The tendency to make this easy assumption about causality is connected to another problem with the study, that there is little sense of what might be called the 'normal' conditions in the village, no base with which to compare the social-psychological conditions studied in 1931-32 (there are some quantitative data, and some narrative, on past *economic* conditions, for example, in the chapter *The Industrial Village*). We do know, however, that the situation prior to the start of the then current period of long-term unemployment was **not** long-term full employment. Unlike its heyday in the second half of the nineteenth century, the recent history of the factory had been characterised by periods of reduced working and industrial unrest, with the factory being closed down progressively during 1929-30 (Jahoda et al., 2002: 13-14). Even in employment, factory workers of that period would hardly be affluent – what might, perhaps, be called 'employed poverty' would be a more normal condition. Indeed, it might well be suggested that, rather than a direct effect of the final closure of the factory, the conditions witnessed in Marienthal are likely to have reflected the cumulative effects, over a considerable period of time, of low income, even when work was available. That the conditions might be the effect of poverty, *as well as* of unemployment, is not considered, yet that may have been of crucial significance, and would have had far-reaching impacts on the conclusions of the study. For example, even if we accept the framework of findings offered by the authors, viewing the specific factors as effects of long-term poverty, rather than of the absence of work, would, in itself, throw very considerable doubt on the later connection of these findings to 'the meaning of work'.

This conflation of unemployment with poverty in the research commits two 'sins'. Firstly, it promotes the view that the *raison d'être* of the less privileged members of society is to work – if the only way that the poor can maintain themselves, materially and, *just as importantly*, socially and psychologically, is through work, then that is what they must need. Being human in their case is the same as being a worker. This is the classic ideology of class, the logic of the workhouse, of workfare – and, indeed, Jahoda did elsewhere argue in favour of welfare-to-work programmes (Fleck, 2002: xii). Secondly, it promotes the idea of the working class as dependent, as requiring the shelter of employers as a kind of patron or guardian. Once denied this benevolence they become socially disoriented, decline into apathy, cease to function properly. Yes, clearly all the worker needs, to be happy and to fulfil his/her social role, is employed work. Indeed, Jahoda later asserted that 'it is only a very small group of psychologically privileged people who can by their own initiative create the latent consequences of employment, outside a compelling manifest [i.e., economic] reason' (Jahoda and Rush, 1980: 29) – and, should technology ever realise its potential to obviate the need for employed work, 'new forms of organized work outside employment' (ibid.: 35) would need to be created.

Sympathy or Empathy, Sentiment or Rationality?

The authors of *Marienthal* are full of *sympathy* for the people of the village, but the bias inherent in this type of interpretation is part and parcel of a general lack of *empathy* with them, symptomatic of their 'cultural blindness' when confronted with the 'strangeness' of typical working class lives. There are many instances of the, apparently unwitting, certainly unacknowledged, predominance of middle class values in interpreting the data. It is well illustrated by one of the 'quantitative studies', that of people walking in the street. The men are observed to walk more slowly than the women. The authors note that, in families where the husband is unemployed, the man may be idle but the work of the wife in the home does not decrease, and may increase, since she now has to make more effort to supply the needs of the family with very little money (Jahoda et al., 2002: 74ff). Thus, women going about their normal business hurry along as usual. Men, on the other hand, do not, because they lack pressing business. But, as there is no denying that the (unemployed) men have no work, we might ask, why should they hurry?

The authors offer the following table, derived from their (covert) observations (Jahoda et al., 2002: 67):

Walking mph	Men	Women	Total
3 or more	7	10	17
2.5	8	3	11
2	18	4	22
Total	**33**	**17**	**50**

It is interesting to note that, in Work Measurement, a person *under incentive conditions* is normally expected to walk at 4 miles per hour. Without incentive, it is 3 mph *when working*. If people not under incentives and not working choose to walk at 2 mph, it is hardly surprising or reprehensible. Just as significantly, as any city-dweller who has spent time in a country village will know, time, and how it should be spent, is regarded differently there – village time is just slower than city time. There is no information on general walking speeds in times of employment in Marienthal, but one might hypothesise that they were always slower than those of ever-hurrying city people, such as the researchers. Despite all this, it is asserted that the men have 'forgotten how to hurry' (ibid.: 66). The Oxford English Dictionary defines hurrying as 'acting with undue or immoderate haste, under pressure, having little time' – one might suggest that, if the men continued to hurry when there was nothing to hurry for, this might itself indicate some underlying emotional problem. The authors themselves note that '(o)nce someone trotted past; it turned out to be the village idiot' (ibid.: 67). Quite!

Apparently, 'the workers of Marienthal have lost the material *and moral* incentives to make use of their time' (Jahoda et al., 2002: 66, our emphasis). The men stand around, carry on leisurely conversations, several smoke pipes, watch the traffic pass. Would the researchers have seen similar problems in the strolling boulevardier, the sauntering flâneur, the idle rich? When workers find that they have free time by force of circumstance not of their making and they use it in such activities, then they are seen as morally degenerate. Truly, it is the absolute duty of the workers to look busy! Indeed, we learn that '… sixty people had already emigrated, which means that the people we found in Marienthal *were the less energetic ones who stayed*' (ibid.: 59, our emphasis). This last, somewhat disparaging, comment illustrates very clearly the normative judgements being made by the researchers. Anyone who had not abandoned the village to find work – possibly non-existent work, bearing in mind that the Great Depression was in full swing – was judged to lack energy. Surely, one could be energetic in seeking work without leaving home – a case in point is noted (ibid.: 52), a man who had written '130 applications for jobs, all of which remained unanswered'. Perhaps some could not leave for other reasons, such as having dependents in need of their immediate presence. Perhaps some thought they might be worse off in abandoning what little security they had amongst friends and family in Marienthal. Perhaps some just weighed all the facts, calculated the pros and cons, and made a *reasoned judgement* that their best interest was served by staying put. Indeed, no evidence is furnished to suggest that those who left fared any better than those who stayed, although there is some comment about the fate of people who emigrated abroad, notably, 'the unhappy experience of some Marienthal families who had gone to France' (ibid.: 57). It is even possible that the researchers themselves were supplying incentives for the villagers to stay in Marienthal, through their welfare and charitable initiatives, though this does not seem to have been considered.

That the unemployed men of Marienthal had adjusted their use of time to accommodate their new experienced reality, as they saw it, seems to the researchers only to indicate despair and moral decay. They demonstrate little understanding of the life of the working class. After all, as previously noted, unemployment, for the villagers, and for workers generally, was part of their normal experience – it was just a fact of life for the working class.

Normality or Abnormality?

Another cogent illustration of this general lack of empathy is provided by the story of '*Family 273*', a one-parent family, with one child: 'The mother had become an alien through marriage and thereupon lost her claim to relief. Immediately after the wedding her husband ran away to join the foreign legion. ... The woman leads a lonely life and is very apathetic...' (Jahoda et al., 2002: 21). Quite apart from the problem of unemployment, this woman would seem to have good cause to feel lonely and apathetic. To marry and then to lose both your husband and your right to relief, and to have a child to support, could be seen as devastating in its own right. As it happens, we do not know what role the factory closure had, if any, in this family and to link her problems to it in this way seems, on the surface, somewhat bizarre[2]. As with the walking speed examples, it is implied that people are just not dealing with their problems 'adequately' – there seems to be an almost Pythonesque requirement to 'always look on the bright side of life'!

A further telling example of the experienced strangeness of the inhabitants of Marienthal is their desire to grow flowers. The authors note the widespread 'ownership' of allotments. Out of the total of 478 families that comprises the village, 392 have *at least* one, and everyone who wanted an allotment got one (ibid.: 23). A typical allotment is about 60 square metres, and the yield of vegetables is 'considerable' (ibid.). Later, they give a number of examples of 'surprising and seemingly irrational spending' (ibid.: 55) that, in their view, represent evidence of either 'a yearning for some remains of joy' or are 'possible symptoms of dissolution' (ibid.). For example:

> Flowers are growing on many of the allotments, although potatoes and other vegetables are vital; beds that could yield some 160 pounds of potatoes are filled instead with carnations, tulips, roses, bell flowers, pansies, and dahlias. When asked why this was so, we were told: "One can't just live on food, one needs something also for the soul. It is so nice to have a vase of flowers at home". (Jahoda et al., 2002: 55)

Presumably our researchers thought that unemployed workers should live by bread, or potatoes, alone – though there is no evidence that more potatoes were needed. Another surprise appears to be the attention given to children. With regard to one family:

> The regular and relatively expensive consumption of 2 liters [sic] of milk per day is also remarkable; it was bought mainly for the children. We noticed time and again, whenever we visited this family, the special concern for the welfare of the children shown by parents who had to forfeit the most elementary amenities of their own. (Jahoda et al., 2002: 30)

This family comprised two adults and *five* children. Other 'irrational' expenditure occurred when some women '…on a birthday or other festive occasion and following a sudden impulse, bought a picture book as a present for a child' (ibid.: 55). Or, again, when 'another family, living only on emergency assistance, *spent good money* on mourning clothes after someone in the family died' (ibid., our emphasis). These comments are redolent of, if not outright disapproval, then incomprehension. That, apart from bringing a little joy into an overwhelmingly depressing situation, the decision to grow flowers might have been taken by a mature, intelligent adult with a competent understanding of the situation in which they find themselves, did not seem to occur to the researchers. That parents do, as part of normal parenting, even under adversity, prioritise their children's needs also escapes them, as does the parental urge to give them an occasional treat. That even poor people have rituals surrounding death and may need to show respect for the dead and show publicly that they are in mourning seems similarly to disturb them.

This incomprehension regarding children is also evident in the attempts to analyse the villagers' use of, and approach to, time. Some were given timetables to complete showing how they spent the day. As presented in *Marienthal*, the data are given in clock-hours: 6-7; 7-8; and so on. Whether by request of, or editing by, the researchers, or just the inclination of those completing the timesheets, (there is evidence for each possibility), the entries for each time slot are somewhat sparse. For example:

A.M.
6-7 Getting up.
7-8 Wake the boys because they have to go to school.
8-9 When they have gone, I go down to the shed to get wood and water. (Jahoda et al., 2002: 68)

This particular example of an unemployed man's expenditure of time is compared to a time sheet by a man who is still in work. Arguing that it is an illustration of the problem with time that unemployment brings, the authors remark that '(w)aking the children certainly does not take up a whole hour' (ibid.: 69). Ignoring the limitations of the method, this suggests that they lack direct experience of having children! In any case, the period in question also seems to cover the entire process of getting them to school, because, in the next period, they have gone. There is a similar sense of incomprehension when encountering the behaviour of the teenagers of Marienthal: despite the activities that the researchers organized for them, '(t)hey disappeared and just "hung around". The leaders of the two youth groups confirmed that their problem, too, was getting hold of the young people' (ibid.: 63). The researchers attribute this to an 'attitude equivalent to resignation' (ibid.). However, it could be suggested that, on the contrary, this is just what teenagers do!

Many of these comments and interpretations are also undermined by the previously noted absence of any sense of what might constitute 'the normal' for the people of Marienthal. Yet this lack may contribute crucially to attributions of abnormality to behaviour that might be entirely normal. The life of the village can never have been luxurious. Add to this the experience of the routine cycle of shorter periods of unemployment and much of the deprivation and coping behaviour identified by the researchers would simply be the lot of the factory worker. Indeed, they note, with regard to the physical condition of the villagers:

> The state of health of the community, despite its rural environment, has never been particularly good, according to the doctor's reports. Work in a spinning or weaving mill is not healthy. (Jahoda et al., 2002: 34)

Regarding one household we are informed that:

> The children are clean and well cared for, the mother told us *she maintained and mended all their things herself. ... She even mended her* husband's *suits.* (ibid.: 46, our emphasis)

And in another,

> The couple is known for its quarrelsomeness. The wife is not too popular. (ibid.: 51)

Much of this behaviour would be normal regardless of the state of employment. It is interesting to speculate who the researchers thought normally repaired the family's clothes, or whether perhaps they threw away damaged or worn garments and simply bought new ones. As regards quarrelsome couples, these may be found even outside of the unemployed working class. It is hard to escape the feeling that the researchers had some idea of a working class idyll where, in return for 'full-ish' employment, workers were diligent, well-behaved, even tempered, and undemanding, gratefully knew their place and were attentive to the needs of their family, the community and their employer.

Solidarity or Friction?

The whole matter of the socio-political relations of the villagers provides yet another very pertinent example of the judgemental naivety of the researchers. Political clubs were an important feature in Austria at the time. Thus the researchers '… knew that the active elements of the population were politically organized and, consequently, we sought to establish political contact with them. Since all shades of political opinion were represented in our research team, we were allowed access to practically all organizations' (Jahoda et al., 2002: 6). However, we learn later, '…when political parties organize charities, people occasionally try to benefit from all sides; a few men had actually become members of both politically opposed organizations. However, … such duplicity was quickly discovered' (ibid.: 41). It is interesting that they use the judgemental word 'duplicity' to describe this behaviour. Perhaps what they were seeing was the rational behaviour of desperate people in distress, seeking to obtain aid for their families as best they could. Even the authors acknowledge that '(a)s privation increases, organization membership becomes less a matter of conviction and more a matter of financial interest' (ibid.: 42). They also note an 'unusual' decline in the normal political hostilities in the village (ibid.: 41), which they see as a manifestation of a moderation of traditional political differences, though they do wonder if this might be challenged by the new National Socialist Party branch (ibid.). Might the arrival of the Nazis even be what caused the reduction in normal political activity? What seems clear is that engagement with village politics was rather more complex than merely gaining access to the political clubs.

The voting pattern in the village (voting being compulsory) remained virtually unchanged in the period 1929-1932, the Social Democrats attracting four times the combined support of all other parties. However, the researchers detect 'a decline from a higher cultural level of political confrontation', in favour of 'a rise in more primitive hostilities motivated by personal malice' (Jahoda et al., 2002: 43). The evidence for this is the increase ('traced with almost documentary precision' (ibid.)) in denunciations to the authorities that people were doing casual work whilst drawing unemployment pay (ibid.):

	Number of Denunciations	Founded	Unfouded
1928-29	9	6	3
1930-31	28	7	21

In an adult population of over 1100 this three-fold increase may or may not be statistically significant as an indicator of increased personal malice, but it must be noted that founded claims remained essentially static. What does seem of significance is that 1928 and the first half of 1929 were 'not bad years for Marienthal… Employment was at its peak' (Jahoda et al., 2002: 14). In other words, the increase in denunciations followed a *major increase* in those claiming. Thus, that the number of denunciations grew is not really surprising, but, of necessity, most claims for relief were genuine and so would be allowable. Denunciations, *as a percentage of those claiming*, almost certainly fell. The researchers do acknowledge, alongside these acts of 'personal malice', 'much willingness of villagers to help those more distressed' and that the balance of 'public spirited and antisocial behaviour' (ibid.: 44) has been unchanged by events. However, they then attribute this lack of 'antisocial impulses', not to neighbourliness, class solidarity or normal humanitarian feelings, but to 'a growing lassitude' (ibid.). Truly, Marienthal is a strange tribe! They can't even be bothered to be nasty to their fellow villagers.

It is worth examining this issue a little further as it does again illustrate the intrusion of the researchers' prejudices into the study. Having asserted that there was an increase in hostilities based on personal malice, a few lines later they state they cannot be sure, due to absence of any historical data (Jahoda et al., 2002: 43). They then acknowledge that various officials with more experience of Marienthal believe that there has been *no increase* in this type of behaviour, which our team then ascribes to a lack of motivation (ibid.: 44). The one piece of 'hard' data on which they base this assertion is the rise, from 3 in the first period to 21 in the second, of *unfounded* denunciations to the Industrial Commission (ibid.: 43). So, how should we understand this seven-fold increase? Firstly, we have no evidence that those with a propensity to denounce their fellow villagers are uniformly distributed amongst the population. It seems equally likely that it is the same few people who have a greater opportunity, and tendency, to 'shop' their neighbours. Secondly, it may be that, given the degree of distress, the authorities were exercising a certain amount of discretion when vetting claims. The researchers themselves note that '(e)ven the officials no longer pretend that it is possible to live on the relief money one may or may not receive… Violations of the fishing laws and even minor thefts of coal from the railways are ignored by the authorities… (P)eople can see the welfare officer and in some cases get permission to take odd jobs for a few hours' (ibid.: 22). That such denunciations were not upheld does not necessarily mean that they were strictly 'unfounded'. Thirdly, as we know from the current furore over MP's expenses claims in the UK, what observers see as outrageous and undeserved might, in fact, be within the rules!

Why then did the researchers claim to have identified an increase in personal malice amongst the villagers, based upon a questionable interpretation of data, then to decide it did not exist, but only because of the 'lassitude' of those unemployed, (as though it should exist!)? The idea that a community in adversity might exhibit solidarity in the face of a common threat (what was later, and in a different context, labelled the Dunkirk spirit) apparently seems strange to them and is, we would suggest, another example of 'cultural blindness'.

Producing the Meanings of *Marienthal*

In the foregoing we have raised some questions about just some of the issues of interpretation that arise from a critical textual reading of *Marienthal* – and it is worth reiterating that the grounds for questioning the interpretations offered by the authors are based on material in the text itself, but generally unexplored by them. The inescapable implication of this reading is that *Marienthal* is, in some respects, a well-intentioned but fundamentally flawed piece of research. We have already suggested some of the factors that seem to have influenced the development of interpretations of the research material. But the inevitable question that follows from that is, how could this have happened? In order to understand this, it is worth looking at some of the characteristics of the research process itself. According to the jacket notes,

> *Marienthal* represents a colossal breakthrough in social research. It provides a combination of quantification and interpretive analysis of qualitative material – an approach that remains in the forefront of present-day research design… The work provides a unique insight into how creative innovations can assist in overcoming collective deprivations [sic].

These are big claims.

The *Introduction* states quite clearly what the research objectives were:

(T)here is a gap between the bare figures of official statistics and the literary accounts, open as they invariably are to all kinds of accidental impressions. The purpose of our study of the Austrian village, Marienthal, is to bridge this gap. [NP] Our idea was to find procedures which would combine the use of numerical data with immersion… into the situation. To this end it was necessary to gain such close contact with the population of Marienthal that we could learn the smallest details of their daily life. At the same time we had to perceive each day so that it was possible to reconstruct it objectively… (Jahoda et al., 2002: 1).

Thus, there is an unequivocal statement about what the research problematic was. What the researchers do not seem to have is some theoretical conceptualisation of how such knowledge could be produced. Fleck (2002: xii) says that '(t)he research group did not waste its time debating preparatory meta-theoretical problems' – or, as it might otherwise be described, developing a methodology. Accordingly, the research is not designed around a set of procedures that have been, at least, hypothesised as epistemologically appropriate to producing the knowledge that they wanted to produce. However, the researchers do have some, apparently intuitive, ideas about what methods to use in the research process. These amounted to what might be called covert participant observation, and what Fleck says is almost action research (although not seeking to stimulate political activism) (2002: xiv). It was essentially *ad hoc*: many techniques were 'discovered' as they went along. This may be highly innovative, as Fleck claims, but it does suggest that there was no possibility, and no attempt, to test such techniques in terms of what kind of knowledge (as opposed to data) they might produce. In other words, they have methods without methodology, techniques without an informing research rationale.

It is noteworthy that none of the authors was at all closely involved in the fieldwork. Fleck points out that this was just the way it happened, rather than being part of the research design (2002: xiv). This is inevitably so, because there really was *no* research design – as he comments, 'the researchers started their project off the cuff' (ibid.: xiii). But, because there was no research design and no *a priori* methodology, there is no indication of what the various techniques that were used were intended to do, or whether they were successful in achieving this intention. Equally, there seems to have been no evaluation, on completion of the project, of how effective the techniques were in producing valid knowledge claims – as opposed to an evaluation based on subjective preference, (for example, whether the resultant knowledge claims had 'fit' with what the researchers believed to be the case and/or wanted to say). The collected research material 'weighed sixty-six pounds' (Jahoda et al., 2002: 9), but is now 'lost due to political circumstances' (Fleck, 2002: xvi). That the material did not survive such turbulent times is hardly surprising and, obviously, by no means the fault of the researchers. It does mean, however, that it is not possible now to re-evaluate how effective the techniques used in the research process may have been.

The researchers did not exactly parachute into the village and start collecting data and interviewing people, they had a policy of active involvement in the life of the village, of contributing some good to the situation:

> If we were to succeed we had to adopt a very special approach: we made it a consistent point of policy that none of our researchers should be in Marienthal as a mere reporter or outside observer. Everyone was to *fit naturally* into the communal life by participating in some activity generally useful to the community. This proved most difficult in the case of the researcher who actually lived in Marienthal. (Jahoda et al., 2002: 5, our emphasis)

This researcher was Lotte Danzinger: there is some confusion about her family name, she is Danziger in the text, but Danzinger according to Fleck. She was a young psychology graduate and lived in Marienthal for about 6 weeks. It was she who established initial contact with the villagers, through the charitable clothing project, which involved a private collection of clothes in Vienna, which were then cleaned and repaired to be distributed by the research team to the villagers, and which was a primary technique for gaining access to the people and to their homes. She later said, in an interview with Fleck in 1988:

> Well, I lived there for a while and did a number of interviews, but I really hated it… I had a terrible, an awful room, really awful. That was for about a week, or perhaps ten days… I left the house in the morning and did a few interviews with different families, and then wrote them down in the afternoon… you could not really write them down in the presence of the people because then they would have immediately stopped telling their stories, so you had to draw up the protocols from memory. (Fleck, 2002: xiii, ellipses in original)

While it is understandable that she would not want to take notes during her interviews, the project was, thus, very dependent on her memory and her interpretation, indeed, on her 'objectivity'. Without wanting to cast doubt on her talents, clearly there is a problem about these field notes being objective accounts, and it may not be inconsequential that she was so very unhappy in Marienthal.

The ambition to integrate themselves into the life of the village is another example of the naivety of the researchers. A total of 120 days (Jahoda et al., 2002: 9) were spent in Marienthal on the project, and it seems 'that "ten psychologists" conducted the field work' (Fleck 2002: xiii), at one time or another. To be useful to the community might have contributed to their being accepted, but it could not contribute to their being integrated – indeed, these very activities may have emphasised their 'outsider-ness' and placed them (perhaps unwittingly) in positions of authority. In any case, it is likely that none of the villagers would have been under the illusion that the visitors were sharing in their situation. In a village the size of Marienthal, to have a team of strangers, city-based professional people, appear suddenly and start asking questions could hardly have realised the intention to 'fit naturally' into the village. This is unlikely to have worked under more normal conditions, but, at that time, the relatively close enquiries into their personal circumstances may well even have seemed quite threatening to some people. Additionally, the special projects had implications for the research process. Apart from the clothing project, these included free medical treatment and parental counselling, a pattern design course, girls' gymnastics, at least one competition offering a prize, and so on. The research team were not just making enquiries into people's circumstances, they were also, through the charitable works that they were engaged in, manipulating those circumstances. It may even have been the case that the villagers were aware that the 'visitors' had access to various kinds of official information about individuals. It may be – indeed, it seems quite likely – that such factors influenced the information given, the behaviour of the villagers and the degree of acceptance of the team in Marienthal. All these factors have a significant bearing on the research process and potentially raise questions about the validity of the data.

The Researchers

Given the many issues that arise from a critical textual reading of *Marienthal*, it is relevant to ask who the authors were. It is worthy of note that '(a)ll three [of the authors], and most of their collaborators, came from fairly well-established, Jewish upper middle-class families' (Fleck 2002: xx). In particular, Lazarsfeld, who was married to Jahoda at the time of the study, was very well connected, socially:

> his father Robert was a lawyer and his mother Sophie ran a salon where leading left intellectuals met regularly. One of them became young Paul's mentor and Paul's mother's lover: Friedrich Adler, the son of the founder of the Social Democratic Party in Austria, Victor Adler. (ibid.)

In their professional lives, they were principally engaged in the application of economic psychology to market research (ibid.: xxii). Their original plan had been to study the leisure activities of workers, who were felt to have been rather ignored by marketing practice. What became the study, *Marienthal*, was suggested to them by a Social Democrat politician, Otto Bauer, who proposed both the topic and the location, but had no further practical involvement in the study (ibid.: xix). As previously noted, none of the authors was directly involved in the field work – during that period, Jahoda was finishing her PhD, Lazarsfeld was busy directing other projects and Zeisel was working in his father's law firm in Vienna. Indeed, there was, apparently, some long-lasting disagreement among the authors about 'the true authorship of *Marienthal*. Evidently the book was the result of a collaborative effort even if it is true that Jahoda wrote the main text' (ibid.: xxx).

The book was published in 1933. On the advice of their German-based publisher, it was published anonymously – at least, the authors' names did not appear on the title page, though it seems that they did appear inside the book (Fleck, 2002: xxv) – on the grounds that their names identified them as Jewish. It was received in a generally positive way but then, in effect, disappeared for about 30 years. It was not translated into English until 1971, because the authors did not wish it. Since its publication in English, *Marienthal* has come to be regarded as a seminal piece of research – the present 2002 edition has warranted at least one reprinting.

Why did the authors not want the study to be translated into English? Lazarsfeld, in his introduction to the first English edition, is quite specific about this:

> For a long time we did not consent to an English translation of our study. Certain aspects of our approach were very naive. We never stated explicitly our sampling procedures and probably never had very good ones; our typologies were developed intuitively and never checked for their logical consistency. We did not use attitude scales – we hardly knew about them. Many of the standards on which my colleagues and I would later insist in our teaching were neglected. I can excuse this only by remembering the adventurous pioneering spirit that propelled us; but it made me uncomfortable enough that for a while I refused any offer to publish a translation. (Lazarsfeld, 2002: xxxv)

Clearly, the authors themselves did not want to make any particular claims about innovative research practices and the centrality of the study. Nonetheless, such claims have been made. They finally agreed to translation into English, apparently, because in the late 1960s and the 1970s unemployment was again rising in the developed countries, and academics were again taking an interest in the phenomenon. Then later, 'social scientists looking for prototypes rediscovered *Marienthal*... Over the next thirty years *Marienthal* functioned as a blueprint for successors' studies. Jahoda's contributions about the latent functions of paid work had a lasting effect on students of work and unemployment from different disciplines and a wide range of countries' (Fleck, 2002: xxvii).[3]

A Contribution to What?

It is precisely this contemporary impact of *Marienthal* that really concerns us. We opened this chapter with Richards' warning about feeding a susceptible audience with superficially plausible, (but ideologically acceptable), explanations as a means of social control. In the uncritical contemporary acceptance of *Marienthal* we have, we would suggest, an outstanding example of these concerns.

We wish to emphasise that we would not seek to deny any utility that *Marienthal* may have had as a pioneering study in the 1930s, and it is certainly an interesting historical document. What we do question is its continuing status as an important piece of informing research. It may well have been innovative in its time but, while such innovation in the research process can be celebrated, it is also attended by risk, especially in terms of establishing the validity of the research claims that ensue. As we have indicated, even the authors did not, apparently, want to make any big claims about the research process. By modern standards, this research process can be seen as rather amateurish, and it is highly unlikely that any contemporary research project would seek to replicate, in detail, that of *Marienthal.* This alone, one might have hoped, would encourage a more careful, and more critical, appreciation. The question is, then, why is it still so uncritically well-regarded? The remarkable thing about *Marienthal* is that its impact has been most significant, not in terms of what ***un***employment *does **to** workers,* but in terms of what *employment can do **for** workers.*

Some of the findings of *Marienthal* are nowadays unsurprising – for example, that the *stress of an endless struggle to survive,* (though this particular characterisation is noteworthy by its absence), might lead to interpersonal friction, an attenuated social life, changed patterns of behaviour, a reorientation of interests in favour of more immediate concerns, self-doubt and uncertainties about the future. One particular finding, however, was most adventitious, namely, the loss of *structure* in the lives of the unemployed. This was most clearly articulated in the chapter entitled *The Meaning of Time.* Of course, free time in conditions of abject poverty is not the same as leisure time, though this is not how the authors see it:

> On examination this leisure proves to be a tragic gift. Cut off from their work and deprived of contact with the outside world, the workers of Marienthal have lost the material and moral incentives to make use of their time. Now that they are no longer under any pressure, they undertake nothing new and drift gradually out of an ordered existence into one that is undisciplined and empty. (Jahoda et al., 2002: 66)

Clearly, and explicitly, for the authors, this 'problem' is caused by the absence of employed work, with the implication that, even if the unemployed workers were not poverty-stricken, they would still not know what to do with their time. In other words, economics aside, workers must have jobs. Thus, the immediate rationale for selling one's labour becomes diluted. In the perpetual struggle between Capital and Labour, the former seeking a minimal outlay, the latter seeking an adequate return, the ultimate burden for Capital has been to pay sufficient for Labour to reproduce itself (that is, to survive).

Contemporaneously with the increase in popularity of defining the labour process in terms of non-material satisfactions, we have seen the formal legitimation, with initiatives in the UK such as Family Income Supplement, of the absence of a requirement on Capital to pay a living wage. The doctrine that there is a moral obligation to have a job, irrespective of how little the wage, preoccupied and energised policy makers in the closing decades of the last century. But the enthusiasm of Capital continually to shift the wage obligation towards welfare payments, minimising costs and improving profits, did see, eventually, the introduction of the much-lauded (though not by employers) Minimum Wage. We should note, nonetheless, that the dissociation from the economic imperative of selling one's labour in order to survive remains intact: the obligation is to pay a *minimum* wage, not a *living* wage. This is, we would suggest, why the findings of *Marienthal* remain so popular: in effect, they substantiate the notion of the non-corporeality, the *immateriality*, of Labour.

Cole (2007: 1135) nicely captures the potency of this study with his characterisation of it as having 'emotional appeal'. It seems almost churlish to question such a sympathetic account of the travails, the emiseration, of the unemployed. However, a critical textual reading of the book has disclosed a range of factors influencing the interpretations of the data – such as, cultural blindness, naivety, the clash of middle class values and the lived experience of the working class – that really ought to excite caution. If it is possible to question the interpretations of the data, this must raise further questions about the findings; if it is possible to question the findings, this must throw doubt onto the later characterisation of these findings in terms of the 'latent functions of work'. That these issues have not been generally developed is, we would suggest, the effect of a more significant aspect of the study, *its ideological fit with dominant views of the value of employed work*. What more could Capital desire, than the belief that Labour should depend on paid work not just for income, but also for its social and psychological infrastructure? The message of *Marienthal* fitted perfectly into the then burgeoning, and still flourishing, literature on 'the meaning of work'. Its principle contribution has been to the idea that paid work has *therapeutic values*, even that these therapeutic values are more significant than its economic value, for workers.

Carey (1977: 34) commented on Herzberg's work that he 'claimed to have found scientific proof that the true human nature and needs of men [sic] comprise just those attitudes and values which fit them ideally for a loyal, subordinate role in a free enterprise system'. In our view, *Marienthal* is precisely another example of this fortuitous phenomenon!

References

Carey, A. (1977): 'The Lysenko Syndrome in Western social science', *Australian Psychologist*, 12(1): 27-38.

Cole, M. (2007): 'Re-thinking unemployment: a challenge to the legacy of Jahoda et al.', *Sociology*, 41(6): 1133-49.

Fleck, C. (2002): 'Introduction to the Transaction edition', in M. Jahoda et al.: *Marienthal: The Sociography of an Unemployed Community*. London: Transaction Publishers.

Jahoda, M. (1979): 'The impact of unemployment in the 1930s and the 1970s', *Bulletin of the British Psychological Society*, 32(August): 309-314.

Jahoda, M., P. F. Lazarsfeld and H. Zeisel (2002 [1971]): *Marienthal: The Sociography of an Unemployed Community*. London: Transaction Publishers.

Jahoda, M. and H. Rush (1980): 'Work, employment and unemployment', *Science Policy Research Unit, University of Sussex, Occasional Paper Series*, 12.

Lazarsfeld, P. (2002 [1971]): 'Forty years later', in M. Jahoda et al.: *Marienthal: The Sociography of an Unemployed Community*. London: Transaction Publishers.

Richards, I. A. (1964 [1929]): *Practical Criticism*. London: Routledge and Kegan Paul.

Notes

[1] Interestingly, and very symbolic of the continuing significance of *Marienthal* in the present, the University of Graz is in the process of constructing a fascinating and very informative website about the book and, especially, about the place, to be found at www.agso.uni-graz.at/marienthal. This site clarifies some of the confusions that arise in *Marienthal*, but fails to clarify others (see below). Confusions have abounded, including disagreements among the authors about when the book was published, who wrote it, even when the study took place.

2   There are a number of tables regarding the demographics of Marienthal, and relating these to numbers of people (or, sometimes, 'consumer units'), in receipt of relief, classified as unemployed, etc. It is, however, very difficult to work out from these tables specific data on these matters, partly because they do not use comparable units of analysis – for example, some refer to individuals, some to families. It seems that 66% of the population of Marienthal was of working age (15-59 years of age) (Jahoda et al., 2002: 15), that 82% of people were dependent on unemployment relief (this figure includes children) (ibid.: 21), that 93 families had at least one member working and a further 18 families had someone who was in receipt of a pension, and that 9 families – of which Family 273 was clearly one – were not in receipt of any relief at all, either because their entitlement had been exhausted or because they were ineligible (ibid.: 19). Trying to elucidate these figures by consulting the website does not help, since those figures also do not appear to stack up.

3   The book has been translated into, *inter alia*, French, Italian, Spanish, Norwegian, Korean, Hungarian, Polish. It seems to have proved to be especially attractive in countries making the transition to capitalism.

4

'Lessons for Managers and Consultants': A Reading of Edgar H. Schein's *Process Consultation*

Nick Butler

Introduction

Perhaps more than anyone else in the field, Edgar H. Schein straddles the divide between academic researcher and organizational consultant. Born in Zurich to Hungarian and German parents in 1928, Schein spent his early years in Switzerland, the Soviet Union, and Czechoslovakia before emigrating to the United States in 1938. Having studied at the Universities of Chicago, Stanford, and Harvard, Schein went on to work in the Neuropsychiatry Division of the Walter Reed Army Institute of Research during the early 1950s. It was here that he conducted research into the effects of communist 'brainwashing' and indoctrination techniques on US prisoners-of-war repatriated from China and North Korea. This research, he writes, first alerted him to the power of 'interpersonal forces' over and above 'the threat of physical force' (Schein, 1993: 39). Fittingly, the theme of 'coercive persuasion' would come to form the basis of his first, co-authored, book (Schein, Schneier, and Barker, 1961). After leaving the Walter Reed Army Institute of Research in 1956, Schein began teaching at MIT's Sloan School of Management and became a Professor of Organizational Psychology and Management in 1964. He has since gone on to work as a consultant for such corporate luminaries as Proctor & Gamble, Citibank, Con Edison, ExxonMobil, Shell, BP, and, in the public sector, the International Atomic Energy Agency. Oil drilling and nuclear fission aside, Schein has written extensively on leadership, corporate culture, organizational development, and career management, and his academic contribution was recently affirmed by his 'Vita Contemplativa' in *Organization Studies* (Schein, 2006). In this chapter, I will focus exclusively on Schein's model of 'process consultation'.

Schein outlines the model of process consultation in a trilogy of practitioner-oriented textbooks written over several decades (1969; 1987; 1999).[1] For Schein, this model is 'a special kind of consultation' (1969: 3) in that it does not require the consultant to possess any technical expertise in a specific organizational area. Unlike conventional content-based consulting, which seeks to make operational improvements to the client organization, process consultation is based entirely on knowledge about how to establish a collaborative consultant-client relation in order to conduct the joint diagnosis of organizational problems and the joint formulation of solutions to these problems. These problems and their solutions, moreover, will be informal and relational, rather than formal and technical, in nature. Process consultation thus seeks to improve interpersonal relations between members of staff in the client organization. For this reason, Schein claims that his model of process consultation can be applied not only by consultants in relation to their clients, but also by managers in relation to their subordinates. The result is as simple as it is seemingly contradictory: by drawing on the model of process consultation, managers are able to act as 'their own consultants' in organizations. The present chapter examines this conundrum by conducting a close reading of Schein's *Process Consultation*, focusing in particular on the first and second volumes.

I will begin by suggesting that the model of process consultation is to be understood primarily in terms of its relation to management. The first section will outline precisely what is meant by the term 'management' by drawing on the work of management theorist Peter Armstrong, which will serve to guide the discussion in the remainder of the chapter. I will conclude by arguing that process consultation allows consultants to gain power over managers whilst simultaneously threatening to undermine the very basis of this power. I want to suggest that this is the *real* lesson to be drawn from Schein's work.

Technical and Relational Components of Management

The meaning and significance of Schein's model of process consultation lies in its relation to management. Before this relation can be brought to light, however, we first need to clarify what we mean by 'management' since, as Grey (1999: 563) points out, 'there are competing claims about what management is and should be'. Some commentators have attempted to define management according to the day-to-day activities performed by managers, often reaching very different conclusions from 'classic' management thinkers such as Fayol and Drucker (see e.g. Carroll and Gillen, 1987; Hales, 1986; Kotter, 1982; Mintzberg, 1973; Watson, 1994; Whitley, 1989). Other commentators, meanwhile, have argued that management has become far more diffused throughout organizations with the shift from a 'command-and-control' to a 'facilitate-and-empower' structure, which means that the task of managing is no longer performed solely by an occupational group of trained managers (see e.g. Barker, 1993; 1999; Ezzamel, Lilley, and Willmott, 1994; Ezzamel and Willmott, 1998; Sewell, 1998; Sewell and Wilkinson, 1992). This argument is extended even further by theorists who suggest that the ideology of management has seeped out of the workplace and entered our everyday lives (see e.g. Hancock and Tyler, 2004; 2008; 2009). The field of management studies, we might be tempted to say, is characterized precisely by this proliferation of perspectives on its object of study. But does this mean that 'management' is fundamentally unstable, ambiguous, and indeterminate?

Perhaps. In any case, this chapter will seek to clarify Schein's model of process consultation by outlining its relation to 'management' as it is understood by Armstrong. Whereas most commentators focus on the (necessarily piecemeal) level of the empirical practice of managing in specific organizations, Armstrong deals with the historical development of prescriptive managerial knowledge as a whole. By reviewing this practitioner literature for managers, Armstrong is able to highlight recurring themes, prevalent trends, and sudden transformations in the body of managerial knowledge (which, no doubt, has come to inform actual management practice over the years). Armstrong's analysis tells us that while managers perform operational tasks as part of their work, they also need to manage the relation with their subordinates. This implies that management, as a body of knowledge, involves two components: technical and relational. As we will see, it is this distinction that allows us to reflect on the meaning and significance of Schein's model of process consultation.

In a series of articles and book-chapters, Armstrong (1987; 1991; 1992; 1996) examines the distinction between the technical and the relational components of management from a historical perspective. He notes that, for some of the earliest proponents of management theory in the late nineteenth and early twentieth century, the right and ability to manage was inextricable from technical expertise. In Frederick Taylor's view, for example,

> the *core* of managerial expertise was the knowledge of productive processes which enabled the industrial engineer to redesign them so as to eliminate 'waste' effort. Indeed, Taylor considered the possession of such knowledge to be the sole legitimate basis on which management could claim authority over the workforce. (Armstrong, 1992: 44; emphasis in original)

Control over labour, in a Taylorist context, is secured by the application of mechanical engineering design principles to the production process (i.e. analyzing and altering factory workers' physical movements to achieve maximum efficiency). Technical expertise, from this perspective, is not separate from managerial practice; the two go hand-in-hand. This means that, for Taylor, '[m]anagement, as a body of knowledge and code of behaviour, remained industry-specific' (Armstrong, 1991: 247).

Beginning in the 1920s, the technical and relational components of management come to be separated. Whereas previously management was conceptualized as practical knowledge of the production process in a particular industry, now management starts to be discussed as an abstract, universal set of skills that is detached from any specific organizational area and therefore applicable in any given industry. As Armstrong (1991: 247) puts it, management is conceptualized as 'a set of techniques which stand in an additive relationship to the technical elements of real-life managerial work'. Such a view finds early expression in Fayol's *General and Industrial Management* (1949: 83), first published in the original French in 1916 and translated into English in 1929:

> For a divisional engineer managerial ability is as important as technical ability. This fact may be surprising but is easily explainable thus: the manager of a metallurgical division, for instance, blast furnaces, steel works, rolling-mills, has not for some years been exclusively concerned with metallurgy – or even with a limited section of metallurgy. All details learnt at college about mines, railways, construction, are no longer any more than vaguely useful for him, whereas handling of men,

planning, in a word, elements of management, are constantly taking up his attention. At the particular level of authority which he has reached the services which he will subsequently be able to render and his own advancement will most likely turn far more on his managerial than on his technical ability.

Fayol makes a clear distinction between knowledge about how to control the production process and knowledge about how to control subordinates, that is to say, the 'handling of men'. For Fayol, unlike Taylor, 'technical ability' and 'managerial ability' do not go hand-in-hand; the former is divorced from, and secondary to, the latter. This means that the relational component of management – forecasting, planning, organizing, commanding, coordinating, and controlling (Fayol, 1949: 5-6; see also Armstrong, 1991: 246-8; 1992: 44-5; 1996: 278-9) – is understood as the *properly managerial* aspect of managers' work whereas the technical component of management is, in turn, understood as the *non-managerial* aspect of managers' work. This conceptualization of management, Armstrong notes (1996: 293-5), is now firmly established in both the practitioner literature for managers and the educational textbooks for students of management.

A number of consequences follow from this conceptualization of management. First, the separation of the technical component from the relational component of management results in a clearer distinction between productive and unproductive aspects of management labour. Armstrong reminds us that, in Marxist terms, productive labour is the part of labour that creates surplus value whereas unproductive labour is the part of labour that serves, among other functions, to direct and control productive labour in order to extract surplus value from it. Broadly speaking, productive labour refers to workers who 'produce a greater value in goods and services than is represented by their wages' while unproductive labour refers to 'all of the tasks within the administrative apparatus [that have] replaced the functions once carried out by the primordial individual capitalist' (1987: 426). Management, along Taylorist lines, is by definition both a part of productive labour (since managers perform operational tasks in the production process) and a part of unproductive labour (since managers direct and control their subordinates in the organizational hierarchy) (1991: 241-4). It becomes possible to separate these types of labour, however, once the technical component of management is divorced from, and made secondary to, the relational component of management. If the former component is viewed as the non-managerial aspect of managers' work, and the latter as the properly managerial aspect, then it is not difficult to see how management can be detached *entirely* from productive labour and come to be situated *exclusively* on the level of unproductive labour (1987: 429). A manager no longer requires any technical knowledge whatsoever; all they need is knowledge about how to control and coordinate staff activities, regardless of the operational area in which they work.

This brings us to a second consequence: the division between different levels of management in the organizational hierarchy. While middle and lower managers continue to perform specific operational tasks in a particular department within the organization (marketing, finance, IT, human resources, etc.) in addition to their general managerial tasks of coordination and control, top managers are concerned almost exclusively with the overall direction of the organization and its members. Put simply, the labour of middle and lower managers will still be productive whereas the labour of top managers will be largely unproductive. As Armstrong notes, it is the latter group that serves as the 'model for managerial excellence': 'Thus, in the same breath as it celebrates its universality, 'management'…comes to identify itself exclusively with the administration of the capitalist enterprise and denies the title of management to authoritative expertise within the productive process' (1987: 428). The 'ideal type' of management, in other words, is now wholly identified with the function of agenda-setting and decision-making at the broadest organizational level, completely disconnected from technical expertise. Such a predicament, of course, would have been unthinkable for Taylor. It becomes possible only once the relational component of management is separated from its technical component, and once the unproductive element of management labour is divorced from its productive element.

Finally, a third consequence: the question of professionalization. Once management is viewed as 'always and everywhere the same in essence' (Armstrong, 1991: 247; 1996: 279), it becomes possible to develop a common body of knowledge that is applicable in every industry and in every department. It is this body of knowledge, moreover, that provides the basis on which management can seek to gain full professional recognition. This was certainly the ambition of British management theorists like Lyndall Urwick (Armstrong, 1991:

250-5; 1996: 279-84). Such a project of managerial professionalization serves to undermine the claim made by engineers that they are more capable of managing an organization than any other professional group. Since performing an operational task is now secondary to dealing with a hierarchical relation, engineers are accordingly relegated to a position that is subordinate to 'managerial specialists' (Armstrong, 1987: 432; 1991: 258). By the same token, the collective interests of managers, as a professional group, are made more secure if management is understood not in terms of industry-specific knowledge of the production process, but rather in terms of abstract and universally-applicable principles for coordinating and controlling staff activities in the organization.

Armstrong's historical analysis of management's technical and relational components allows us to bring into focus the meaning and significance of Schein's model of process consultation. The next section will show that process consultants have also been able to detach their work from the operational tasks of productive labour. This opens up the possibility for consultants to position themselves at the top-most level of organizational hierarchies and, moreover, to secure their collective interests as a professional group on the basis of a body of knowledge. To this extent, the model of process consultation mirrors the 'ideal type' of management. But the divorce of the relational component of consultancy from its technical component has profound, indeed paradoxical, implications. We will examine these implications by describing, first, how the model of process consultation differs from conventional content-based consulting and, second, how Schein encourages managers to act as 'their own consultants' in organizations.

The Model of Process Consultation

At the beginning of the first volume of *Process Consultation*, Schein contrasts the model of process consultation with two 'more traditional consultation models' (1969: 4): the 'purchase model' and the 'doctor-patient model'. This allows Schein to tell us what is unique and distinctive about the model of process consultation in relation to other types of organizational consulting.

The purchase model, Schein says, is based on the idea that the client[2] purchases a service from a consultant that is based on technical expertise in a specific organizational area. This model of consultancy assumes that the client knows what the problem is and how it can be resolved: 'The buyer, an individual manager or some group in the organization, defines a need – something he wishes to know or some activity he wishes carried out – and, if he doesn't feel the organization itself has the time or capability, he will look to a consultant to fill the need' (1969: 5). This might involve hiring a consultant to find out how a group of customers feel, to help in the design of a new plant, or to put into operation a new accounting system (1969: 5). The effectiveness of this model depends on the client being able to conduct an accurate diagnosis and to communicate the organizational problem clearly to the consultant. For this reason, Schein says, the purchase model often fails to deliver improvements to the client organization (1969: 5).

The doctor-patient model, meanwhile, involves the client hiring a consultant to conduct a general diagnosis, to identify any organizational problems, and to propose possible solutions. Schein elaborates:

> One or more executives in the organization decide to bring in a consultant or team of consultants to 'look them over', much as the patient might go to his doctor for an annual physical. The consultants are supposed to find out what is wrong with which part of the organization, and then, like a physician, recommend a program of therapy. (1969: 6)

This model is based on the notion that the organization is dysfunctional in some way and that the client requires a consultant to find out what the disorder is and how it can be remedied. Its effectiveness depends on the client's willingness to allow the consultant access to information about the organization as well as the client's disposition to accept or reject the consultant's diagnosis. For this reason, the doctor-patient model also often fails to deliver improvements to the client organization (1969: 6-7).

Both the purchase model and the doctor-patient model involve some basic assumptions about the relation between the consultant and the client. In the first model, the consultant is construed as a passive 'seller' whereas the client is construed as an active 'buyer'. In the second model, meanwhile, the consultant is construed as an active 'doctor' whereas the client is construed as the passive 'patient'. Both the purchase model and the doctor-patient model, however, are variations on the same basic model: in both cases, the consultant plays the role of a vendor (as a provider of managerial services) and the client plays the role of a customer (as a purchaser of managerial services). In effect,

Schein is outlining *the model of conventional content-based consulting*, which involves the provision of outsourced expertise to a client organization.

Against the purchase model and the doctor-patient model, Schein proposes a third model: 'process consultation' (or 'P-C').[3] In contrast to the purchase model and the doctor-patient model, the model of process consultation emphasizes the need for a collaborative consultant-client relation in order to conduct the joint diagnosis of problems and the joint formulation of solutions. As Schein puts it: 'The client must learn to see the problem for himself, to share in the diagnosis, and to be actively involved in generating a remedy' (1969: 8). Since the publication of *Process Consultation*, it has become commonplace for the practitioner literature to encourage consultants to establish a collaborative relationship with the client. What is novel and interesting about the model of process consultation, however, is the fact that it does not necessarily involve any technical expertise in a specific organizational area.[4] Schein explains:

> It should be emphasized that the process consultant may or may not be expert in solving the particular problem which is uncovered. The important point in P-C is that such expertise is less relevant than are the skills of involving the client in self-diagnosis and helping him to find a remedy which fits his particular situation and unique set of needs. The process consultant must be an expert in how to diagnose and how to develop a helping relationship. He does not need to be an expert on production, marketing, finance, and the like. (1969: 7)

While Schein does not discount the possibility that the process consultant may well possess technical expertise, he makes it clear that this is not a prerequisite for process consultation. The process consultant, on this view, need only possess the skills for establishing a collaborative consultant-client relation (what Schein calls here a 'helping relationship') in order to engage the manager in joint problem diagnosis and joint solution formulation. The purpose of process consultation, for Schein, is to 'help the manager become a sufficiently good diagnostician himself', since 'problems will stay solved longer and be solved more effectively if the organization solves its own problems' (1969: 6). The process consultant, then, 'should not work on the actual concrete problem himself', but should instead play 'a role in teaching diagnostic and problem-solving skills' to the manager (1969: 6). The actual *content* of the problem is less important, for Schein, than the *process* by which this problem is identified and remedied.

Schein is actually equivocal about whether or not technical expertise plays a role in process consultation at all. Whereas, in the above passage, he suggests that the process consultant 'may or may not be [an] expert' and 'does not need to be an expert' in an organizational area – which implies that technical expertise *can* play a role – he later goes on to say that it *cannot*, in fact, play a role in process consultation:

> Actual solutions to management problems…would not be considered valid interventions in a P-C model. If I permitted myself to become interested in a particular management problem in sales, marketing, or production, I would be switching roles from that of process consultant to that of expert resource. Once I have become an expert resource, I find I lose my effectiveness as a process consultant. (1969: 103)

Schein says that any application of technical expertise in a client organization would detract from the function of the process consultant. By solving a particular managerial problem in a specific organizational area – such as sales, marketing, or production – the process consultant becomes an 'expert resource', thus falling into either the purchase model or the doctor-patient model. As Schein notes, the application of technical expertise in a specific organizational area is, for the process consultant, 'very rare, largely because it violates some of the basic assumptions of the process consultation model' (1969: 118). Such comments serve to emphasize the fact that process consultation can be – perhaps *must* be – devoid of all technical expertise.

Let us pause for a moment to reflect on the consequences of Schein's model of process consultation. We previously said that the relational component of management has come to be separated from its technical component. Whereas management was once conceptualized as practical knowledge of the production process in a particular industry, management is now understood as an abstract, universal set of skills that is detached from any specific organizational area and therefore applicable in any given industry. In the same way, our preliminary analysis of process consultation suggests that the technical component of consultancy has become divorced from, and made secondary to, its relational component. Whereas consultants working within the purchase model or the doctor-patient model must possess technical expertise in a specific organizational area (such as sales, marketing, or production), process consultants need only possess knowledge about how to establish a collaborative relation with their clients in order to engage them in joint problem diagnosis and joint solution formulation. This means that the model of process consultation is conceptualized by Schein as an abstract, universal set of skills that is detached from any specific organizational area and applicable in any given industry. In this respect, the model of process consultation can be completely divorced from the operational tasks of productive labour and come to be situated exclusively on the level of unproductive labour. This presents an opportunity for consultants to position themselves at the top-most level of organizational hierarchies, since it is here that the task of management is disconnected from any technical expertise and wholly identified with the relational processes of coordination and control. By gaining access to and exerting influence over senior executives in organizations, process consultants will no doubt be able to raise their occupational status and, consequently, secure a higher asking-price for their services.[5] This could conceivably offer one explanation why Schein is so keen to detach the model of process consultation from the operational tasks associated with conventional content-based consulting.

But if the model of process consultation does not involve any content whatsoever, what purpose does it serve for client organizations? The next section will show that process consultation seeks to improve interpersonal relations between members of the client staff. For this reason, Schein claims that the model of process consultation can be applied not only by consultants in relation to clients, but also by managers in relation to subordinates.

'Lessons for Managers and Consultants'

The primary objective of process consultation, as we said, is to establish a collaborative consultant-client relation that permits the joint diagnosis of problems and the joint formulation of solutions. But that is not all. Schein states that such a 'helping relationship' is of practical use only to the extent that it permits the consultant and the client to deal with interpersonal relations in the organization, such as communication between individuals, group problem-solving and decision-making, and inter-group cooperation and competition (1969: 13). This means that process consultation is concerned not with delivering technical expertise into the client organization, but with changing the way its employees relate to and communicate with each other. Although Schein initially claims that the purpose of developing a collaborative consultant-client relation is to help the manager 'find a remedy which fits his particular situation and unique set of needs' (1969: 7), it is readily apparent that he has a very specific idea about the kinds of issues that must be addressed in a client organization in order to improve its effectiveness. For the process consultant, the organizational problem and its solution will always be relational, rather than technical, in nature.

It should be said that Schein does not deny the merit of making operational improvements to a client organization. He emphasizes the need, rather, to deal first and foremost with 'the processes which occur between people and groups' (1969: 11) before dealing with technical content. He elaborates:

> I am not contending that focusing on human processes is the *only* path to increasing organizational effectiveness. Obviously there is room in most organizations for improved production, financial, marketing, and other processes. I am arguing, however, that the various functions which make up an organization are always mediated by the interactions of people, so that the organization can never escape its human processes. (1969: 9; emphasis in original)

For Schein, there is always an underlying relational dimension to any technical problem. On this view, the 'how' of management (its process) is just as important, if not more so, than the 'what' of management (its content). Schein admits that this might seem counterintuitive to some managers, who 'tend to focus much more on the content of decisions, interactions, and communications' (1969: 124). In this respect, it is part of the task of process consultants to demonstrate to managers that '[human] processes in the organization follow patterns which can be studied and understood, and which have important consequences for organizational performance'. Managers must be shown, moreover, that these 'processes can be rationally changed and adapted to increase the effectiveness of performance' (1969: 124). Whereas conventional content-based consulting – such as the purchase model or the doctor-patient model – focuses principally on the formal aspects of client organizations by seeking to improve technical content, the model of process consultation targets the informal aspects of client organizations by seeking to improve relational processes between members of the client staff.

It is for this reason that the model of process consultation can be put to direct use not only by consultants, but also by managers. This point, it should be said, remains largely implicit in the first volume of *Process Consultation*. But when the second volume appears in 1987, with its revealing subtitle *Lessons for Managers and Consultants*, there can be no doubt about the wider applicability of process consultation that Schein envisages. In the preface, he describes the genesis of the second volume:

> My original intention had been simply to revise the 1969 book. However, as I began to write, I realized that most of what I was saying was an elaboration and that the new ideas were intended for a much different audience. Whereas my original book was a primer for consultants, the present book is much more a new approach for experienced consultants and a prescription for effective management…Line managers often have to function as process consultants vis-à-vis their subordinates, peers, and bosses…I believe that all managers can become more effective if they adopt some of the concepts of process consultation and learn some of the skills associated with that concept. (1987: vii-viii)

While Schein had initially sought only to amend the first volume of *Process Consultation*, he says that the second volume extends beyond that work. Most significantly, he came to realize that the model of process consultation can be applied by managers as well as consultants. But what does it mean for managers to 'learn some of the skills' associated with process consultation? On a basic level, it means that managers will come to deal with their subordinates (as well as their peers and bosses) in the same way that consultants deal with their clients, namely, by establishing a collaborative relation in order to conduct the joint diagnosis of problems and the joint formulation of solutions. The purpose of such an undertaking, moreover, is to improve relational processes between members of staff in an organization. This allows Schein to call the model of process consultation a 'prescription for effective management' as well as a 'new approach for experienced consultants'.

Schein admits that managers and consultants appear, on the surface, to differ considerably. Managers, on the one hand, exercise formal authority over their subordinates and remain inside their organization. Consultants, on the other hand, do not exercise formal authority over their clients and, on the whole, remain outside the client organization (1987: 5). Beyond these superficial differences, however, there are certain shared characteristics that belong equally to managers and consultants. Schein explains: 'People who are perceived by their colleagues, bosses, and subordinates to be *effective* managers and *effective* consultants have in common that, when they relate to others whom they are trying to influence, they both take the stance of trying to *help*' (1987: 6; emphasis in original). Managers and consultants both attempt to help the people with whom they are dealing, whether these people are clients or subordinates; their basic task, therefore, is the same.[6] For Schein, it is not a case of arbitrarily imposing on managers the model of process consultation, but of drawing attention to the similarities between managers and consultants in order to improve the effectiveness of both:

> Managers reading this book may find at first that some of the ideas seem less applicable to them, but the more they think about the managerial role, the more they will come to recognize how much of their own behaviour resembles that of consultants, and therefore, how much they might increase their own effectiveness if they learned some of the philosophies, concepts, and skills that consultants, especially process consultants, use. (1987: 9)

Schein seeks to reassure sceptical managers about the feasibility and value of adopting the tenets of process consultation. While it might at first seem counterintuitive to think of the managerial role as a consultancy role, Schein insists that the latter in fact resembles the former since they each share the same task of 'helping'. Managers, on this view, can be said *already* to act as consultants in their own organization and should therefore draw on consultancy knowledge to improve their managerial effectiveness. Schein emphasizes, moreover, that process consultation is his favoured 'model of helping', over and above the purchase model (now called the 'expert model') and the doctor-patient model (1987: 8; see also 22-34). We will recall that, in the first volume of *Process Consultation*, Schein said that both the purchase model and the doctor-patient model often fail to deliver improvements to the client organization and so, for this reason, they should be avoided by the consultant. Likewise, in the second volume, Schein asserts that it is rarely ever appropriate for the manager to adopt either of these models:

When should a manager be an expert, a doctor, or a process consultant? The formal authority of a manager makes it easy for him to fall into the expert or doctor role, especially when help is being sought by a subordinate. But if the goals of the manager are to teach the subordinate problem-solving skills and to ensure that the solutions developed will be the right ones and will be implemented correctly, then being a [process] consultant is by far the preferable way to begin. (1987: 35)

A manager should not act as an expert or a doctor, then, but as a process consultant. This involves establishing a collaborative relation with subordinates in order to conduct the joint diagnosis of problems and the joint formulation of solutions. It is worth pointing out that these problems and solutions will be informal and relational, rather than formal and technical, since 'effective managers spend far more time intervening in *how* things are done than on *what* is done' (1987: 39; emphasis in original). The consequences are clear: a good manager, for Schein, is one who has the ability to be a process consultant.

What is most striking about Schein's line of reasoning in the second volume of *Process Consultation* is the way it undermines the conventional primacy of management over consultancy. Managers resemble consultants, not the other way around. It is no longer enough, it seems, for a manager to be effective at carrying out their managerial responsibilities; a manager must now also act as 'their own consultant' in the organization. We might wonder whether an actual consultant (such as Schein) needs to be present in the client organization to ensure that the manager properly adopts a consultancy role, or whether a manager is able to function as a consultant without the help of such an external adviser. We might also wonder whether the manager-as-consultant, if he or she follows the model of process consultation strictly enough, will succeed in transferring diagnostic and relationship-building skills to their subordinates (thus turning them into de facto consultants as well). In any case, it is clear that Schein views his model of process consultation as a set of guidelines for managers, as well as consultants, to draw on in order to improve interpersonal processes in organizations. To this extent, the model of process consultation serves to modify the relationship between consultancy and management: the former, with a curious twist, becomes the 'ideal type' of the latter — consultancy as a 'model for managerial excellence'.

Discussion

We previously said that management theorists such as Urwick sought to develop a body of managerial knowledge that is based entirely on abstract and universally-applicable principles for coordinating and controlling staff activities in the organization, thus undermining the claim made by trained engineers that they are more capable of managing an organization than any other professional group. The conceptual framework of process consultation can be understood in much the same way. Consultancy thinkers such as Schein seek to develop a body of consultancy knowledge that is similarly stripped of all technical expertise, based solely on abstract and universally-applicable guidelines for dealing with interpersonal relations in the client organization. This serves to undermine the claim made by managers – from whichever background and training – that they are the group most capable of managing organizations effectively. On this view, process consultation challenges the very grounds of the managerial revolution in the twentieth century, namely, the assumption that salaried executives are inherently suited to the task of overall agenda-setting and decision-making in organizations. Although process consultants are by no means alone in contesting this assumption – activist shareholders and financial intermediaries have also worn away some of the autonomy that managers have traditionally enjoyed – what is most interesting about Schein's work is the fact that it explicitly aims to replace the relational component of *management* with the relational component of *consultancy*.

The peculiarity of this situation cannot be overstated. On the one hand, the model of process consultation seeks to transform the traditional manager-subordinate relation into an entirely new relation, the 'consultant-client relation'. This serves to change the way we understand modern management by prioritizing the consultancy role over and above the managerial role. On the other hand, it is not difficult to see how the model of process consultation could become separated from the occupational group to whom it properly belongs (i.e. consultants) and come to fall securely within the province of management. From this perspective, the relational component of consultancy would simply *turn back into* the relational component of management as soon as it is installed in the client organization. This alerts us to the paradox at the heart of *Process Consultation*. Schein makes the model of process consultation indispensable for managers, thus advancing the collective interests of consultants; but in doing so, Schein risks turning the model of process consultation into a form of managerial knowledge, thus impairing the collective interests of consultants. This paradox does not imply a 'flaw' or an 'error' in the model of process consultation, but in fact provides the source of process consultants' power over managers even as it simultaneously threatens to undermine the very basis of this power.

We would be mistaken to think that this view of consultancy is limited to Schein's work. Indeed, it is becoming increasingly common in the practitioner literature for managers to be encouraged to act as 'their own consultants' in organizations. This implies that the paradoxical idea of the manager-as-consultant has become too widespread for it to be dismissed as an isolated case. One well-known consultancy textbook asserts that 'a manager can also act as a consultant if he or she gives advice and help to a fellow manager, or even to subordinates rather than directing and issuing orders to them' (Kubr, et al., 2002: 3). The same point is made by Margerison (2001: 4), who suggests that, like consultants, 'line managers also spend a good deal of time advising and using consulting skills'. Markham (1997) also sees the consultancy role as one that has a wider applicability in organizations: 'consultancy skills are increasingly seen as an important element of every business person's toolkit' (1997: xiii). It is not only consultants, then, who are engaged in consultancy activities: 'nowadays, staff functions have increasingly to engage with their colleagues in a consultancy fashion. Competence in consultancy skills is vital to all' (1997: 1). Such 'consultancy skills' must be applied not only by consultants in dealing with clients, but also by managers in dealing with subordinates. This approach to management consultancy is even more pronounced in Markham's (2001) edited collection *How to Be Your Own Management Consultant*. The very title of this book – which serves as a succinct summation of Schein's main argument in the second volume of *Process Consultation* – explicitly emphasizes the need for managers to adopt the consultancy role in their own organization.

The fact that managers can – indeed, *have to* – adopt a consultancy role suggests that the very meaning of consultancy is currently being modified:

The word 'consultation' has always implied giving advice…Today, the concept of consultation and consultancy is changing rapidly. It is a set of activities designed to improve things. This can be and is done by managers as well as consultants. The role of consultancy is now multi-faceted. It now involves relationships between manager and subordinate just as much as it involves relationships between clients and consultants. (Margerison, 2001: 10)

Whereas management consultancy once referred solely to forms of business counselling, it now refers to establishing and maintaining relationships in organizations, whether between consultants and clients or between managers and subordinates. While this certainly entails a shift in the way we understand consultancy, more importantly it also implies a shift in the way we understand management itself. A manager must draw on consultancy knowledge (such as the model of process consultation) in addition to, or even in the place of, managerial knowledge. Margerison (2001: 104) directly echoes Schein on this point: 'An effective manager is increasingly an effective consultant'.

Admittedly, the notion of the 'manager-as-consultant' represents the extreme end of the consultancy spectrum. Most consultants, it should be said, simply provide technical expertise to managers in a specific operational area and do not seek to transform the traditional manager-subordinate relation into a 'consultant-client relation'. But this does not detract from the meaning and significance of Schein's model of process consultation. As we have shown, this model provides a way for consultants to deal with clients as well as a way for managers to deal with subordinates. To this extent, process consultation serves not only as the 'ideal type' of consultancy but also as the 'model for managerial excellence'. By replacing the relational component of management with the relational component of consultancy, however, the model of process consultation risks becoming a form of managerial knowledge; the power of consultants over managers is thus jeopardized by the very same factor that underwrites its success. Such is the real lesson to be drawn from Schein's work, which brings with it both a promise and a threat to the future profession of organizational consultancy.

Conclusion

In his autobiographical essay 'The Academic as Artist: Personal and Professional Roots', published in the *Management Laureates* series, Schein (1993: 50) states that '[t]he most consistent feedback I get on my writing is that I am somehow able to make things clear'. Having examined the first and second volumes of *Process Consultation*, we might wonder whether we would be tempted to give Schein slightly different feedback on his work. While his style of writing is certainly clear enough, the ideas he expresses in his books are characterized by considerable ambiguity. By unsettling the conventional distinction between 'consultancy' and 'management', it is impossible for us to say conclusively whether the model of process consultation is a part of consultancy knowledge, a part of managerial knowledge, or somehow a part of both. But perhaps this is the point. As Armstrong reminds us, an occupational group must maintain 'a certain mystique and indeterminacy' around their knowledge base so as to retain exclusive control over it, thus preventing other occupational groups from using the same set of techniques (1984: 101; 1985: 134; see also Larson, 1977: 31-2). Analogously, if Schein's work possesses a somewhat elusive quality, then it is not difficult to see how this might allow process consultants to retain a monopoly over the model of process consultation, thereby rendering it inaccessible to managers – even at the same time as managers are entreated to apply it themselves in their own organizations. In any case, what *is* clear from the preceding discussion is that Schein's work is worthy of extensive 'practical criticism' in its own right (see Armstrong and Lilley, 2008). Such a task, it should be said, can be undertaken without either betraying the strictures of a disciplinary field (in this case, the sociology of management) or by reducing the 'applied' intent of *Process Consultation*. It is in this spirit that we have sought to engage with the work of Schein, encompassing as it does both the realm of academia and the world of business.

References

Armstrong, P. (1984) 'Competition between the organizational professions and the evolution of management control strategies', in K. Thompson (ed.) *Work, Employment and Unemployment: Perspectives on Work and Society*. Milton Keynes and Philadelphia: Open University Press.

Armstrong, P. (1985) 'Changing management control strategies: The role of competition between accountancy and other organizational professions', *Accounting, Organizations and Society*, 10(2): 129-148.

Armstrong, P. (1987) 'Engineers, management and trust', *Work, Employment and Society*, 1(4): 421-440.

Armstrong, P. (1991) 'The divorce of productive and unproductive management', in C. Smith, D. Knights, and H. Willmott (eds) *White-Collar Work: The Non-Manual Labour Process*. Basingstoke and London: Macmillan.

Armstrong, P. (1992) 'The engineering dimension and the management education movement', in G. L. Lee and C. Smith (eds) *Engineers and Management: International Comparisons*. London: Thomson Learning.

Armstrong, P. (1996) 'The expunction of process expertise from British management syllabi: An historical analysis', in I. Glover and M. Hughes (eds) *The Professional-Managerial Class: Contemporary British Management in the Pursuer Mode*. Aldershot: Ashgate.

Armstrong, P. and S. Lilley (2008) 'Practical criticism and the social sciences of management', *ephemera: theory & politics in organization*, 8(4): 353-370.

Barker, J. R. (1993) 'Tightening the iron cage: Concertive control in self-managing teams', *Administrative Science Quarterly*, 38(2): 408-437.

Barker, J. R. (1999) *The Discipline of Teamwork: Participation and Concertive Control*. London: Sage.

Carroll, S. J. and D. J. Gillen (1987) 'Are the classical management functions useful in describing managerial work?', *Academy of Management Review*, 12(1): 38-51.

Ezzamel, M., S. Lilley, and H. Willmott (1994) 'The "New Organization" and the "New Managerial Work"', *European Management Journal*, 12(4): 454-461.

Ezzamel, M. and H. Willmott (1998) 'Accounting for teamwork: A critical study of group-based systems of organizational control', *Administrative Science Quarterly*, 43(2): 358-396.

Fayol, H. (1949) *General and Industrial Management*, trans. Constance Storrs. London: Pitman.

Grey, C. (1999) '"We are all managers now"; "We always were": On the development and demise of management', *Journal of Management Studies*, 36(5): 561-585.

Hales, C. P. (1986) 'What do managers do? A critical review of the evidence', *Journal of Management Studies*, 23(1): 88-115.

Hancock, P. and M. Tyler (2004) '"MOT your life": Critical management studies and the management of everyday life', *Human Relations*, 57(5): 619-645.

Hancock, P. and M. Tyler (2008) 'Beyond the confines: Management, colonization and the everyday', *Critical Sociology*, 34(1): 29-49.

Kotter, J. P. (1982) *The General Managers*. New York: Free Press.

Kubr, M., et al. (2002) *Management Consulting: A Guide to the Profession, 4th Edition*. Geneva: International Labour Office

Larson, M. S. (1977) *The Rise of Professionalism: A Sociological Analysis*. Berkley: University of California Press.

Margerison, C. J. (2001) *Managerial Consulting Skills: A Practical Guide, 2nd Edition*. Aldershot: Gower.

Markham, C. (1997) *Practical Management Consultancy, 3rd Edition*. Milton Keynes: Accountancy Books.

Markham, C. (ed.) (2001) *How to Be Your Own Management Consultant: Consultancy Tools and Techniques to Improve Your Success, 2nd edition*. London and Milford: Kogan Page.

Mintzberg, H. (1973) *The Nature of Managerial Work*. London: Harper Collins.

Schein, E. H. (1969) *Process Consultation: Its Role in Organization Development*. Reading, Mass.: Addison-Wesley.

Schein, E. H. (1987) *Process Consultation, Volume II: Lessons for Managers and Consultants*. Reading, Mass.: Addison-Wesley.

Schein, E. H. (1993) 'The academic as artist: Personal and professional roots', in A. G. Bedeian (ed.) *Management Laureates: A Collection of Autobiographical Essays, Volume 3*. Greenwich and London: Jai.

Schein, E. H. (1997) 'The concept of 'client' from a process consultation perspective', *Journal of Organizational Change Management*, 10(3): 202-216.

Schein, E. H. (1999) *Process Consultation Revisited: Building the Helping Relationship*. Reading, Mass.: Addison-Wesley.

Schein, E. H. (2006) 'From brainwashing to organizational therapy: A conceptual and empirical journey in search of 'systemic' health and a general model of change dynamics. A drama in five acts', *Organization Studies*, 27(2): 287-301.

Schein, E. H. (2009) *Helping: How to Offer, Give, and Receive Help*. San Francisco: Berrett-Koehler.

Schein, E. H., I. Schneier, and C. H. Barker (1961) *Coercive Persuasion: A Socio-Psychological Analysis of the 'Brainwashing' of American Civilian Prisoners by the Chinese Communists*. New York: W.W. Norton.

Sewell, G. (1998) 'The discipline of teams: The control of team-based industrial work through electronic and peer surveillance', *Administrative Science Quarterly*, 43(2): 397–428.

Sewell, G. and B. Wilkinson (1992) 'Someone to watch over me: Surveillance, discipline and the just-in-time labour process', *Sociology*, 26(2): 271–289.

Watson, T. J. (1994) *In Search of Management: Culture, Chaos and Control in Managerial Work*. London: International Thomson Business Press.

Whitley, R. (1989) 'On the nature of managerial tasks and skills: Their distinguishing characteristics and organization', *Journal of Management Studies*, 26(3): 209-224.

Notes

[1] Schein's original 1969 book was revised and republished in 1988 under the title *Process Consultation, Volume I: Its Role in Organization Development.*

[2] Schein (1987: 117) writes that 'the question of who is actually the client can be ambiguous and problematical', since a variety of people can be designated as 'the client' in an organization. For the most part, 'the client' refers to an employee in a managerial position who 'owns' the organizational problem and who is able to pay for consultancy services with a part of their departmental budget (Schein, 1987: 117-8; see also 1997). Our use of the term 'client' will be restricted to this meaning.

[3] The model of process consultation has its roots in a variety of disciplines, including social psychology, sociology, and anthropology, as well as organizational areas such as leadership, training, and mentoring (1969: 12-3). Unfortunately, there is no space here to describe the interconnections between process consultation and these other fields of knowledge.

[4] It is for this reason that Kubr, et al. (2002: 72) assert that '[w]hile any consulting involves some collaboration with the client, the process approach is a collaborative approach par excellence'.

5 This is what Armstrong (1984; 99: 1985; 132), following Larson (1977), calls the advancement of a 'collective mobility project' by an organizational profession.

6 In *Process Consultation Revisited*, Schein (1999: 1-2) expands this concept of 'help' so that '[t]he ability to be an effective helper also applies to spouses, friends, managers vis-à-vis their superiors, subordinates, and peers, parents vis-à-vis their own parents and children, and teachers vis-à-vis their students'. His most recent book pushes the boat out even farther: the concept of 'help' now applies not only to 'the *consultant* trying to improve the functioning of an organization', but also to 'the *friend* supplying the word that is on the tip of your tongue', 'the *suicide hotline operator* assisting someone in distress', 'the *funeral director* helping the grieving family cope with death', and 'the *nurse* assisting a patient with the bedpan' (Schein, 2009: 5-6: emphasis in original).

5

Multiple Failures of Scholarship: Karl Weick and the Mann Gulch Disaster

Thomas Basbøll

'If now the dead of this fire should awaken and I should be stopped beside a cross…' Norman Maclean

Introduction

The 2006 Academy of Management meeting included a preconference professional development workshop (PDW) on 'richness'. 'The intent of this PDW,' wrote Sara Rynes, the editor of the *Academy of Management Journal*, 'was to remedy the paucity of formal instruction in qualitative methods at many universities' (2007: 13). Karl Weick was invited as one of 'the world's best qualitative researchers in the field of management and organizations' and his contribution (Weick, 2007) was printed in a special editors' forum of AMJ the following year. He chose to talk about 'the generative properties of richness', and used what Rynes described as 'his own experiences in studying wildland firefighters' as the core of his presentation, the most notable example of which is of course his 'reanalysis' of the 1949 Mann Gulch disaster (Weick, 1993). That paper, which he had originally presented as a keynote address, was published in the *Administrative Science Quarterly* at the request of one of its editors (Weick, 2007: 15). The editor has since identified himself as Bob Sutton, who recalls that Weick had been hesitant to publish it because it was perhaps 'too weird' for what Sutton describes as a 'respectable' and 'rather stuffy' journal. But Sutton 'begged a little', and the paper ultimately 'got rave reviews from distinguished peers and was soon published' (Sutton, 2009). It has since become one of Weick's most famous studies, and is, indeed, often counted among not only his own

85

finest work but, as Rynes (2007: 13) put it, 'the best of the best' in qualitative methodology. Moreover, following John van Maanen's (1995) use of it in his famous exchange with Jeffrey Pfeffer during the so-called Paradigm Wars, the success of Weick's Mann Gulch analysis can be taken as a major contribution to what Michael Rowlinson (2004: 617) has called 'the victory of style over theory' in sensemaking research. The paper is in every respect a seminal contribution to the managerial sciences, having affected both our perception of organizations and our approach to scholarship.

In the history of wildland firefighting, and in the local history of west-central Montana, Mann Gulch, August 5, 1949, marks the time and place of the tragic deaths of thirteen young men. The story of the crew of smokejumpers who lost their race against the forest fire they were fighting has been told and retold, both in prose (Maclean, 1992) and in song (Keelaghan, 1995). In the literature of the managerial sciences, meanwhile, it represents a 'cosmology episode' occasioned by 'multiple failures of leadership' (Weick, 1993: 650). Although one may always quibble about the nuances in an interpretation of a discipline's consensus about a particular event, it is safe to say that the received view in the management literature is that the disaster resulted from a lack of leadership and, more profoundly, a lack of wisdom. This interpretation of the actions and attitudes of Wagner Dodge and his crew has been canonized in Michael Useem's collection of 'stories of triumph and disaster', *The Leadership Moment* (1998). Citing both Weick and Useem, Glynn and Jamerson speak straightforwardly of 'Dodge's failure'; he failed 'quite literally' to 'breathe life' into his organization, we are told. Under his leadership, Dodge's men grew increasingly confused and ultimately panicked instead of following his instructions; their organization was a mere 'shell' that, for lack of 'heedful interrelating', was disposed to disintegrate at the critical (i.e., leadership) moment (Glynn and Jamerson, 2006: 156). If he had taken his role as leader more seriously, built his team properly, and maintained his authority throughout the ordeal, it is argued, his men might well have survived. The lesson that is most often emphasized by readers of Weick's analysis is that what was missing in Mann Gulch was an 'attitude of wisdom', a kind of epistemic humility. Because Dodge was taciturn about the unfolding crisis, his crew was overly confident that they would get the fire under control before morning. In his contribution to Cameron, Dutton and Quinn's *Positive Organization Scholarship*, Weick emphasizes the related 'breakdown of trust' (Weick, 2003: 75), which can of course be traced back to Dodge's failure as a leader. In the eyes of organization theorists, then, Wagner Dodge must bear a great portion of the responsibility for the deaths of thirteen young men under his command.

Since Dodge himself died only a few years later, long before Weick's article was written, he has not been able to defend himself against the charge. Indeed, the author of the most detailed attempt to understand Dodge's situation, Norman Maclean, died before his book, *Young Men and Fire* (1992), had even been published, and that book was Weick's sole source of factual information about the disaster. Interestingly, immediately after restating his claim that the Mann Gulch disaster resulted from 'multiple failures of leadership' that unleashed 'senselessness, panic, and cosmological questions', Weick proposed to conclude his analysis 'just about where Maclean would want us to end' (1993: 650). My aim here is essentially to challenge that closing claim. I suspect there are several points at which Norman Maclean would have liked Weick to end his analysis, certainly points at which he would have encouraged him to pause for reflection. Ultimately, I think he would have wanted us to stop well short of concluding that Wagner Dodge failed as a leader. Indeed, my rereading of Maclean's book suggests that we must replace our current sense of Dodge's failure as a leader with a much more accurate sense of Weick's failures of scholarship.

Mann Gulch and the Leadership Moment

Maclean's book is about both social and natural forces, and we can provisionally distinguish the Mann Gulch 'disaster' from the Mann Gulch 'fire'. The *fire* started on August 4, 1949, when lightning struck the ridge between Mann Gulch and Meriwether Canyon, in the Helena National Forest of west-central Montana. It burned for five days and spread to over 4500 acres before it was finally brought under control. The *disaster*, meanwhile, occurred shortly before 6:00 pm on August 5, 1949, when a crew of smokejumpers was caught in a 'blowup'; three survived, thirteen died. The fire had been spotted on August 4 by a forest ranger stationed in Meriwether Canyon and, following standard procedure, the crew of smokejumpers parachuted into the Gulch at around 4:00 pm the next day. It spent its first hour in the Gulch calmly collecting its gear in an area that would be covered in flames at the end of the second. The crew ultimately had no influence on the development of the fire in that time; the firefighters and the fire had simply been brought together at the worst possible moment, a fateful one for most of them. It is no wonder, then, that Maclean describes the event as a *tragedy*.

Weick's contribution is to construe the tragedy as what Useem (1998) would later call a 'leadership moment'. This is, at first pass, a natural way to build on Maclean's dramatic interpretation of the disaster: a meeting of 'young men and fire', man and nature. By focusing on the leader of the crew, we have a way of personifying the event in a 'tragic figure', i.e., an *individual* who 'loses' what was ultimately a *collective* struggle. The event now becomes *his* story; it becomes history. Just as the Battle of Little Big Horn is *Custer's* Last Stand, the Mann Gulch disaster has become *Dodge's* ultimate failure as a leader, his 'leadership moment' gone wrong. While Maclean himself makes the comparison to Custer's fateful battle on several occasions, however, he ultimately abandons what he calls 'the disgraced officer's plot', which is, he argues, more useful for making films than for explaining what actually happened in 1949 (Maclean, 1992: 155-6). As Maclean saw it, the events in Mann Gulch were best understood, not in terms of organizational behaviour, but in terms of what we might call *infernal* behaviour, i.e., the behaviour of the fire. It was Weick's 're-analysis' – hot off his reading Maclean's just-published book – that appropriated the tragedy for the managerial sciences by placing the emphasis on *organizing* and *leadership* in explaining the deaths of the firefighters. While the *fire* was caused by a lightning strike, 'the *disaster* at Mann Gulch,' says Weick, 'was produced by the interrelated collapse of sensemaking and structure' (2001: 105, my emphasis). This is clearly presented as an *empirical* conclusion that can be drawn from the facts of the case, and we can see that it is not a trivial claim by imagining its negation. According to Weick, the disaster could have been averted; the sensemaking and structure of the crew could have been prevented from collapsing. Adequate leadership, which would have fostered 'resilience', he argues, is what would have made the difference.

It is this claim that I want to subject to critical scrutiny. To do so, it is fortunately not necessary to investigate the facts of the Mann Gulch disaster at first hand. After all, Weick claimed only to have read Maclean's book before arriving at his empirical conclusions, and we can do the same. On the basis of that book, then, Weick makes two key claims about the behaviour of the crew of firefighters. The death of thirteen firefighters is explained by their 'stubborn belief' (Weick, 1993:

636) that the fire they were fighting would be under control by the next morning and their subsequent 'panic' (ibid.: 637-8) when this belief was confronted with the realities of the fire. At the decisive moment, Weick claims, with both their role structure and their worldview in ruins, they were unable to understand an instruction from their foreman that might have saved them. It is easy to see how these two claims support a conclusion about an 'interrelated collapse of sensemaking and structure'. It is also easy to see how this analysis might locate a 'failure of leadership', since a good leader would presumably know how to temper the crew's beliefs about the fire with, say, an 'attitude of wisdom' and would, certainly, inspire the sort of confidence that would be required to keep the crew from panicking. The important question is whether Weick's source, Maclean's book, licenses the necessary conclusions.

The answer, as I have already suggested, is no – in fact, not at all. Weick distorts key facts in Maclean's account, and omits others, in order to get the story of Mann Gulch to serve his ends and thereby illustrate his theory of sensemaking in organizations. According to Maclean, the fire fighters quickly abandoned their view of the fire as one they would soon have under control; they did not panic and, indeed, experienced real fear only after it was too late to affect their sensemaking. More generally, it is clear that Maclean ultimately exonerates the sensemaking of the crew, and Dodge's leadership, finding instead that what happened in Mann Gulch cannot be attributed to organizational behaviour but resulted from the behaviour of the fire. When all the factors are properly weighed, the crew was essentially doomed from the start to be caught up in what Maclean calls a 'conflagration of forces', neither material nor social but, simply, infernal. No amount of resilience, sensemaking, or organizing of any kind could have saved them. To show this, I will compare Weick's paper with Maclean's book in regard to their answer to three key questions about the Mann Gulch disaster. First, did the smokejumpers panic? Second, did 'positive illusions' about the seriousness of the fire kill the smokejumpers? Finally, would wisdom and heedfulness have saved the smokejumpers? Weick answers yes to all three. Maclean, as I want to show, clearly answers no.

Did the Smokejumpers Panic?

As mentioned, Weick's analysis identified two factors that 'produced' the disaster in Mann Gulch: a collapse of sensemaking and a collapse of structure. Though he emphasizes that they are 'interrelated', each of these general explanations are tied to specific facts that Weick adduces about what happened in the gulch. Thus, the collapse of sensemaking was tied to 'positive illusions' about the seriousness of the fire, which I will deal with in the next section, and the collapse of structure precipitated panic among the members of the crew, which I will deal with here.

Weick theorizes the 'panic' of the crew with a passage from Freud's *Group Psychology and the Analysis of the Ego* that, as Weick puts it, 'reversed' the then commonly held view that panic causes group disintegration (Weick, 1993: 638). Rather, argued Freud, group disintegration causes panic; it is when members of a group suddenly lose their role structures (such as those tied to command) that 'a gigantic and senseless fear is set free'. This is of course exactly what Weick needs in order to make his argument that what went wrong in Mann Gulch was a 'collapse of sensemaking': poor leadership caused group disintegration, and group disintegration caused panic, which, in turn, is tantamount to senselessness. Accordingly, he describes the minutes leading up to the disaster in terms that resonate with Freud's account of panic in military groups:

> As the crew moved toward the river and became more spread out, individuals were isolated and left without explanations or emotional support for their reactions. As the ties weakened, the sense of danger increased, and the means to cope became more primitive. The world rapidly shifted from a cosmos to chaos as it became emptied of order and rationality. (Weick, 1993: 638)

While this does indeed describe the preconditions of panic suggested by Freud, it is hard to find support for it in Maclean's account. Here, for example, is his description of the crew at about the same time that Weick described as a world quickly shifting 'from a cosmos to chaos':

> Now that they weren't going to hit the fire head on, some of the excitement was gone. ... The crew, though, was still happy. They were not in that high state of bliss they had been in when they expected to have the fire out by tomorrow morning and possibly be home that same

night to observe tall dames top-heavy with beer topple off bar stools. On the other hand, attacking the fire from the rear would make the job last longer and mean more money… (Maclean, 1992: 66)

I will return to this clear indication that the crew's belief that they would have the fire out by morning was anything but 'stubborn'. What is interesting here is that the mood of the crew is described in such radically different terms. Like us, Maclean and Weick know that the crew is in real danger; indeed, most of them will be dead not much more than fifteen minutes later. But in his analysis Weick simply projects (to use a Freudian notion) this knowledge onto his interpretation of the crew's emotional state, while Maclean, who has formed a detailed sense of what the crew would have thought and felt about what they were experiencing at the time, notes that they were not only unafraid but 'happy', not only not irrational but thinking about how they would spend their paychecks when they got back to the base. Though it is true that the crew was getting spread out and confused on the slope of the gulch (Maclean, 1992: 65), there is simply no indication that the group is disintegrating in the manner Freud described.

The most important difference between Weick's account and Maclean's is that the former posits both fear and panic in the Gulch, and the latter explicitly concludes the opposite. Here's how Maclean discusses the question of whether the crew panicked:

The survivors say they weren't panicked, and something like that is probably true. Smokejumpers are selected for being tough but Dodge's men were very young, and as he testified, none of them had ever been on a blowup before and they were getting exhausted and confused. (Maclean, 1992: 72)

Rumsey and Sallee say the men did not panic, but by now all began to fear death and were in a race with it. (ibid.: 93)

The first quote describes how they felt at the beginning of their race with the fire; the second quote how they felt as they neared the end. Perhaps the most categorical rejection of the panic thesis, however, comes in Maclean's conclusion. We here find all the relevant notions of structure and disintegration *in precisely the wrong order* for the thesis to hold:

> As the smokejumpers went up the hill *after leaving Dodge* it was like a
> great jump backwards into the sky – they were suddenly and totally
> without command and suddenly without structure and suddenly free to
> disintegrate and free to finally be afraid. *The evidence is that they were not
> afraid before this moment*, but now great fear suddenly possessed the empty
> places. (ibid.: 297, my emphasis)

Freud's theory (and therefore Weick's) requires that the crew be without
command, without structure, free to disintegrate, and free to feel fear
before reaching Dodge and his famous escape fire, which the crew, in its
panic, did not understand. Maclean tells us quite clearly that these
preconditions for panic only arose after it was too late. According to
Weick's only source of information about the disaster, then, it was *not*
'produced by a collapse of structure', as he claims. In any case, contrary
to Weick's major empirical claim, the evidence suggests that the crew
did not panic.

Did 'Positive Illusions' Kill the Smokejumpers?

We saw above that Maclean mentions in passing that the crew was 'not
in that high state of bliss they had been in when they expected to have
the fire out by tomorrow morning' (1992: 66). With this in mind,
Weick's second major empirical claim becomes quite puzzling.
According to Weick, the crew maintained a 'stubborn belief that it faced
a 10:00 fire' (1993: 636), i.e., a fire that it would have under control by
ten o'clock the next morning. Part of the confusion that ultimately led
to disaster, he argues, is that the crew grew uneasy because the imagined
ten o'clock fire 'did not act like one' (ibid.: 635). Even in the face of
this, he says, 'People rationalized this image until it was too late. And
because they did, less and less of what they saw made sense' (ibid.: 635).
He takes this as 'a powerful reminder that positive illusions can kill
people' (ibid.: 636). Maclean's account, meanwhile, contradicts this
explanation of what happened on virtually every point.

Weick argues that if the crew had not been so stubborn in its belief
that the fire would be under control by ten o'clock the next morning
they would have communicated more about what was going on:

> It is striking how little communication occurred during the three and a
> half hours of this episode. There was little discussion during the noisy,
> bumpy plane ride, and even less as individuals retrieved equipment
> scattered on the north slope. After a quick meal together, people began

hiking toward the river but quickly got separated from one another. Then they were suddenly turned around, told to run for the ridge, and quickly ran out of breath as they scaled the steep south slope. (Weick, 1993: 644)

We must note in passing that Weick here gets the slopes of the Gulch wrong. The crew fled up the *north* slope of the Gulch, not the south slope (though perhaps he means the south slope of the *ridge*). What is much more important is that a crucial conversation did take place while the cargo was collected and the meal was eaten. Dodge and a fireman who was already on the scene decided that the vegetation on the south slope (where the fire was) posed a danger to the crew. They then abandoned the idea of fighting it head on like a ten o'clock fire and decided to get out of what Dodge described as a 'death trap' (Maclean, 1992: 63-65). It should be noted that these details are in Weick's account of the incident (Weick, 1993: 628-9) but are then ignored in his analysis. One must conclude that Weick likes the drama of words like 'death trap' but would not grant that this showed that Dodge (and the crew) had revised their opinion of the fire and their situation. When we read Maclean for ourselves, however, we learn quite unambiguously that they had no 'stubborn beliefs' and no 'positive illusions'.

Perhaps the source of Weick's misreading lies in a sentence on page 34 of Maclean's book. Like most fires, the Mann Gulch fire began as a 'ground fire' and the basic approach to fighting such a fire is to get to it early, while it is still small, surround it (by clearing flammable materials around it), and then keep it contained until it burns itself out. 'Until an hour before the end, that is what the smokejumpers expected the fire to be—hard work all night but easing up by morning' (Maclean, 1993: 34). This sentence must be understood in the context of the timeline of events for the whole disaster, however. Taken out of context, it does seem like the crew 'held onto' a belief in a fire they would have out by morning until the end of the ordeal (i.e., the final hour). But to properly understand its significance we must keep in mind that they did not begin to approach the fire during their first hour in the gulch. More importantly, they had been in the gulch only two hours when disaster struck. That is, as soon as the crew began to engage with the fire, they realized it would not be out by morning. Moreover, even at that time there was no objective indication of anything other than the *risk* of a blowup, and that risk was immediately spotted by Dodge and the forest ranger on the scene; they evaluated the situation together and took the only appropriate course of action. In fact, the phrase 'ten o'clock fire' is less an expression of an empirical assessment of a fire, as Weick seems to think, and more an expression of an attitude (Maclean, 1992: 19), a kind of watchword, and, in fact, a policy (Omi, 2005: 94); it was simply their job to do everything they could to get the fire under control before morning. Weick distorts, not the times themselves, but our sense of the timing of events, by getting us to think that the whole last hour was an unfolding crisis. What in fact happened, as Weick fondly cites (but does not understand) Maclean to say, was that 'the upgulch breeze suddenly [turned] to murder' (Maclean, 1992: 217; Weick, 1993: 641). This happened at a moment when they did not have a clear view of the fire, which means that they were at first, and unwittingly, walking towards the fire, and then forced to turn around and run away from it.

While the crew did not hold positive illusions about the fire, then, they did lack knowledge and, for a few unavoidable minutes, perceptual input. At the time, fighting forest fires was a relatively new trade, and there was little scientific research into the behaviour of fire in a wildland setting. Tellingly, while Weick (1993: 650) notes the possibility that an 'inadequate understanding of leadership processes in the late [19]40s' may share part of the blame, he leaves Maclean's observations about fire science out of the account. Maclean notes, for example, that early fire researchers worked with relatively simple models based on what were essentially laboratory experiments to test how various materials burn. This leaves many complexities out of account and, as Maclean puts it, you end up trying to 'approach infinity with nothing more than a mishmash of little things you know about a lot of little things—certainly with nothing that could have been put in a hand calculator and dropped with Wag Dodge into Mann Gulch to avert his tragedy' (Maclean, 1992: 262). Dodge was approaching infinity with decidedly finite means and at this clear marker of the limits of his knowledge we may turn to the question of his judgment. After all, Weick often leaves us with the impression that 'sensemaking' is tantamount to 'wisdom' (see Weick, 2004, for example).

Would Greater 'Wisdom' have Saved the Smokejumpers?

Weick defines wisdom as 'an attitude taken by persons toward the beliefs, values, knowledge, information, abilities, and skills that are held, a tendency to doubt that these are necessarily true or valid and to doubt that they are an exhaustive set of those things that could be known'

(Weick, 1993: 641, quoting Meacham, 1983: 187). We have already seen that the crew revised its beliefs about the fire and was now working with the (unfortunately all too valid) idea that they should get out of the way of the fire as quickly as possible. Indeed, Dodge wanted to get to the river (instead of the top of the south ridge as originally planned) because he wanted a good escape route: 'If worse came to worst and the wind changed and blew downgulch, the crew could always escape into the river' (Maclean, 1992: 64). This was clearly a rather 'wise' view, which took into account that he could not know exhaustively how the wind and, consequently, the fire would behave. Wisdom could not have made difference because, on Weick's own definition, the crew and its leader were already wise.

But there is a still deeper problem with the call for greater wisdom among smokejumpers. Weick ties the lack of wisdom to the lack of communication among the members of the crew. Simplifying somewhat, the received view is essentially that Dodge should have been more talkative (Useem, 1998: 54; Jamerson and Glynn, 2006: 156). Since Maclean is Weick's only source of information about Mann Gulch one would expect him to consult Maclean's book for suggestions about whether things like 'the attitude of wisdom' and 'heedful interrelating' would have worked there. More specifically, we want to know whether more 'communication' would have helped the crew? As it turns out, Maclean deals with this possibility in his discussion of how Mann Gulch changed how crews were selected and trained:

> the greatest concern was to remove the contradiction between training men to act swiftly, surely, and on their own in the face of danger and, on the other hand, training men to take orders unhesitatingly when working under command. *On a big fire there is no time and no tree under whose shade the boss and the crew can sit and have a Platonic dialogue about a blowup. If Socrates had been foreman on the Mann Gulch fire, he and his crew would have been cremated while they were sitting there considering it.* Dialogue doesn't work well when the temperature is approaching the lethal 140 degrees. (Maclean, 1992: 220, my emphasis)

This clear rejection of the subtler and more nuanced forms of communication that Weick proposes might have strengthened 'sensemaking' in Mann Gulch is left entirely out of Weick's discussion of the case, although it appears in the only book on the subject he had at that time read. It is not for me to decide whether it is Maclean or

Weick who is right; as a reader, however, one expects to be told when a conclusion conflicts with the conclusions of relevant experts. Indeed, my complaint here is not that Weick does not understand what happened in Mann Gulch; it is that he does not respect the views of the very expert he props his own authority up with. He does not understand, and does not seem to care, what is happening on the pages of Maclean's book.

The Disgraced Officer

Let us return to the question of where Maclean would have wanted us to end. Weick tells us that the essential components of his analysis 'flowed from a single book [he] consumed while acting as an armchair ethnographer' (Weick, 2007: 16). It is easy to imagine how this approach might get a number of critical details wrong, and in his book Maclean mentions another account that does just that: a movie 'supposedly based on the Mann Gulch fire' called *The Red Skies of Montana*. It fuses, he says, 'small broken pieces of truth' with a 'worn-out literary convention' (Maclean, 1992: 155) and it was his goal to recover the truth that had been covered over with convention, myth, and legend, supported only by the 'immortality' that accrues to a story that is 'rerun several times a year on TV'. There is a tendency, he noted, to impose a plot.

> This added life-giving plot is the old 'disgraced officer's plot', the plot in which the military leader has disgraced himself before his men, either because his action has been misunderstood by them or because he displayed actual cowardice, and at the end the officer always meets the same situation again but this time heroically (usually as the result of the intervening influence of a good woman). By the way, this plot has often been attached to movies and stories about Custer Hill. Perhaps this is a reminder to keep open the possibility that there is no ending in reality to the story of the Mann Gulch fire. If so, then let it be so—there's a lot of tragedy in the universe that has missing parts and comes to no conclusion, including probably the tragedy that awaits you and me. (Maclean, 1992: 155-6)

The ironies accumulate here. Jamerson and Glynn speak of how Dodge's leadership should have 'quite literally ... "breathed life" into [his] organization' (2006: 156), while in fact rehearsing what Maclean disparages as the 'life-giving plot' of a 'worn-out literary convention'. They may, perhaps, be excused for taking Weick's analysis on trust, as

Barbara Czarniawska (2005: 273), for example, says we must. Indeed, Weick assures us that Maclean's 'data' not only 'combat 12 of the fifteen sources [of invalidity] listed by Runkel and McGrath and are only "moderately vulnerable" to the other three', they are also drawn from the work of 'an experienced woodsman and storyteller [i.e., Maclean], who has "always tried to be accurate with the facts"' (Weick, 1993: 632; quoting Runkel and MacGrath, 1972: 191 and Maclean, 1992: 259). But after all Maclean's hard work, Weick's reanalysis returns us squarely to the tired plot we can see on TV, not just about firefighters, but police officers, soldiers, school teachers, and every other hero we might imagine. Maclean urges us to leave other possibilities open because, as he puts it, 'there's a lot of tragedy in the universe that has missing parts and comes to no conclusion'. Weick will not 'let it be so'. In his armchair, the Mann Gulch Disaster is once again Dodge's Leadership Failure, as the Battle of Little Big Horn is Custer's Last Stand.

Indeed, since Weick is trying to locate the cause of the disaster in the organizational sensemaking of the crew, he does very little to help us to understand the fire itself. This despite the fact that Maclean's conclusion is actually that Useem's 'leadership moment' is not very relevant in the case of Mann Gulch. Instead of retelling the cinematic plot of the 'disgraced officer', Maclean spent years trying to understand both the organizational *and infernal* behaviour that produced the outcomes that day. On this basis, he explains that the members of the crew were, for too long unwittingly, participants in a simple race against the fire. When they jumped, 'they were leaving an early station of the cross, where minutes *anywhere along the way* would have saved them' (Maclean, 1992: 57, my emphasis). It was only at the very last minute that 'leadership' might have been an issue, and at that same moment, as Maclean makes clear, neither causes nor responsibility can be confidently assigned to human agency or natural forces (1992: 289, see below).

Instead of noticing this, Weick makes an elaborate effort to establish the obvious point that a crew of firefighters is 'an organization' (1993: 632). He also dwells a bit strangely on the question of whether to describe the crew as an 'outfit' or 'nondisclosive intimacy' (ibid.: 647-8) – strange because these 'alternatives' are not grammatically interchangeable (and may be empirically compatible). Most surprisingly, however, he makes no effort at all to understand the relationship of the crew to the larger organization of the U.S. Forest Service, nor, though it turns out to be a relevant part of how they make sense of their job, the relationship of the firefighters to the U.S. government (Maclean, 1992: 51-2). While it ultimately made no difference, the disaster would have been easy to understand from an organizational point of view simply by noting the U.S. Forest Service's budget at the time (Maclean, 1992: 40-1). Crews were selected to fight particular fires by choosing names off the top of a list and seeing if they were currently in camp. After fighting a fire, the fire fighter was moved to the bottom of the list. The reason for this way of doing things is that they did not have the budget to keep crews together and on call in camp, but had to send individuals (not whole crews) out of camp to do various more menial tasks while waiting for fires to break out. This fact about the larger organizational structure in which Dodge's leadership was embedded is mentioned in passing in Weick's analysis and then, it seems, ignored in drawing his conclusions.

Although Maclean tells us about the 'prohibitive costs' (1992: 40) of alternative organizational schemes, this fact is left entirely out of Weick's study. This is a significant oversight, one would think, in the pages of the *Administrative Science Quarterly*. Indeed, while Maclean (1992: 41) notes that 'you don't have to be an administrative genius, to see in this organizational scheme of things the possibility of calamity in a crisis', Weick leaves the economics of the disaster entirely on the side, including, as is apparent in the quote above, the role of money as a motive for the firefighters. Indeed, the motives of the firefighters do not figure very seriously in Weick's analysis at all. This is unfortunate because the key moment in the episode, at least as history remembers it, is perhaps best understood by reference to the reasons the firefighters gave themselves for participating in such dangerous work, their 'character' if you will.

Only one or two minutes before the men died, Dodge invented a possible means of escape. As they ran out of the trees and into an open area of dry grass, he stopped and lit a match, with which he set the grass on fire. This cleared an area of flammable material where the men could lie down (albeit in still hot ashes), and this is in fact what Dodge did. It saved his life. But his crew did not heed his orders to follow him into the space cleared by his escape fire. Some may not have heard him and others may have believed that Dodge had lost his mind. This is significant because, as Maclean suggests, there was both a widespread belief and a 'high probability' that some smokejumpers were 'at least a little bit nuts' (Maclean, 1992: 20). Additionally, as we have seen, there was a necessary tension between a respect for authority (following a superior's orders) and the need for smokejumpers to 'act swiftly, surely, and on their own in the face of danger' (Maclean, 1992: 219). Only a particular kind of organization, would employ such men and organize them in the manner that it did. There is good reason, then, to believe that Mann Gulch was what Perrow aptly called a 'normal accident'. That is, given the organizational constraints (both psychological and economic) wildland firefighting was bound to face tragedy and disaster on occasion. It is only in the movies that the actions of a single participant make the difference between success and failure. Maclean, in any case, did not find the organizational issues, and certainly not the leadership issues, especially important or difficult to understand. By the time the story reaches Glynn and Jamerson (2006) through Useem (1998), however, Mann Gulch can unequivocally be referred to as 'Dodge's failure'.

I have been arguing that this is not just a dramatic simplication but a radical distortion of the facts. Interestingly, Maclean is very certain that much the story of what happened in Mann Gulch has been covered up or distorted by interested parties, and is in general very suspicious of the U.S. Forest Service, despite his overwhelming respect for the men and women who work for it. Weick, however, makes almost nothing of the subsequent efforts of the U.S. Forest Service to make sense of the disaster, nor of Maclean's struggle to come to terms with a difficult and elusive truth. (By contrast, he has no reservations about impugning the honesty and self-respect of firefighters (Weick, 2003: 75)). So while Weick finds 'Then Dodge saw it,' (Maclean 1992: 70) to be 'the most chilling sentence in the book' (1993: 629) – so chilling, indeed, that he embellishes it with an exclamation point that is not found in his source – an organization theorist might have found another sentence more salient: 'The Forest Service knew right away it was in for big trouble' (Maclean, 1992: 146). After all, it is here that we get an indication of the organizational problem implicit in the disaster rather than its Hollywood potential. It is ironic that Maclean, who took a much more critical view of the organizational structures that were involved in the Mann Gulch disaster, ultimately found that it was the behaviour of the fire, not the behaviour of the men, that needed explaining. It is less ironic that an 'armchair ethnographer' (Weick, 2007: 16) who is happy to rely on 'moves of the imagination made within soft constraints' (Weick, 2004: 654) would then leave his source's analysis and conclusions entirely on the side and essentially make up a story of his own to validate his theory.

Conclusion

Recalling everything he had learned through his study of the Mann Gulch disaster, Maclean offers a sobering thought experiment to prime the reflections of the would-be analyst. 'If now the dead of this fire should awaken and I should be stopped beside a cross, I would no longer be nervous if asked the first and last question of life, How did it happen?' (1992: 87) These words remind us that there is a human, even moral, dimension to the stories we tell about each other, especially stories about how people die. Can we, as organization scholars, the heirs of Weick's reanalysis, pretend not to be nervous about the prospect of meeting the dead young men of Mann Gulch? After all, as Mark Anderson (2006) has noted, organization scholars are not often critical of Weick's results. His equivocations and hedges notwithstanding, Glynn and Jamerson's (2006) perfectly reasonable, if wholly uncritical, reading of his analysis, for example, puts the blame squarely on Dodge. On Weick's version of the story, it was Dodge who failed to keep his men together; this failure was fatal, and the men died because they lost their heads in a crisis. Is that what we would tell them if they stopped us beside one of their crosses on the slope of Mann Gulch?

According to Maclean, the men were doomed from the moment they landed in the Gulch. As I noted above, abandoning the gulch at any moment, even a few minutes sooner 'anywhere along the way would have saved them' (Maclean, 1992: 57). Tragically, they had no way of knowing that that is what should have done. Even at the one point where Dodge had in fact been accused of erring, namely, his possibly endangering the crew by lighting the escape fire, Maclean settles on an aptly infernal image: a conflagration of causes. Shortly after the escape fire was lit,

> ...no component any longer had any individual responsibility for the simple reason that in a moment there were no individual components. Just conflagration. What was happening was passing beyond legality and morality and seemingly beyond the laws of nature, blown into a world where human values and seemingly natural laws no longer apply. (Maclean, 1992: 289)

It is the sort of verdict that perhaps only 'an experienced woodsman and storyteller, who has "always tried to be accurate with the facts"' (Weick, 1993: 632; quoting Maclean, 1992: 259) can make. And it is here, I think, and not with a judgment about Wagner Dodge's failure as a leader, that Maclean would have wanted us to stop, if at all. Though it took Weick a few hours in his armchair to 'make sense' of the tragedy (Weick, 2007: 16), Maclean himself never did stop trying to understand it. Perhaps that was because he half-expected one day to be held accountable before the ghosts of the men who died that day. Or perhaps he simply hadn't suffered from a 'paucity of formal instruction in qualitative methods' when he went to school.

References

Anderson, M. (2006) 'How can we know what we think until we see what we said? A citation and citation context analysis of Karl Weick's *The Social Psychology of Organizing*', *Organization Studies*, 27(11): 1675-1692.

Czarniawska, B. (2005) 'Karl Weick: concepts, style, reflection' in C. Jones and R. Munro (eds.) *Contemporary Organization Theory*. Oxford: Blackwell.

Glynn, M.A. and H. Jamerson (2006) 'Principled leadership: A framework for action' in E. D. Hess and K. S. Cameron (eds.) *Leading with values: positivity, virtue, and high performance*. Cambridge: Cambridge University Press.

Keelaghan, J. (1995) 'Cold Missouri waters'. *A Recent Future*. Tranquilla Music.

Maclean, N. (1992) *Young Men and Fire*. Chicago: University of Chicago Press.

Meacham, J. (1983) 'Wisdom and the context of knowledge: knowing that one doesn't know' in D. Kuhn and J.A. Meacham (eds.) *On the Development of Developmental Psychology*. Basel: Karger.

Omi, Philip N. (2005) *Forest Fires: A Reference Handbook*. Santa-Barbera: ABC-CLIO.

Rothermel, Richard C. (1993) 'Mann Gulch Fire: A race that couldn't be won', United States Department of Agriculture, Forest Service

Intermountain Research Station, General Technical Report INT-299, May 1993.

Rowlinson, M. (2004) 'Challenging the foundations of organization theory', *Work, Employment and Society*, 18(3): 607-620.

Runkel, P. J. and J. E. McGrath (1972) *Research on Human Behavior: A Systematic Guide*. New York: Holt, Rinehart & Winston.

Rynes, Sara L. (2007) 'Editor's foreword', *Academy of Management Journal*, 50(1): 13.

Sutton, R. I. 'Wisdom, randomness, and the Naskapi Indians', blogpost at *Work Matters*. July 06, 2009. Available at: http://bobsutton. typepad.com/my_weblog/2009/07/wisdom-randomness-and-the-naskapi-indians.html.

Useem, M. (1998) *The Leadership Moment: nine true stories of triumph and disaster and their lessons for all of us*. New York: Three Rivers Press.

Van Maanen, J. (1995) 'Style as theory', *Organization Science*, 6(1): 133-143.

Weick, K.E. (1989) 'Theory construction as disciplined imagination', *Academy of Management Review*, 14(4): 516-531.

Weick, K.E. (1993) 'The collapse of sensemaking in organizations: The Mann Gulch disaster', *Administrative Science Quarterly*, 38(4): 628-652.

Weick, K.E. (1995) 'What theory is not, theorizing is', *Administrative Science Quarterly*, 40(3): 385-390.

Weick, K.E. (1996) 'Drop your tools: An allegory for organization studies', *Administrative Science Quarterly*, 41(2): 301-313.

Weick, K.E. (2003) 'Positive organizing and organizational tragedy' in K. S. Cameron, J. E. Dutton, and R. E. Quinn (eds) *Positive Organizational Scholarship: Foundations of a New Discipline*. San Francisco: Berrett-Koehler Publishers.

Weick, K.E. (2004) 'Mundane poetics: Searching for wisdom in organization studies', *Organization Studies*, 25(4): 653-668.

Weick, K.E. (2007) 'The generative properties of richness', *Academy of Management Journal*, 50(1): 14-19.

6

The 'Nature of Man' and the Science of Organization

Jeroen Veldman

Introduction

In this chapter I will address the explicit assumptions about the nature of man as stated by Jensen and Meckling (1994). I have chosen their 'Nature of Man' article for a close reading because of the influential position that Jensen and Meckling occupy in agency theory and because of the effects of agency theory on organization theory. This article clearly shows the behavioural assumptions behind that theory and the effects of the way they use these behavioural assumptions to construct a tautological theory of organization.

Jensen and Meckling's 'The Nature of Man' (1994) is widely read and often cited. It was first published in the top-tier *Journal of Applied Corporate Finance* and was then reprinted in two widely used textbooks: *Foundations of Organizational Strategy* (Jensen, 1998) and *The New Corporate Finance – Where Theory Meets Practice* (Chew, 2001). Today it is also available through the Social Science Research Network online repository. Its influence no doubt owes much to the position that Jensen and Meckling themselves occupy in the economic discipline. Jensen and Meckling's 1976 article 'Theory of the Firm: Managerial Behavior, Agency Costs and Ownership Structure' is widely credited with first formulating the nexus of contracts theory (Bolman and Deal, 2008). They have pioneered new methods for determining executive compensation, especially the idea of linking their performance to stock market performance (Cassidy, 2002). Jensen has published on a number of occasions with Fama, on stock pricing (Fama and Jensen, 1969) and the separation of ownership and control (Fama and Jensen, 1983) and has also published with Black and Scholes (Black, Jensen and Scholes, 1972). These articles are widely cited in the areas of corporate governance and finance. 'The Nature of Man', then, is interesting in terms of its behavioural assumptions and the influences these assumptions have had on wider economic scholarship.

The article is also of interest to organization scholars, because it is very explicit in its statements on organizations and the way these assumptions relate to behavioural assumptions about individuals. In 1976, Meckling stated that

> there is a real possibility for developing 'A Science of Organizations,' a unified body of social science theory. It will be unified by use of the same model of the individual across organizations. Indeed, if I were certain that freedom to pursue social science research would survive the next 100 years, I would confidently predict that this is where the social sciences would go, hopefully, with a very sophisticated REMM. (Meckling, 1976: 559)

Indeed, the 'Science of Organizations' that Meckling describes has come to be. When Jensen and Meckling state in their introduction to 'The Nature of Man' that their ideas about the ontological status of organizations and the relation of individuals to organizations constitute 'the foundation for the agency model of financial, organizational, and governance structure of firms' (Jensen and Meckling, 1994: 1), they are not exaggerating. The REMM (Resourceful, Evaluative, Maximizing Model), which lies at the heart also of 'The Nature of Man' has become an important basis for thinking about organization in economics, finance and legal scholarship and has thereby fostered a common basis from which the REMM can be used across these disciplines. This can be seen in the various contexts in which the wider assumptions underlying the text have been exported. According to a list provided in the article, these assumptions have also been used in the fields of political studies to explain voter behaviour and the behaviour of regulators and bureaucrats (Jensen and Meckling, 1994: 35). In particular, it has been used to understand the constitution of the firm (Alchian and Demsetz, 1972; Arrow, 1971) where it informs issues of governance (Butler, 1989; Fama, 1980; Williamson, 1996) and intra-firm structures (Jensen and Meckling, 1976). More generally, the building blocks provided by REMM have been influential in economic and legal scholarship through their use in agency theory (Bratton, 1989). Considering this wide influence, Jensen and Meckling's understanding of the 'nature of man' then becomes important to consider, both for its behavioural assumptions and for its assumptions about the nature of organizations.

The Nature of Man

Jensen and Meckling's model of the nature of man is based on REMM: the Resourceful, Evaluative, Maximizing Model. This model 'best describes the systematically rational part of human behaviour.' (Jensen and Meckling, 1994: 1). In this model

> individuals are resourceful, evaluative maximizers. They respond creatively to the opportunities the environment presents, and they work to loosen constraints that prevent them from doing what they wish. They care about not only money, but about almost everything — respect, honor, power, love, and the welfare of others. The challenge for our society, and for all organizations in it, is to establish rules of the game that tap and direct human energy in ways that increase rather than reduce the effective use of our scarce resources. (Jensen and Meckling, 1994: 1)

REMM thus consists of a number of postulates regarding their nature: the individual cares and is an evaluator; each individual's wants are unlimited; the REMM is a maximizer, who 'acts to enjoy the highest level of value possible', and the REMM is a resourceful individual (the slippage from 'model' to 'individual' is in Jensen and Meckling's article). Rather than the mechanical behaviour that is generally attributed by economists to economic agents who follow the first three assumptions, REMM is gifted with ingenuity and creativity. On the basis of these postulates, they posit the existence of four different models of the nature of man: the economic, sociological, psychological and political model. These are 'pure types' described 'in terms of only the barest essentials' (Jensen and Meckling, 1994: 2-3). According to Jensen and Meckling, all these models are reductionist in one sense or another. The sort of reduction that is applied takes out essential characteristics of the models that have been developed so far and do not capture the essence of the Nature of Man:

> The usefulness of any model of human nature depends on its ability to explain a wide range of social phenomena (...) We want a set of

characteristics that captures the essence of human nature, but no more. (Jensen and Meckling, 1994: 2)

The question then becomes how Jensen and Meckling reject these models, how their own alternative model is constructed and what type of reductionism they apply to capture the essence, but no more.

They start by addressing the economic model of man. According to Jensen and Meckling, their REMM is very different from the short-run money-maximizer. The traditional economic model is just 'a reductive version of REMM' (Jensen and Meckling, 1994: 15) because REMM is willing to trade off short-run gains for long-term gains, including non-financial ones. However, the examples provided in the economic and psychological model fail to show how exactly REMM deals with or is concerned with 'goods' such as solitude, companionship, honesty, respect, love, fame, immortality, art, morality, honour, power, love, and the welfare of others (Jensen and Meckling, 1994: 1, 4, 15, 35). Moreover, the kind of creativity employed in their examples does not set the REMM apart from the standard economic model as a creative individual. Given the examples provided, the 'creativity' of REMM is constrained to the function of creating 'new opportunities' and mainly applied to circumvent the constraints of law or policy on human behaviour (Jensen and Meckling, 1994: 5). REMMs are therefore guided by a very narrow set of behavioural constraints, which we will also find in its economic nature.

In REMM, the word 'need' and its emotional impact is substituted by 'want' or 'desire' in order that we focus on 'alternatives, substitutes, and costs in a productive manner.' (Jensen and Meckling, 1994: 10). Removing the word 'need' creates never satiated individuals who are always willing to substitute. As a result, it is only cost that determines the amount of want, desire or demand for a good (Jensen and Meckling, 1994: 10). 'Needs' can then be considered in light of the want or desire of the asking party, rather than the need of the party 'selling'. In this way, everything becomes a negotiable object, as long as the right price is offered.

The acronym REMM fulfils two roles. Initially, it is a model for a complete description of human behaviour as a Resourceful, Evaluative, Maximizing *Model*. Through the addition of ingenuity and creativity, REMM turns out to be a description of individuals who need to make choices as well. REMM thus turns into a Model of generalized behaviour, conflated with the actions and nature of very concrete individuals in very particular settings. In this way, REMM as a model assumes that the behaviour of individual human beings can be mapped and used for a complete description of an (economic) system, while REMM as a description of individuals making individual choices simultaneously assumes that these individual human beings also express traits that escape this modelling exercise. The acronym REMM then assumes that it is both a complete description of a system, based on behavioural assumptions, while it simultaneously assumes the position of red-blooded individuals that somehow escape this model, presumably by those same behavioural assumptions.

This double setup with REMM is mirrored in the nature of man that Jensen and Meckling assume to be the basis of 'the sociological model'. Jensen and Meckling depict sociology as a system-approach, reducing individuals to system agents. The existence of social theory itself works to keep people in a state of lack of responsibility by the fact that social theory has either given the legitimation for or actually held them in a position where they would not take responsibility. Rather than providing a critique of social theory, 'sociological man' itself is turned from a theoretical system agent into a concrete individual through several examples. Sociological man turns out to be a victim by the fact he has been made able by sociologists to reduce himself to a victim, which then leads to an automatic disavowal of responsibility. Social theory itself, then, is responsible for a lack of responsibility on the part of the actors that it posits and for the state of the lives of those actors. According to Jensen and Meckling, their observations on the consequences of social theory and the nature of sociological man are based on social science literature and on public discussion (Jensen and Meckling, 1994: 2). However, they reference not one basic textbook that underpins these theoretical insights.

Like REMM, the sociological model is thus rendered as a simplified set of behavioural assumptions, which is then conflated with the actions of a red-blooded 'sociological man'. Unlike REMM, the behavioural assumptions that are projected onto sociological man leave no room for the same escape route through ingenuity and creativity.

From the sociological model it is a small step to the political model. We are warned to be extremely wary of this political model, since its logic does not withstand 'careful scrutiny' (Jensen and Meckling, 1994:

28). When government steps in, it is because individuals do not take responsibility for themselves (which can largely be attributed to the same behavioural assumptions underlying the sociological model) or because it is in the self-interest of politicians and bureaucrats (Jensen and Meckling, 1994: 29). The concept of the state subordinates human individuals, providing 'an example of the most extreme anti-individualist position, one which makes the organization itself the ultimate end.' (Jensen and Meckling, 1994: 23). As a result of this subordination 'Individual purpose is not only unimportant, it is an evil that must be stamped out.' (Jensen and Meckling, 1994: 23), a view that they trace back to Platonic origins. It must be noted, moreover, that 'Plato's views are not very different from those of most Marxists.' (Jensen and Meckling, 1994: 23). The circle is then closed by stating that 'In the Marxist model, individuals (…) behave according to the sociological model.' (Jensen and Meckling, 1994: 23). The philosophical-political alliance between Plato and Marx therefore leads to a sociological model that is meant to subordinate human individuals to organizations and states (Jensen and Meckling, 1994: 23).

In the light of this philosophical-political alliance and the antecedents of the sociological model it is not surprising that neither the state nor professional planning can be entrusted with economic matters. Instead, the price mechanism should determine how to relate needs or wants to available manpower, plant and material (Jensen and Meckling, 1994: 11). It is not made clear in this article, how these ideas relate to the fact it is still the state that is obliged to take necessary strong action to keep REMMs in check through harsh penalties on undesirable behaviour. As they state: 'as [education and rehabilitation programs] are accompanied by a reduction in the penalties and other "costs" of criminal behavior, we should not be surprised to find that REMMs more frequently choose to be criminals… it is not surprising from the viewpoint of REMM that Singapore has no drug problem… as illustrated by the recent caning of an American youth for vandalism, punishment for infraction of Singapore law is carried out swiftly and publicly' (Jensen and Meckling, 1994: 20). The interesting upshot from these remarks is, that criminal behavior is apparently a rational and defensible choice from the point of view of the REMM in the face of reduced costs for such behaviour. Moreover, this quote clearly shows the kind of 'costs' that Jensen and Meckling have in mind to effectively deter an individual REMM from criminal behaviour.

The article thus posits a Nature of Man that first pays lip service to an expansion of the economic model of man, then denounces the sociological, psychological and political models of man, finally to return to an REMM that functions both as a model and as an individual. This REMM in the end answers uncannily well to the behavioural assumptions that ordinarily underlie economic modelling (Bratton, 1989). REMM, then, appears very much like a construct that filters out sociological, psychological and political aspects from an ideal-type actor, assuming that ingenuity and creativity can only be applied to the remainder. Since REMM can be seen as a construct that hardly deviates from the standard behavioural assumptions that underlie economic modelling, the remainder that ingenuity and creativity can be applied to is simply the economic part of this ideal-type actor. REMM is therefore created by Jensen and Meckling through a crude sort of economic behaviourism at the expense of other scholarly disciplines.

However, the question remains why the explicit disavowal of organizations is necessary and how the conjunction of this disavowal with these behavioural assumptions is related to the wider success of agency theory in organization studies and more specifically in theories of governance. For these questions I will turn to the second part of the article.

A Science of Organizations

In the second part of the article, the postulate of 'creativity' and the straw man version of social theory turns into a denial of the existence of organizations. According to Jensen and Meckling, the general failure of the social sciences is that individuals are reduced to system-agents or 'atoms'. The undesirability of this position provides the hinge for a discussion of the nature of organization with methodological individualism as an ontological starting point. Methodological individualism posits that the agency of all associations, including the state, should be understood as attributable to individuals only in social science (Elster, 2007). In legal scholarship, this approach takes the human individual as the sole possessor of rights and duties. For this reason 'the only real starting point for political or legal theory is the individual' (Horwitz, 1985: 181).

In 'The Nature of Man', Jensen and Meckling invoke methodological individualism not to prioritize the theoretical attribution of agency to human individuals, but rather to dispel the organization itself. They posit that preferences cannot exist on the level of organizations or groups, but only on the level of individuals. In their view, organizations are purely conceptual artefacts and cannot really have purposes (Jensen and Meckling, 1994: 24). In addition, organizations do not want, need or suffer; organizations or groups of individuals cannot have preferences; organizations cannot be exploited, have conflicts, make war or be objects of compassion (Jensen and Meckling, 1994: 11). Jensen and Meckling are very insistent that all these properties should be attributed to individuals only:

> Concepts such as exploitation and conflict can be used in a group context to refer to more than one individual, but such language has meaning only in terms of individuals. Organizations cannot be exploited any more than machines or rocks can be exploited. Only individuals can be exploited, can suffer, can make war; only individuals can be objects of compassion. Organizations are purely conceptual artifacts, even when they are assigned the legal status of individuals. In the end, we can only do things to and for individuals. (Jensen and Meckling, 1994: 24)

The central statement is therefore that 'organizations are purely conceptual artifacts'.

The question is why Jensen and Meckling would be so vocal about this issue in an article on the Nature of Man and why they would explicitly add the statement 'even when they are assigned the legal status of individuals'. An answer to this question can be found in the wider assumptions about governance and the nature of man in agency theory.

In agency theory, it is assumed that any type of organization can be constructed as a nexus-of-contracts. At the basis of the nexus of contracts approach stands the contract. All types of relations within any type of organization are predicated on a contractual basis. This position advocates a free functioning of contracting individuals (including corporations) to order their affairs how they choose. The law then only sets rules, which actors can follow or choose to contract around. The 'firm' thus consists of a collection of rational contracting individuals with equal starting positions: '(...) the nexus of contracts consists of discrete contracts among rational economic actors, and the firm springs up as a spontaneous productive order.' (Bratton, 1989: 451). The 'organization' or 'firm' is now no longer an entity that exists in itself and can no longer be attributed with agency. As a result, the type of contractual agency that first adhered to the 'agents' can then be prioritized to establish the organization itself as a contracting 'nexus'. The image of the contracting individuals then reflects the REMM, both as a model of man and as a model of organization. Agency theory thus constructs a particular view of organization by explicitly rejecting the organization itself as a valid level of analysis.

This rejection of the organization becomes even more interesting in the context of Jensen and Meckling's addition of the words 'even when they are assigned the legal status of individuals', which means that agency theory not only attempts to construct the corporation as an aggregation of contracting individuals, but wants to reduce the separate legal entity that is created by incorporation in the same way. This is important, because the separate legal entity is not the same as the emergent identity of an aggregation of individuals constituting the corporation. The separate legal entity is different because it is a reified singular representation that sues, hires, fires and generally *contracts* in its own name. As a result, this representation of 'the firm' has a singular type of contracting agency. However, in the language of agency theory, the separate legal entity (understood as the nexus) can be reduced in the same way as any type of organization. As a result, it does not appear as a reified entity, but rather as a 'convenient fiction' (Bratton, 1989).

This idea is such a 'convenient fiction' for a number of reasons. First, it denies the fact that the separate legal entity as a contracting entity positions the separate legal entity as a type of contractual agent that is fundamentally different from other agents in the nexus. the separate legal entity appears as a 'legal fiction' with a singular contracting agency. The use of methodological individualism subsequently introduces the assumption that the separate legal entity itself has a theoretical position, comparable to that of a human being as a singular contracting agent. This leads to a position that both entities are equal and contract from an equal starting position. This equality in contracting possibilities is not reflected in business practice, where the constitution of the separate legal entity means that it can contract from a very different position to an individual human being in terms of agency, ownership, legal protection, liability, lifespan, access to information and access to organizational resources. The dismissal of the separate legal entity as a 'convenient fiction' therefore prioritizes the separate legal entity as a contracting agent over others by making human actors and the separate legal entity equal in theory, although their de facto economic and legal position are quite different.

Second, if the separate legal entity is dispelled as a 'fiction', this allows the corporation to be constructed as a generic 'firm', consisting of voluntary contractual relations between homogeneous and equal partners. By focusing on such voluntary contractual relations between ontologically homogeneous actors, this position effectively dispels the special position of the managerial conception of the corporation and the connected centralization of power and hierarchical connections within the corporate structure (Bratton, 1989). The intriguing remark of Jensen and Meckling that neither the state, *nor professional planning* can be entrusted with economic matters (Jensen and Meckling, 1994: 11) makes sense in this regard.

Third, the ownership of the corporation is held in legal theory by the separate legal entity in itself. The fact that the separate legal entity is a reified concept and is specifically what allows for a number of attributions, like those of ownership and purpose to this entity (Berle, 1997). Since the attribution of ownership is based on the legal reification of the separate legal entity, its implicit dismissal leads to an attribution of ownership to a constituent group within the corporate structure, rather than to the separate legal entity itself. In agency theory, this is used to argue for shareholder primacy on the basis of their 'ownership' of the corporation. The attribution of ownership to shareholders is a very debatable claim, because the increasing distance between the shareholders and their factual position within the corporation was the reason for the use of the separate legal entity in the first place (Ireland, 1999). Moreover, this attribution of ownership to a constituent group, rather than to individuals, is hardly compatible with methodological individualism.

Fourth, the use of the separate legal entity as a reified entity is what makes the concept of the holding company possible (Horwitz, 1985). To obfuscate the existence of the separate legal entity dismissal therefore means that the principles underlying the holding company become virtually invisible, both in economic and in legal discourse.

The separate legal entity thus fulfils a large number of important functions in economic theory. However, an explicit acceptance the separate legal entity as a reified construct would undermine the homogeneity of actors and agency that agency theory assumes and threaten the level playing field between all contractual actors in the market or in the firm. This undermines the reconstitution of the management corporation into a flat firm of voluntary contractual relations and it the attribution of ownership to a singular group within the corporate constituency. It is therefore necessary for agency theory to argue that the separate legal entity is 'merely' a convenient fiction in order to retain the homogeneity of its actors and to create a very specific theory of governance that disregards the specifics of the corporation.

Methodological individualism is therefore not the philosophical starting point for agency theory, but rather a necessary complement that is used to create a tautology: by denying the reification of any type of organization, an alternative idea of organization can be created that is simply the reflection of the assumptions posited on the level of the individual. This is where the double position of the REMM as both a model of red-blooded human individuals and as a model of organizations shows its importance. By conflating the two, Jensen and Meckling can invoke methodological individualism to produce this tautology.

The rejection of the organization in combination with this particular usage of methodological individualism has one more effect that should be noted. As argued above, the fact that the separate legal entity is included in the same capacity as human beings into legal and economic scholarship as a singular representation means that they can be constituted as *equal* entities. As a result the notion of a singular economic or legal 'actor', 'agent', 'person' or 'entity' can shed any explicit reference to a human being by reference to all types of agents as similar contractual system-agents in a legal and economic system (Macey, 1991). This notion turns the idea of a 'person' around, because the category of the 'person' now includes the incorporated entity unless otherwise posited. The representation of the 'person' in a legal and economic setting is then similar to, but not necessarily the same as that of a human being. The representation of singular legal representations as contractual agents through their legal and economic representations becomes the primary and inevitable shared mode through which the representation of both the individual human being and the separate legal entity is constructed.

All legal and economic 'persons' can then be reconstituted as contracting agents that answer to a narrow set of behavioural and political constraints (Bratton, 1989). In this way, 'persons' become reconstituted as their ideal-type economic counterparts, producing a representation of rational, informed, economically motivated, utility-maximizing agents that can be used as a representation for human beings and the separate legal entity alike: '(...) rational economic actors denuded of significant human characteristics' (Bratton, 1989: 462). As a result, the definition of the 'individual' or 'person' and its agency in legal and economic scholarship shifts towards that of a paradigmatic legal and economic contractual legal subject (Naffine, 2003). Agency theory thus constitutes the person as an ideal-type contractual agent in a very one-sidedly defined economic-legal system (Ireland, 2003).

The reconstitution of the notion of the legal and economic 'person' then creates a very versatile idea about how human beings and separate legal entities create 'firms' as contractual 'agents', operating in a level contractual playing field. In the larger economic landscape, these 'firms' again contract in a similar capacity with individual human beings and 'firms' around them. Both the internal governance of the corporation and the wider marketplace thus become constituted in terms of ideal-type legal and economic actors. In this way, the assumptions behind REMM become unavoidable building blocks for the understanding of organizations and society, just as Meckling predicted in 1976.

Conclusion

What is called 'the nature of man' by Jensen and Meckling becomes the nature of purely conceptual agents with very narrow behavioural constraints in a closed theoretical system. These conceptual agents are legal and contractual entities that are 'denuded of any human characteristics' (Bratton, 1989: 462). Because the constitution of the organization cannot be understood beyond the agency of these entities, the organization becomes the tautological result of these economic and legal 'agents'. Jensen and Meckling's 'Science of Organizations' thus introduces the REMM as an ideal-type actor that constitutes the Nature of Man as well as the Nature of Organization.

When used for the separate legal entity REMM becomes much more than a descriptive model of the Nature of Man. Jensen and Meckling construct an idea of organizations and their representation through the use of methodological individualism, explicitly dismissing all types of representation over and above the human individual. However, in the context of incorporation they cling to the reified separate legal entity with singular agency for its 'convenience'. This pragmatic exception produces a reification of the separate legal entity against a theoretical and normative background that explicitly prohibits the acceptance of such reifications.

Jensen and Meckling therefore produce a theory of organizations that initially refers to methodological individualism to deny all types of reification of representation, but is quick to abandon this theoretical position when the reified separate legal entity with singular agency shows its 'convenience' in issues like hierarchy, power relations, unequal contracting positions, the continued existence of holding companies and the attribution of ownership. The use of methodological individualism in agency theory is therefore not meant to understand all aspects of organizations and governance through the agency of human individuals, but rather to take the focus away from the separate legal entity as a constitutive factor in the governance structure of the corporation and to refocus on the specific rules for organizing that appear in the postulates of REMM.

Considering the aspirations of Jensen and Meckling to develop a 'Science of Organizations' and the success they have had in producing an ideal-type contractual actor for legal and economic scholarship, considering that this ideal-type actor is produced at the expense of a gross reduction of human agency and a lack of evidence for its behavioural assumptions (Bratton, 1989), considering that their ideal-type actor is produced by using politically charged statements and by a simplistic and unfounded dismissal of other scholarly disciplines, considering that the theory behind REMM amounts to an abuse of methodological individualism in the light of the specifics of the separate legal entity, considering that REMM leads to a gross misrepresentation of the governance of the corporation in organization theory and finally, considering that Jensen and Meckling produce a one-sided attack on the state and its institutions, while defending a privileged position for the corporation as a reified representation of association for its 'convenience', it becomes clear why the acceptance of the 'Nature of Man' article in textbooks on finance and strategy is important to study for its effects on theories of organization and governance.

It is time to rethink these behavioural and political assumptions and work on a Science of Organizations from a perspective that understands the Nature of Man and the Nature of Organizations quite differently.

References

Alchian, A.A. and H. Demsetz (1975) 'Production, information costs, and economic organization', *Engineering Management Review, IEEE*, 3(2): 21-41.

Arrow, K.J. (1964) 'Control in large organizations', *Management Science*, 10(3): 397-408.

Baysinger, B. D. (1991) 'Organization theory and the criminal liability of organizations', *Boston University Law Review*, 71: 341.

Baysinger, B. D. and H. N. Butler (1985) 'Role of corporate law in the theory of the firm, The', *Journal of Law and Economics*, 28: 179.

Berle, A. A. (1997) *The Modern Corporation and Private Property*. Rev. edn, New London: Transaction.

Black, F., M. C. Jensen and M. Scholes (1972) 'The capital asset pricing model: Some empirical tests', *Studies in the Theory of Capital Markets*, 81: 79-121.

Bolman, L. G. and T. E. Deal (2008) *Reframing Organizations: Artistry, Choice, and Leadership*. San Francisco: Jossey-Bass Inc Pub.

Bratton Jr, W. W. (1989) 'The nexus of contracts corporation: A critical appraisal', *Cornell L.Rev.*, 74: 407.

Butler, H. N. (1988) 'Contractual theory of the corporation, The', *Geo.Mason UL Rev.*, 11: 99.

Cassidy, J. (2002) 'The greed cycle', *The New Yorker*, 23: 64-77.

Chew, D. H. (2001) *The New Corporate Finance : Where Theory Meets Practice*. 3rd edn, Boston, Mass./London: McGraw-Hill/Irwin.

Elster, J. (2007) *Explaining Social Behavior: More Nuts and Bolts for the Social Sciences*. Cambridge: Cambridge University Press.

Fama, E. F., M. C. Jensen, L. Fischer and R. Roll (1969) 'The adjustment of stock prices to new information', *International Economic Review*, 10.

Fama, E. F. (1980) 'Agency problems and the theory of the firm', *Journal of Political Economy*, 88(2): 288.

Fama, E. F. and M. C. Jensen (1983a) 'Agency problems and residual claims', *Journal of Law and Economics*, 26(2): 327-349.

Fama, E. F. and M. C. Jensen (1983b) 'Separation of ownership and control', *The Journal of Law and Economics*, 26(2): 301.

Horwitz, M. J. (1985) 'Santa Clara revisited: the development of corporate theory', *West Virginia Law Review*, 88: 173.

Ireland, P. (1999) 'Company law and the myth of shareholder ownership', *Modern Law Review*, 62(1): 32.

Ireland, P. (2003) 'Property and contract in contemporary corporate theory', *Legal Studies*, 23: 453.

Jensen, M. C. and W. H. Meckling (1976) 'Theory of the firm: Managerial behavior, agency costs and ownership structure', *Journal of Financial Economics*, 3(4): 305-360.

Jensen, M. C. and W. H. Meckling (1994) 'The Nature of man', *Journal of Applied Corporate Finance*, 7(2). Available at: http://papers.ssrn.com /sol3/papers.cfm?abstract_id=5471&rec=1&srcabs=94032.

Jensen, M. C. (1998) *Foundations of Organizational Strategy*. Harvard: Harvard University Press.

Macey, J. R. (1991) 'Agency theory and the criminal liability of organizations', *Boston University Law Review*, 71: 315.

Mackenzie, D., F. Muniesa and L. Siu (2007) *Do Economists Make Markets? On the Performativity of Economics*. Princeton: Princeton University Press.

Meckling, W. H. (1976) 'Values and the choice of the model of the individual in the social sciences', *Schweizerische Zeitschrift für Volkswirtschaft und Statistik*, 112(4): 545-565.

Williamson, O. E., S. G. Winter and R. H. Coase (1993) *The Nature of the Firm: Origins, Evolution, and Development*. New York: Oxford University Press, USA.

Williamson, O. E. (1996) *The Mechanisms of Governance*. New York: Oxford University Press, USA.

7

Performativity:
From J.L. Austin to Judith Butler

Alan McKinlay

Introduction

'Performativity' is fast emerging as a key concept in critical management studies. Yet while the concept's originator, J.L. Austin, is often cited there has been no serious engagement with his concept, far less how it has made the perilous journey from mid-century philosophical debate, through literary and then feminist theory, to arrive in the business school. We begin by providing a summary and discussion of J.L. Austin's concepts of ordinary language philosophy. Specifically, we outline the development of Austin's concept of 'performativity'. Austin's notion of 'performativity' stressed the necessary entanglement of words and action in everyday speech. We will ask why this term has travelled such a distance from its origin as a highly specific philosophical intervention to contemporary studies of, for instance, esoteric economic instruments. We then turn to Judith Butler, by far the most influential post-Foucault theorist, again someone whose work on gender and identity is increasingly being appropriated by organizational studies. Here we summarise Butler's key concepts and suggest where they draw on Austin and where they go beyond his concept of 'performativity'.

Foucault's importance to Butler has been much discussed but much less well understood is Austin's contribution to her thinking, despite her repeated acknowledgement of her debt, particularly in *Excitable Speech* (1997). Finally, we offer some preliminary, critical comments on the ways that the term 'performativity' has been assimilated into organization studies. We contrast Austin's philosophical imagination and literary wit with the highly partial and confused version of 'performativity' that is becoming common currency in critical management studies. Understanding the subtleties of Austin's reflections on how to categorise ordinary language philosophy is important not just in tracing the development of Judith Butler's theorising of identity but should also sound a cautionary note against bastardised notions of 'performativity' claiming Austin as an authority.

A Few Poorly Attended Lectures?

> You are more than entitled not to know what the word 'performative' means. It is a new word and an ugly word, and perhaps it does not mean anything very much. But at any rate there is one thing in its favour, it is not a profound word. (Austin, 1970: 233)

Why have a dozen lectures delivered at Harvard about linguistic theory by an Oxford philosopher in 1955 provided a central concept for contemporary social sciences? After all, Austin published little during his short life (1911-60), and only a little more posthumously (Warnock, 1989: 1-10). His most famous book – *How To Do Things With Words* – began as a lecture series, rewritten but still bearing the hallmarks of public oratory. Nor was Austin a public intellectual, although he was massively influential within his Oxford circle and did make the odd foray into the mass media. In his bearing and manner he was a man of his time and place, thoroughly wedded to the conventions of Oxford philosophy: 'J.L Austin… tended to write and speak of Aristotle as though he were an interesting but slightly exasperating colleague living on the next staircase' (Harris, 1994: 233). There is little to suggest that Austin used philosophical controversy to seek fame or notoriety beyond Oxford. Indeed, Austin claimed that he had little interest in launching his own school of philosophy. During his closing remarks to what was left of a dwindling audience for his Harvard lectures he claimed, perhaps disingenuously, that his aim merely had been to clarify some important points of linguistic philosophy 'rather than proclaiming an individual manifesto' (Austin, 1975: 164). Of course, this is precisely what he intended. Colleagues and critics, notably his life-long adversary, A.J Ayer, were not convinced by Austin's claim to modesty. Indeed, Ayer's return to Oxford was partly motivated by his desire to counteract Austin's hegemony (Ayer, 1984: 160; Annan, 1990: 410-11; Ignatieff,

1998: 84). And with good reason: Austin was advocating a particular type of linguistic turn that spoke to academic philosophy's inability to hear the profound moral and ethical issues of everyday life and, most importantly, that were understood, conveyed and contested through ordinary language. Moreover, analytical philosophy was not just indifferent to its inability to hear ordinary language but dismissive of the need to address the philosophical complexities of ordinary language (Laugier, 2005: 97). Of course, these were not merely philosophical controversies but bound up with ferocious personal rivalries amongst Oxford philosophers. Famously, Ayer – publicly, personally and later in print – accused Austin of being nothing more than a destructive critic: 'you are like a greyhound that refuses to race but bites other greyhounds to prevent their racing either' (Ayer, 1977: 160; Berlin, 1980: 109). Similarly, Ayer argued that Austin gathered Oxford's young, ambitious philosophers to regular Saturday morning seminars to cement his influence, not to stimulate debate (Ayer, 1977: 295-6). One admirer of Austin saw this practice not just as a continuation of a pre-war Oxford tradition but as a direct result of his career in army intelligence: well-drilled investigators working steadily through minutely detailed tasks in order to uncover important, large truths (Warnock, 1969: 12-3). However, even one of Austin's most ardent – and life-long – admirers, Stanley Cavell, conceded that the many charms of Austin's writing were a poor guide to the lack of warmth he demonstrated during his informal Saturday salons:

> Austin was, in my eyes, a forbidding, cold man. He famously gathered the young teachers of philosophy at Oxford together each week for a session of Austinian exercises and some of them, some very brilliant young thinkers, chafed under the treatment. (Cavell, 1995: 73)

Austin extended his practice of convening informal Saturday morning seminars for young faculty during his stays in America. We can gauge something of the intellectual and emotional intensity that these seminars were designed to produce from Cavell's reflections on his agonised reading of his own interactions with the man he referred to as 'my teacher' throughout his career (similarly, Pitcher, 1973: 20-1). During one session, one of Cavell's papers was the subject for discussion. Or, rather, Austin placed Cavell's typescript in front of him at the start of the seminar, and then studiously avoided discussing it. Initially disturbed by his mentor's silence, Cavell much later discovered that Austin had approved of his work and had even recommended it to other Oxford scholars. This proved to be cold comfort for Cavell. For many years, Cavell pondered the way that his work was initially – and so intimately – passed over, and, later, publicly praised in his absence, with no apparent thought to its impact on the young American philosopher or even if this praise would ever reach his ears, far less compensate for his silence during the Saturday seminar. Austin's deliberate, hurtful – literal – speaking *over*, but not through Cavell's words during the seminar, was not, he concluded, a slight or sign of disapproval; rather, it indicated that 'Austin's silence was …establishing a private and sincere moment of acceptance of the work I had done. Perhaps I found this behaviour too formal or hidden, to take in at a glance; but I seem to have found it also too familiar to take kindly, since my reaction on hearing of his praise was anger: Just like my father, I told myself; public praise and private denial' (Cavell, 1994: 56-7). We will never know whether Cavell's reading of 'my teacher' was accurate or well wide of the mark, not that this mattered much to Austin. Nor can we know whether Austin's behaviour was a haughty slight, a harsh form of moral education or a mere oversight. Contemporary accounts of Austin tell us of an intensely private man, besotted by order and detail to the point of easy caricature, and not someone prone to mistake the meaning attached even to small-talk (Rogers, 2000: 146). Cavell's huge emotional investment in trying to understand the meaning of this exchange provides a sense of the intensity of the relationship for the younger man whose exposure to Austin and his ideas redefined him as a follower and a son as much as a philosopher.

The structure of Austin's famous Harvard lectures traced the broad definitions of two forms of ordinary language: 'constative' and 'performative'. The Harvard lectures were not, however, conventionally structured, moving from critique to hypothesis, then drawing to a definitive conclusion. Rather, Austin moved obliquely, developing what seemed to be a series of powerful, definitive statements, only to almost immediately erode any sense of certainty by hesitation, question and uncertainty. He finished each lecture expressing doubts, not conclusions. This structure was a deliberate attempt to signal both the radical and provisional nature of his proposals. Nevertheless, Austin defined two categories of 'utterance' – he deliberately limited himself to the spoken word – 'constative' and 'performative'. Constative utterances are descriptive and so amenable to empirical verification. For

Austin, constatives are not philosophically interesting or, more accurately, have constituted philosophy's foreground since the ancient Greeks, a pre-eminence that merely reflected 'the philosophers' preferred sense of simply uttering something whose sole pretension is to be true or false' (Austin, 1975: 72). While constative utterances were not necessarily substantively banal they were most definitely philosophically uninteresting. As Austin was well aware, to accept his straightforward definition of constative redefined truth as an empirical rather than a philosophical question, a move which called into doubt the central planks of western philosophy. Even on this central issue Austin hesitated. Towards the end of his lectures Austin even disowned this foundational distinction by defining *all* utterances as performative. Constatives then become a sub-set of performatives, in that the function of the declarative statement is not descriptive but brings an act into being (Fish, 1989: 37-67). However, we do not need to follow Austin in dispensing with the distinction between constative and performative (Recanati, 1987: 20, 67-70; Bach, 1975). A performative is *always* more than words. Quite simply, a performative is not a description 'or to state that I am doing it: it is to do it' (Austin, 1975: 5-6; Furberg, 1971: 193-200). Of course, the paradigmatic case is to make a promise. As Junge (2006: 286) puts it, 'it is not the will that creates the obligation, but the utterance of the promise, may we will it or not. The performative act itself creates the motive to honour the promise ...Whenever we say something that somehow affects others, we might be held responsible for having said it, and knowing this, we will feel committed to our words'. To issue a performative, then, is both 'a creative and a mapping operation' (Graham, 1977: 85). Performativity is inescapably social since it establishes, confirms, questions, or subverts a social relationship. Austin concluded on the impossibility of a clear, abstract, and sustainable definition of 'performativity'. Being forced to coin such 'a new and ugly word' was doubly disappointing for Austin (Austin, 1970: 232). First, to resort to technical terms or, much worse, a clumsy neologism, was to risk the premature closure of philosophical debate. Second, each new conceptual coinage was, in no small measure, to admit a defeat for ordinary language, to register that ordinary language had been tried and found wanting in terms of clarity or precision. As a mainstream Oxford philosopher, a thoroughgoing empiricist and pragmatist, Austin was suspicious even of his own conceptual innovation. Austin thought of language in an empiricist, not abstract way. This is not to say that his logic is commonsensical, no matter how prosaic his exemplars or how determinedly peculiar his metaphors.

Through the course of his twelve Harvard lectures Austin rehearsed the possible grammar of performatives: active verb, indicative, first person, present tense. This grammatical form makes performativity explicit and obvious but, concluded Austin, these conditions are neither grammatically necessary nor socially sufficient. For the first, well-attended, half of Austin's twelve Harvard lectures he pondered such linguistic issues, then, at every opportunity, unpicked his initial solutions: six or so inconclusive lectures is more than enough for even the most patient audience (Petrie, 1990: 118-9). The collapse of attendance was not due to Austin's poor delivery: even Austin's bitterest critics acknowledged that he was a gifted public speaker, albeit one with a flat, toneless voice (Rogers, 2000: 255). Through the second six – and ever-more sparsely attended – lectures of the series, Austin turned to his attempt to produce a working definition of performativity. Austin puzzled at just what grammatical structures were both necessary and sufficient for a statement to be performative. This was an issue that he failed to resolve to his satisfaction. The deterioration in Austin's Harvard audience was surely only partly offset by the ardour of some of those that remained, and can be attributed to his cautious, inconclusive style of posing problems, suggesting solutions, only for these to be found wanting and discarded. Perhaps, on the other hand, the intellectual and *personal* challenge of Austin's approach to the preoccupations of analytical philosophy, was dawning on his audience.

> His aim in his study of performatives is at once to lift the nondescriptive or nonessential or nonconstative gestures of speech to renewed philosophical interest and respectability, and to bring, or prepare the ground on which to bring, the philosophical concern with truth down to size. (Cavell, 2005: 180-1)

A performative is more than a statement but is also an action appropriate to time, place and wider social context. The statement is immanent in the action and vice-versa; both are essential and necessary one to the other and neither makes sense independently. The entire performative must conform, to a greater or lesser degree, with social convention. *All* performatives, in other words, *must* have a social as well as a linguistic content, be comprehensible, and 'felicitous' – in Austin's phrase – in a given social context. *All* performatives are, then, socially contingent rather than definable exclusively by their grammatical structure.

In all his writing and, just as importantly, his lecturing, Austin used an Oxford 'house-style' form of plain prose. Complex philosophical points were conveyed in stripped down terms, accompanied by everyday homilies and commonplace expressions. Ironically, many of the phrases Austin used to illustrate his lectures retain their warmth and charm but can also seem arcane, outmoded or reeking of donnish sensibilities. But it is a rare etymologist that illustrates 'a putative description of a physical action' with putting in a golf tournament (Austin, 1970: 258). In this case, he was – perhaps – making very erudite mischief at the expense of his arch-rival Ayer (1952: 35) who used the phrase 'putative proposition' in a central passage about the verifiability of truth – and the futility of listening for philosophical meaning in ordinary speech – in his most important book, *Language, Truth and Logic*. There was, then, much more to this terrible pun than artifice: Austin's peculiar metaphors and striking phrases are central to how he developed his argument, engaged his audience and allowed his readers to follow his line of thinking. Or a much simpler explanation is possible: Austin was both a golfer and a philosopher (Stroll, 2000: 163). It is perfectly plausible to read Austin as deliberately using jokes to draw attention to areas where he felt his ideas were not fully worked out or where paradoxes remained (Felman, 2002: 71-5). In person as well as in prose, he occasionally took a childlike, but never malicious, delight in the absurd or in gently leading questioners into untenable or ridiculous positions (Picker, 1973: 19-23). Donnish humour was always polished and generally had an acerbic, sly quality that could not easily be mistaken for charm or naivete, certainly not by other Oxford insiders, perhaps the only audience that really mattered to Austin. Cruel slights and juvenile puns were rehearsed, polished and retold in this insular world (Mitchell, 2009). Austin was notorious for his rigour and his austere debating style but stood apart from the refined cruelties of high table conversation. When rehearsing a disagreement about the nature of truth he suggested that 'comments on comments, criticisms of criticisms, are subject to the law of diminishing fleas' (Austin, 1970: 154). Nor was this an affectation that he dropped when confronted with a high-minded professional audience. Throughout his Harvard lectures Austin revelled in playful and accessible language. Elsewhere, during a typically intricate discussion of 'responsibility' and 'intentionality', one discovers that to feed peanuts to a penguin is to endanger their life: 'Did I feed the peanuts intentionally? Beyond a doubt: I am no casual peanut shedder' (Austin, 1970: 275). During an aside pondering the distinction between 'inadvertently and 'automatically', we learn that he was 'partial to ice cream' and often day-dreamed about the limits to self-control and his liking for a second helping of dessert while at high-table dinners (Austin, 1970: 198). Of course, there is no way of knowing whether Austin is allowing us a glimpse of his personality and life-style or whether his personal asides were no more than stylistic conceits. Such ambiguities are inherent in Austin's theory as much as in his style. Even the title of his most famous work, *How to Do Things with Words*, can be read as both a promise and a description:

> *How to Do Things with Words* is a great work of ironic philosophical speculation. It demands and repays the closest attention to its details of language. Meanwhile, on the brink of that, Austin's title hovers there on the cover or title page, faintly smiling, enigmatic, quizzical, ironical, a little like the photograph on the fron cover of the paperback edition of his *Philosophical Papers*. That photograph shows Austin as the patriarch, grandfather, or *capo* of speech-act theory. Austin's title for *How to Do Things with Words* is the first joke among many jokes in this admirable joke book. One wonders if any library or bookstore has ever filed this book among the how-to books. That would no doubt have pleased Austin. (Miller, 2001: 11)

To be sure, these moments of levity served an immediate purpose: they were designed to put his audience at ease but they were also the prelude to the deconstruction of his metaphor or example. In a famously acerbic denunciation of the dead hand of linguistic philosophy, Ernest Gellner (1959: 260) condemned Austin's pathological pedantry and his espoused reverence for ordinary language as a smoke-screen for a retreat from the world rather than an engagement with it: 'a philosophic form eminently suitable for gentlemen. ...no vulgar new revelation about the world, no guttersnipe demands for reform'. The use of exemplars also signalled the philosopher's conventional means of discussing first principles and not a substitute for even the beginning of empirical analysis. Every metaphor has a precise purpose: to consider, refine, or reject a way of thinking through the metaphorical clarification of a philosophical issue. Austin's superficiality was deliberate, measured and used to signal, if seldom to resolve, new issues that his approach had surfaced. Equally, by leavening his Harvard lectures with classical, poetic, literary and philosophical allusions – in several languages – Austin left no doubt about the weight of his learning, no matter how lightly borne (Cavell, 1994: 124-5).

Speech act theory stands to one side of the opposition between structuralism and post-structuralism. For speech-act theory regards society and speech acts as mutually constitutive, in much the same way as Marx considered his infamous metaphor of 'base-superstructure' (Sayer, 1983). Speech act theory escapes from the prison house of language and the solipsism of psychoanalysis by accepting the collective determinants of human speech and actions. The validity of performatives cannot be assessed in terms of their correspondence with an action or event in the same way as a constative. That is not to say that performatives cannot be assessed for their validity or, as Austin would have it, their 'appropriateness'. 'Appropriateness' simply signalled that the performative statement must be appropriate to its social context. The limit case is easily identified. To reverse two of Austin's most famous illustrations: it would be as ridiculous to say 'I do' when naming a ship as it would to say 'I name this ship the Queen Elizabeth' during a wedding ceremony. However, Austin was not content to rely on absurdities and proceeded to carefully elaborate six conditions that must be met for a performative to be entirely successful: there must be a robust framework of conventions; all participants must act according to these conventions; complete the act and live out its consequences; and their behaviours must be paralleled by an endorsement of the thoughts or feelings demanded by convention (Austin, 1975: 15).

So, Austin established a complex and comprehensive set of necessary conditions for a speech act to be performative: he was careful not to suggest that even if all these necessary conditions were met that this was sufficient for an utterance to be deemed performative (Searle, 1969: 137-40). For Austin, typologies of this sort were always imperfect, always incomplete and their categories never mutually exclusive. Given such a demanding set of conditions performatives can only rarely, if ever, be fully successful. My lack of clarity here is deliberate for, as we shall see, this is an issue which has intrigued later readings of Austin. Parenthetically, we would add that although Austin offers neither guidance nor comment here, it is the manner of their failure that offers the most room for theoretical development and empirical debate in organization studies. Some performatives are only partially successful due to, flawed acts or misunderstandings or bad faith by one or more participants. In highly ritualised ceremonies, an incomplete or flawed performative is extremely rare: again a marriage or the launch of a ship. But these are hardly everyday occurrences. Equally, minor flaws in a ritual need not undermine its meaning or prejudice its outcome: a groom may stumble over his vows or a bride may have private reservations, but that seldom halts the ceremony although it may later alter the course of the marriage. In 1956 Austin provided a British radio audience with an unscripted but clearly well-rehearsed example of the difficulties associated with the classification of infelicities. Again, Austin used one of his favourite examples, the naming of a ship, an *explicit* performative.

> Suppose that you are just about to name the ship, you have been appointed to name it, and you are just about to bang the bottle against the stern; but at that very moment some low type comes up, snatches the bottle out of your hand, breaks it on the stern, shouts out 'I name this ship the *Generalissimo Stalin*', and then for good measure kicks away the chocks. Well, we agree of course on several things. We agree that the ship certainly isn't now named the *Generalissimo Stalin*, and we agree that it's an infernal shame and so on and so forth. But we may not agree as to how we should classify the particular infelicity in this case. (Austin, 1970: 239-40)

Elements of the ceremony were fully felicitous. Even the 'low person's' words were grammatically and socially, if not politically, correct, except for the fact that he was not authorised to say them. There is a further possible reading, however. The 'low person's' disruption would certainly have run counter to the normal conventions of a launch. Neither conformity of word nor deed alone is sufficient for a performative to be felicitous. Indeed, the invocation of the wrong name, quite apart from the nature of the invader, could invalidate much of what followed. For the ship would be launched but the vessel's name would always be followed by some smiling, perhaps incredulous, reference to its temporary 'alternative' name and the principals would never quite outlive the memory of their part in the day's events. In that sense, Austin depicts the launch as unambiguously 'unfelicitous' in word and deed. Of course, here felicitousness depends on the politics of whoever is applying Austin's tests: for the energetic young communist and her or his comrades would surely regard this as an audacious assertion of an alternative set of conventions, entirely contrary to the immediate context of the ceremony and established authority more generally. 'Low persons' might laugh and applaud the felicitousness of their comrade's intervention, just as it was being rued by the launch party and deprecated by stuffy Oxford philosophers. Here we collide with Austin's peculiar sense of the fixity of the social: he begins from an understanding that the felicity of performatives is assessed against deep-set social conventions. Here Austin seems uncomfortably aware that he is straying over the boundaries of his discipline into, as he puts it, anthropology. He recognises that he cannot settle this to his satisfaction and it seems as if he decides almost to put this matter to one side. He does this by invoking a conservative kind of social Darwinism that asserts that long usage embeds social conventions: only those that fit some purpose and display sufficient practical precision survive in the long-run. Austin is conscious of the conservatism of his position but regards it as consistent with the logic of ordinary language philosophy and, indeed, the robust subtlety of everyday speech.

> our common stock of words embodies all the distinction men have found worth drawing, and the connexions they have found worth making, in the lifetimes of many generations; these surely are likely to be more numerous, more sound, since they have stood the test of the survival of the fittest, and have subtle, at least in all reasonably practical matters, than any you and I are likely to think up in our arm-chairs of an afternoon – the most favoured alternative method. (Austin, 1970: 182)

To say the least, this leaves Austin unable to think about ways that authority may be challenged by acts – words and deeds – that flout established power in the most visible way possible. To usurp the launch, to name a ship after a communist rather than the monarch, especially at the height of the cold war, is to cleave open a space for dissent, albeit momentarily. Now, Austin would reply that this moment of resistance would be closed down immediately, not just by the 'low type' being manhandled off the launch platform by security, accompanied by the catcalls or, at least, the horrified gasps of the crowd. To Austin there would be little likelihood of any cheers for the mischievous, perhaps threatening, interloper. As the platform party regained its composure, so the weight of authority was reasserted. Indeed, perhaps the dignified bearing of the launch party in the face of such adversity would enhance the authority of the ceremony. The same disruption to the same performative ceremony can, therefore, be judged to have quite different forms of meaning and felicity.

More generally, then, Austin's definition – and his illustrations – suggest that performatives are often associated with – or are essential to – rituals and that there is an almost infinite variety of ways in which performatives can be flawed without failing completely. Nonetheless, flaws, whether slight or serious, are not restricted to words but could just as easily involve actions, demeanour, or thoughts. The performative can, in other words, be undone by thought, speech or deed, or, indeed, by inaction. As a former army officer, Austin would be acutely aware of the potency of the dumb insolence of subalterns. Nor is this vulnerability restricted to relatively unscripted everyday life. The most profound ceremonies can be compromised if not wholly undone by the smirk of a cynical groom or the laughter of a nervous bride. Here Austin raises a point that was to move centre-stage during contemporary discussions of identity. In general, utterances have to be 'serious' for them to be performatives. This is a crucial philosophical point. The word is not an outward sign of 'an inward or spiritual act: from which it is but a short stop to go on to believe or to assume without realising that for many purposes the outward utterance is a description, *true or false*, of the occurrence of the inward performance' (Austin, 1975: 9). One can safely infer that for Austin 'identity' was necessarily socially constructed, socially enabled and collective by nature, even though it is normally experienced – and most often articulated – individually.

Austin's main concern was to identify the conditions necessary for 'felicitous' or 'happy' performatives. Identifying would-be performatives that violate all of his conditions is straightforward: 'it is like a marriage with a monkey' (Austin, 1975: 25). Necessarily, then, he recognises that not all performatives fully satisfy these conditions but do not fall completely short. While he takes the *fact* of failure for granted, the *nature* of this failure can take many forms. Austin does not allow this recognition to delay him in his clarification of performative speech acts. Nevertheless, almost parenthetically, he uses several terms for performatives that fail to satisfy these conditions: unhappy, abuses, misfires, disallowed, botched, void, without effect, purported, hollow (Austin, 1975: 14-5, 17-8).

Austin provides a rich and provocative account of what it is to be social. He provides a way of rethinking the operation of ordinary language that demands that we attend to its conditions of possibility – social as much as linguistic; that the most subtle ethical questions are asked – and answered, however partially – in everyday life; and that understanding ordinary language should be the prime objective of philosophy rather than a second order matter. That said, Austin leaves critical issues unresolved. This he acknowledged, indeed signalled, throughout his Harvard lectures. First, the force of any performative is not determined by its internal logic but by its congruence with its social setting. So there is uncertainty over who judges the felicity of a performative (see Massen, 2006: 170-1). Determining such issues is an empirical, not theoretical, matter. Austin offers a few methodological hints about how one would conduct empirical research but he does not take this very far. Second, there is an instinctive conservatism in Austin that does not just recognise but positively *values* the stability of ordinary language, a stability that he regards as a precondition of the subtle and robust ethical judgements that can be made through ordinary language. As we shall see, this conservative stress on the internal and social stability of ordinary language has been turned on its head by contemporary theorists, most notably Judith Butler.

Butler and Performativity

Performativity or, more generally, speech acts formed one of the key battlegrounds for literary theory for over two decades before the 'theory wars' abated in the mid-1980s. Indeed, it would have been all but impossible for a literary theorist of Judith Butler's generation to avoid becoming embroiled in the paradigm wars around speech-act theory in its various, sometimes virulent, forms. Butler played little direct part in these debates, and while her texts often critically engage with other scholars, this is always performed in a measured tone, bereft of personal or political invective. That said, there is none of Austin's playfulness or quirky use of metaphors in Butler. Quite the reverse: her prose is dense and unforgiving. A charitable reading would locate Butler's work in a hostile academic and political climate and so register her prose as marked by a constant wariness, a guardedness that each point had to be made meticulously lest it become a hostage to political opponents We should be wary, then, of criticising Butler *solely* in terms of style for this can often be a code for a deeply conservative disdain for any deviation not just from plain prose, but from entrenched – and politically deadening – commonsense (Lakoff, 2000: 58-9; Ferguson, 2003: 17-9). For it is precisely such unspoken, commonsensical assumptions about gender that Butler is trying to disrupt. Nevertheless, Butler makes few concessions to her reader: there is little chance of finding an aside about the digestive weaknesses of penguins, far less her fondness for ice cream.

Butler arrived at Austin via Derrida's interpretation of performativity, an interpretation that, observed Stanley Cavell (1995: 44), lay somewhere between 'an attack' and 'a sort of celebration or homage'. Philosophically, Derrida was drawn to Austin's open, and his elliptical, yet precise, style. Derrida is far from unique in being enchanted by Austin as a writer of literature as much as a philosopher of language. In an important sense, Derrida's commentary was much closer to eulogy than critique. And we know that Derrida was capable of the most withering of criticisms. Indeed, the title of Derrida's collection of essays – *Limited Inc* – can, perhaps, be read as a pun on one of Austin's most celebrated essays, "Three Ways of Spilling Ink'. Derrida's comments on Austin were part of a contribution to a conference on communication. In one sense, Derrida offers a summary, albeit selective, of Austin's ordinary language philosophy. He develops his contribution by contrasting the performative utterance which, unlike the constative

> does not have its referent (but here that word is certainly no longer appropriate, and this precisely is the interest of the discovery) outside of itself or, in any event, before and in front of itself. It does not describe something that exists outside of language and prior to it. It produces or transforms a situation, it effects; and even if it can be said that a constative utterance also effectuates something and always transforms a situation, it cannot be maintained that that constitutes its internal structure, its manifest function or destination, as in the case of the performative. (Derrida, 1988: 13)

Derrida compliments Austin for 'an analysis which is patient, open, aporetical, in constant transformation, often more fruitful in the acknowledgement of its impasses than in its positions' (Derrida, 1988: 14).

The hesitations that thinned out Austin's Harvard audience were precisely what Derrida found most attractive. But he was much less convinced by Austin's retention of the self-aware individual at the author of the performative. What Austin took to be unlikely, the moments which rendered a performative infelicitous, should, countered Derrida, be considered quite differently. For Derrida, the possibility of failure is a necessary and defining element of *every* performative, not just those that proved infelicitous. So, Derrida argued, Austin regarded failure as an external 'trap into which language may *fall* or lose itself as in an abyss situated outside of or in front of itself?' (Derrida, 1988: 17). Derrida mocked this timidity: language becomes something surrounded by risk, a kind of 'perdition which speech could never hope to leave, but which it can escape by remaining 'at home,' by and in itself, in the shelter of its essence or *telos*?' Risk – infelicity – is not, insists Derrida, external to language but internal and a condition of its possibility. *All* performatives are flawed in some way or other, to a greater or lesser extent. The truly successful performatives offered by Austin – the naming of a ship – or by Derrida – Paul Ricouer calling a meeting to order – are exceptional, highly ritualised, with scripted roles for all, and clearly structured authority. For Derrida, these are not exemplars of performatives in general but limit cases. Derrida marks the importance of context for Austin's notion of performative but retaining intentionality and the singularity of meaning renders Austin a metaphysician of the ordinary. Derrida's reading of Austin is by no means uncontested. On the contrary, Culler (1983: 114) insists that Austin regards the possibility of failure as an integral part of performatives and, indeed, that 'something cannot be a performative unless it can go wrong'. Substantively, however, we can differ from Derrida's reading of Austin and agree with his suggestion that some degree of risk – or danger – of failure is inherent in every performative utterance. Certainly, it is this sense of infelicity inscribed in *every* performative that Butler adopts from Derrida's comments on Austin (see Felman, 2002: 44-5). It is precisely the *possibility* of failure that is inherent in the unremarkable routines that define gender from which Butler derives political hope.

Irrespective of the path to *How to Do Things with Words*, a close reading of Butler reveals just how great is her debt to the Oxford philosopher. This debt was made explicit in *Excitable Speech* (1997), in which she explores and develops Austin's notion of performative, a term that does not appear in her previous work (Lloyd, 2006: 36). This is not to say that Austin and performativity are not implicit and pervasive in how she had considered gender previously. For Butler, gender is not constative – a fact to be confirmed – but always, to some extent, performative, a way of speaking and a way of acting in and on the social world. Gender identity is not a more or less accurate referent of the real but something that is made through words and deeds. Now, only a gross misreading of Butler would conclude that she proposes that *only* words produce gender: subjectivity arises with, through and against gestures, routines, the stuff of gender in everyday life. Indeed, Butler's novelty was in taking sociality seriously (Cusset, 2003: 210-12). In two important respects, then, Butler remains close to Austin. First, Butler, like Austin, emphasises the open-ended, the potentiality inherent in *all* identities. Second, Butler stresses the inescapable role of the social in the construction of identity, an echo of Austin's (1970: 178) insistence on social context and his scepticism of excessive materialism, of any sense of an ultimate, even visceral, practice being a sufficient explanation of discourse. In important way, Butler both remains faithful – felicitous – to Austin and uses his notion of performativity as a starting-point. Butler remains close to Austin in her emphasis on the indeterminancy and contingency of language, action and meaning. Identity is *always* unfinished business. She shares with Austin a belief in the importance of the taken-for-grantedness of everyday life and the ways it shapes identity (Loxley, 2006: 14). Importantly, this is where Austin stops and where Butler begins. Butler employs Austin to consider the nature of gender as a *social* grammar.

Echoing Foucault's instinct and – sometime – methodology, Austin (1970: 179-80) looked to the unusual, the abnormal, to 'throw light on the normal, will help us to penetrate the blinding veil of ease and obviousness that hides the mechanisms of the natural successful act'. Similarly, in his remark that aesthetics should occasionally put aside 'the beautiful' to explore 'the dainty and the dumpy' of the everyday, so Austin asks us to consider the extraordinary riches of ordinary language (Austin, 1970: 183). In seeking to establish the necessary conditions – the conditions of felicity – for ordinary language (Cavell, 2002: xx), Austin is on similar terrain to Foucault who sought the linguistic categories and institutional logics that produced certain behaviours, certain subjectivities. Of course, Foucault's histories often involved a double move, placing the 'abnormal' centre-stage while turning unquestioned routines of, say, prisoners or army cadets into something strange. In *Excitable Speech* Butler uses empirical material to develop her theoretical position. Specifically, she examines public testimonies of one kind or another, as forms of confession, moments which, of course, Foucault regarded as symptomatic of modernity. Butler's political objective is to question and help destabilise gender identities. Again, there is a consistency with Foucault, in that both sought to overcome what they regarded as the stultifying effect of Marxist politics, in favour of the proliferation of identities and resistance, a kind of hyper-radical pluralism (Gaussot, 2006: 86-7).

What then did Butler make of her relationship with Austin? Like many others, she found Austin's writings charming and amusing. In *Excitable Speech* (1997) she points to at least three important senses in which her notion of performativity accords with that of Austin. First, and this is a point that is explicitly reinforced several times in the text, that a performative utterance is not simply discourse but has some kind of impact on the world, even if only to reinforce existing conventions, hierarchies and identities. Second, that she shares Austin's stress on the absolute need to contextualise speech and much of his uncertainty about how this could be done theoretically and empirically. Again, this insistency on the sociality of speech means that she remains faithful to Foucault in escaping the illusion of the sovereign individual (Butler, 1997: 3, 16, 80-2). Third, and bearing in mind the importance of Derrida's reading of Austin for the development of Butler's theory, she goes beyond Austin in highlighting the ambiguity and instability of performativity. Austin points to the ambiguity and instability of performativity as an analytical category which Butler summarises as, 'actions that are performed by virtue of words, and those that are performed as a consequence of words' (Butler, 1997: 44). This tension at the centre of every *performative* Butler takes to the heart of every *identity*. Identities become deeply performative, expressed, reinforced and projected by every felicitous gesture and brought into question by every ill-chosen joke or gesture. Of course, the sense of self-doubt inherent in *every* identity, the way individuals and institutions monitor, police and manage identity is the crucial connection she makes between Austin, Foucault and psychoanalysis. Fourth, the authority of every performative utterance is determined by social structure and convention, by the power and legitimacy bestowed by consistent and unremarkable repetition. Even here, Butler is careful to stress the provisional nature of every performative, no matter how dully uncontroversial (Butler, 1997: 51).

For Butler, gender is performative in the sense that 'it is real only to the extent that it is performed' (Butler, 1990: 278-9). This has led to much serious misunderstanding since it collapses performativity into performance. Butler is arguing that what we say about ourselves and how we act does not represent a fixed underlying identity. Our words, gestures and actions are not expressions of – or even merely constitutive of – who we are. In fact, Butler's controversial and, she later added, somewhat ill-chosen account of drag was presaged by Austin on forms of 'pretending', especially exaggeration (Austin, 1970: 258). In no small measure, her – later regretted – conflation of 'performance' and 'performativity' betrays the Derridean route she took to Austin. That is, Derrida's partial reading of Austin stresses performance in an extremely literal sense that is incompatible with the balance of his writings (Hammer, 2002: 158-62). For Austin, 'pretending' involves some degree of extemporisation, perhaps spontaneity, a knowing approximation rather than guileless mimicry, and a readiness to drop the pretence, not to extend it indefinitely nor even necessarily to await discovery. To pretend is, then, neither a disguise nor a serious attempt at deception. Here Austin (1970: 268-9) is sensitive to the ambiguities of pretence. Similarly, far from drag being a deceit, it is a pretence that is intended not just to blur perceptions of gender but to compel everyone to consider these ambiguities: whether they be an actor, watcher or participant; whether with empathy, delight, uneasiness or revulsion.

Another reading of Butler's remarks on drag, however, produces a different kind criticsm, and one that is not so easily disposed of. Even if one discounts Butler's commentary on drag as an ill-advised metaphor, this does not eliminate the sense of constant change, of the instability of identity that pervades her work. This instability is politically important to Butler since it allows questioning, resistance, and change. Theoretically, the cost of Butler's tight focus on the *moment* is a peculiar ahistoricity. She is left with a theoretical and stylistic difficulty that is by no means unique to Butler but which is, nonetheless, particularly acute in her work. That is, how to maintain a robust constructivist position while at the same time acknowledging the inescapable, visceral, fragile materiality of the body (Kirby, 2006: 66).

In *Gender Trouble*, there is no mention of Austin but the notion of performativity, refracted through Derrida, is clear enough in her insistence that conventional gender identities are endlessly, inventively generative and inherently unstable: 'The injunction *to be* a given gender produces necessary failures, a variety of incoherent configurations that in their multiplicity exceed and defy the injunction by which they are generated' (Butler, 1990: 145). In an important sense, Butler's voluntarist position represents the other side of the coin from Austin's linguistic conservatism, his position that the structures of ordinary language – and the conventions of ordinary life – were, if not timeless, then certainly changed only at the most glacial pace. Butler implicitly acknowledges the difficulties of her position and draws on Derrida's essay on Austin to provide a way out of her theoretical dilemma. In this important sense, Butler goes beyond Austin by offering concepts about *how* speech acts reproduce established conventions, social structures and identities. Following Derrida, Butler argues that the key is the *repetition* of the thoroughly unremarkable daily routines of gender which both produce a sense of individual choice and reproduce conventional identities and hierarchies (Lloyd, 2007: 61-6; McKinlay, 2010). Butler, like Austin, stresses the sociality of identity, not its psychology. Establishing and sustainining – far less modifying – an identity is a complex process of negotiating and reflecting upon, innumerable, demanding routines. Understanding that process, insists Butler, is a theoretical process that cannot begin from the individual, the moment of performance, or abstract notions of 'structure'.

Conclusion: The Peculiar Journey of 'Performativity'

If J.L. Austin coined the concept 'performativity' as a way of understanding the social embeddedness of everyday language, then this proved to be only the beginning of the concept's journey. If much of Austin's initial appeal lies in the verve and humour of his writing then its lasting influence is attributable to its open-endedness. However, for all the ease with which some of Austin can be read and enjoyed this never detracts from the care he took about the substance of his argument or the intensity and precision of his thinking. Austin's Harvard lectures were an illustration of what he meant by performativity and, as it turned out, were themselves performative in their effect on all forms of literary and social theory. Performativity is a simple enough idea, plausible as a theory and is intuitively convincing in terms of everyday experience. And it is this ease, the taken-for-grantedness that has allowed Austin's original concept to travel so far from his very specific grammatical objective. 'Performativity' was a key term in the paradigm wars that revolutionised literary theory, is inescapable in any contemporary discussion of gender and is becoming increasingly common in organization studies. In particular, 'performativity' is becoming an important term in 'critical management studies'. In some ways this is not surprising. Perhaps the two defining characteristics of 'critical management studies' has been its openness to new ways of theorising management, work and organization and, second, an insistence that they way we talk about our working lives, employment and organization is the way we come to understand and act upon ourselves and each other. Naturally, Judith Butler, J.L. Austin and their 'shared' concept of performativity are becoming increasingly important resources for critical management studies. Indeed, in an important intervention Spicer, Alvesson and Karreman (2009) issue a clarion call for a simultaneous rethinking and remaking of critical management studies. Performativity – as a concept and as a practice – is placed at the centre of this project. Their aim is nothing less than to provide a *unifying* intellectual and political agenda for critical management studies. Critical management studies has adopted something of a cynical distance from political or ethical engagement, distrustful or dismissive of anything that smacks of assuming a 'normative' position. The alternative to being *against* performativity – the dominant position in critical management studies – is, they argue, to embrace performativity and render it critical, engaged and pragmatic. In short, they demand that critical management studies will become *more* performative. Now, one can only applaud this rekindled appetite for political engagement, however ill-defined. But we can question their reading of performativity which, despite their attempt to distance themselves from the disengaged mainstream of critical management, remains unchanged. Disappointingly, Spicer, Alvesson and Karreman (2009) offer only a bowdlerised notion of performativity that owes much more to Lyotard than it does to Austin. Admittedly, in a footnote Lyotard claims proximity to and distinctiveness from Austin's notion of performativity: 'the two meanings are not far apart. Austin's performative realizes the optimal performance' (Lyotard, 1984: 88). In Lyotard, then, performativity is a catch-all term that refers to any system that maximises outputs as it minimises inputs. This is close to the meaning of performative that so exercises Spicer, Alvesson and Karreman (2009), but it is far from consistent with Austin. Following Austin, one can be no more 'anti' performative than one can be 'against' verbs or give only qualified approval to nouns. There is a real danger that doing things with words is morphing into doing anything – everything – with *his* word, performativity. This abuse of Austin would surely have tested the limits of his prickly Donnish civility. If critical management studies must define new ways of political, ethical and pragmatic engagement, then it surely must also attend to the ethics of scholarly production, an ethics which demands that we take care with our appropriation of concepts. There is more to this than scholarly nit-picking. The power of Austin and Butler lies in the way they prepare the ground for historical and empirical research, the way that both avoided premature theoretical closure and, in Butler's case, acknowledged the obstinate power of established gender identities as she celebrated their inherent uncertainties and malleability. The ways that performatives fail are their most interesting theoretical and empirical feature, not the limit cases where there is near perfect citation of established rituals and identities.

References

Austin, J. L. (1970) *Philosophical Papers*. Oxford: Oxford University Press.

Austin, J. L. (1975) *How to Do Things with Words: The William James Lectures delivered at Harvard University in 1955*. Oxford: Oxford University Press.

Ayer, A. J. (1952) *Language, Truth and Logic*. Second edition, New York: Dover.

Ayer, A. J. (1977) *Part of My Life*. London: Collins.

Ayer, A. J. (1984) *More of my Life*. London: Collins.

Bach, K. (1975) 'Performatives are statements too', *Philosophical Studies*, 28: 229-236.

Berlin, I. (1980) *Personal Impressions*. London: Hogarth Press.

Butler, J. (1990) *Gender Trouble: Feminism and the Subversion of Identity*. London: Routledge.

Butler, J. (1997) *Excitable Speech: A Politics of Performativity*. London: Routledge.

Cavell, S. (1994) *A Pitch of Philosophy; Autobiographical Exercises*. Cambridge, Mass: Harvard University Press.

Cavell, S. (1995) *Philosophical Passage: Wittgenstein, Austin, Derrida.* Oxford: Blackwell.

Cavell, S. (2002) *Must We Mean What We Say?* Cambridge: Cambridge University Press.

Cavell, S. (2005) 'Passionate and performative utterance: Morals of an encounter', in R. Goodman (ed.) *Contending with Stanley Cavell.* Oxford: Oxford University Press.

Culler, J. (1983) *On Deconstruction: Theory and Criticism after Structuralism.* London: Routledge & Kegan Paul.

Cusset, F. (2003) *French Theory: Foucault, Derrida, Deleuze & Cie et les Mutations de la Vie Intellectuelle aux Etats-Unis.* Paris: La Decouverte.

Derrida, J. (1988) *Limited Inc.* Evanston, IL: Northwestern University Press.

Felman, S (2002) *The Scandal of the Speaking Body: Don Juan with J.L. Austin or Seduction in Two Languages.* Stanford, CA: Stanford University Press.

Ferguson, M. (2003) 'Difficult style and "illustrious" vernaculars: A historical perspective', in J. Culler and K. Lamb (eds) *Just Being Difficult? Academic Writing in the Public Sphere.* Stanford, CA: Stanford University Press.

Fish, S. (1989) *Doing What Comes Naturally: Change, Rhetoric, and the Practice of Theory in Literary and Legal Studies.* Durham NC: Duke University Press.

Furberg, M. (1971) *Saying and Meaning: A Main Theme in J.L. Austin's Philosophy.* Oxford: Basil Blackwell.

Gaussot, L. (2008) 'Le Sexe/Genre comme Discours et comme Asujettisement: Usage de Foucault', in J.-C. Bourdin, F. Chauvaud, V. Estellon, B. Geay, B. and J.-M. Passerault (eds) *Michel Foucault: Savoirs, Domination et Sujet.* Rennes: Presses Universitaire de Rennes.

Gellner, E. (1959) *Words and Things: A Critical Account of Linguistic Philosophy and a Study in Ideology.* London: Gollancz.

Graham, K. (1977). *J.L. Austin: A Critique of Ordinary Language Philosophy.* Brighton: Harvester.

Hammer, E. (2002) *Stanley Cavell: Skepticism, Subjectivity and the Ordinary.* Cambridge: Polity Press.

Harris, J. (1994) 'The arts and social science, 1939-1970', in B. Harrison (ed.) *The History of the University of Oxford, vol. viii, The Twentieth Century*. Oxford: Clarendon Press.

Ignatieff, M. (1998) *Isaiah Berlin: A Life*. London: Chatto & Windus.

Junge, K. (2006) 'The promise of performance and the problem of order', in J. Alexander, B. Giesen and J. Mast (eds) *Social Performance: Symbolic Action, Cultural Pragmatics, and Ritual*. Cambridge: Cambridge University Press.

Kirby, V. (2006) *Judith Butler: Live Theory*. London: Continuum.

Lakoff, R. (2000) *The Language War*. Berkeley, CA: University of California Press.

Laugier, S. (2005) 'Rethinking the ordinary: Austin *after* Cavell', in R. Goodman (ed.) *Contending with Stanley Cavell*. Oxford: Oxford University Press.

Lloyd, M. (2006) *Judith Butler: From Norms to Politics*. Cambridge: Polity.

Loxley, J. (2006) *Performativity*. London: Routledge.

Lyotard, J.-F. (1984) *The Postmodern Condition: A Report on Knowledge*. Manchester: Manchester University Press.

McKinlay, A. (2010) 'Performativity and the politics of identity: Putting Butler to work', *Critical Perspectives on Accounting*, forthcoming.

Massen, S. (2006) *Narrative Dimensions of Philosophy: A Semiotic Exploration of the Work of Merleau-Ponty, Kierkegaard and Austin*. Basingstoke: Palgrave Macmillan.

Miller, J. Hillis (2001) *Speech Acts in Literature*. Stanford CA: Stanford University Press.

Mitchell, L. (2009) *Maurice Bowra: A Life*. Oxford: Oxford University Press.

Petrie, S. (1990) *Speech Acts and Literary Theory*. London: Routledge.

Pitcher, G. (1973) 'Austin: A personal memoir', in I. Berlin et al. *Essays on J.L. Austin*. Oxford: Clarendon Press.

Recanati, F. (1987) *Meaning and Force: The Pragmatics of Performative Utterances*. Cambridge: Cambridge University Press.

Rogers, B. (2000) *A.J. Ayer: A Life*. London: Vintage.

Sayer, D. (1983) *Marx's Method: Ideology, Science and Critique in Capital*. Brighton: Harvester.

Searle, J. (1969) *Speech Acts: An Essay in the Philosophy of Language.* Cambridge: Cambridge University Press.

Spicer, A., Alvesson, M and D. Karreman (2009) 'Critical performativity: The unfinished business of critical management studies', *Human Relations*, 62: 537-560.

Stroll, A. (2000) *Twentieth-Century Analytic Philosophy.* New York, NY: Columbia University Press.

Warnock, G. (1969) 'John Langshaw Austin, A biographical sketch', in K. Fann (ed.) *Symposium on J.L. Austin.* London: Routledge & Kegan Paul.

Warnock, G. (1989) *J.L. Austin.* London: Routledge.

8

Four Close Readings on Introducing the Literary in Organizational Research

Christina Volkmann and Christian De Cock

Introduction

In this chapter we will make a case that organization studies texts have tended to reduce literary theory to a static repository of concepts from which argumentative 'tools' or theoretical 'back-up' can be picked up as and when necessary. A discrete field of study like literary theory thus becomes a kind of supermarket full of material from where individual aspects are taken to reflect on methods for researching organizational 'reality' or to theorize on organization in general. Examples include using literary theory as a text-structuring device (e.g. through a 'checklist' or a set of labelling devices), as a way of distinguishing 'good' from 'bad' texts, or as a fixed status symbol by alluding to a string of theorists, novelists or poets whose writings only readers with a sound knowledge of literary theory will be able to appreciate fully and which presupposes a degree of consensus amongst literary scholars which does not exist.

The initial focus of our close reading will be on three texts published in respected organization studies journals during the 1990s (respectively Easton and Araujo, 1997; O'Connor, 1995; Hatch, 1996). Here the authors argue for different, open research approaches and discuss the implications of not being able to fix organizational reality in a way akin to the natural sciences. Yet, at the same time the texts under consideration tend to treat literary theory as a fixed entity which provides an infinite amount of typologies and frameworks (including 2x2 matrices!), thus denying the very implications they aim to discuss

143

for their own discipline. This reduction seems to be symptomatic of the quest for some solid ground to anchor the field of organization studies to. However, because the reduction is just that, and because it fails to take into account the complexity and constant flow and flux within the discipline it is 'using' (in this case literary theory), the attempt to find solid ground is doomed to failure.

We will then move on and perform a fourth close reading on the 'application' of the work of Wolfgang Iser in organization studies; a body of work which explicitly aims to move beyond typologies in order 'to produce an alternative pattern that can do justice to literature, the fictive, and the imaginary by bringing their limitless aspects into focus' (Iser, 1993: xiv). Iser's work (e.g. on Reception Theory/Reader Response Theory or Games/Play in the literary text) stands out in that it seems to be quoted frequently from paper to paper with a lack of argumentative purpose, thus excluding it from further engagement and consigning it to a kind of shorthand or code for 'those in the know'. Examples we will investigate in some detail include Golden-Biddle and Locke (1993), Czarniawska (1999) and Linstead (2000).

Overview of Terminology

In the knowledge of possibly oversimplifying literary terms, we shall attempt a brief clarification of our terminology. *Literature* denotes fictional texts such as novels, unless stated otherwise, for example, when 'literature' might stand for the body of texts produced on a certain subject, as in 'the literature on discourse'. *Literary theory* will refer to what is thought, written, and debated about literature, and the person engaged in such activity will be referred to as 'literary scholar'. Culler provides the following definition in a classic text:

> Literary theory is [...] the study of problems about the nature of literature: its forms, its components, their relations. Literary theory is not a set of competing methods for the analysis of literary works – methods that are to be judged by their relevance to problems [...] any more than linguistics is a set of competing models that are to be judged by their success in helping puzzled listeners understand obscure utterances. (Culler, 1981/2001: 244)

A term related to, and indeed often used synonymously with, literary theory is that of *literary criticism*. Following Culler's definition, however, we view the latter as closer to a 'set of competing methods for the analysis of literary works' and hence prefer the broader term of *literary theory*. Moreover, the term *literary criticism* is often ambiguous as it can suggest a degree of terminological closeness to specific theoretical directions such as New Criticism[1] with its text-immanent interpretation. Such connotation would be unfortunate, especially as the somewhat opposing concept of *Reception Theory/ Reader Response Theory* (RRT) will be discussed later. *Literary criticism* is also often connected with the evaluation of literary texts as good or bad literature, a connotation we wish to avoid.

It is in connection with RRT that the concept of the *reader* will be considered, with 'reader' referring to the way the reader is inscribed in a text, the way in which the text only happens when being read. Our discussion of the *reader* and RRT in Organization and Management Theory (OMT) texts represents another example of the way in which this concept is used in an isolated way. In organization studies, the concept of the *reader* is a potentially complex one in that it comprises several 'readers': Managers (or employees in general) 'read' organizations, and so do researchers in the field. There is an interesting twist here in that organizational researchers read as text what managers and employees produce (and read).[2] The researchers are in turn readers of the texts in their academic community, texts that they themselves contribute to.

Our preliminary reflections on terminology also have to draw attention to a concept central to literary theory and also to organization studies, that of the *text*. Nünning gives the following definition: '[Text is] an instrument of communication through language; colloquially used for the coherent written representation. [...] It comprises the written, printed, spoken word, pictorial illustrations, or linguistic conventions which are interpreted by literary scholars' (Nünning, 2001: 625-626; our translation).

In our chapter 'text' denotes two things, covering both aspects of this definition, although we point out here that we do not wish to conflate literary and non-literary texts. The first aspect is that of 'text as organizational reality'. This follows DeVault's (1990: 888) idea of 'examining society as text' and also Atkinson and Coffey (1997: 46), who point out 'the pervasive significance of documentary records, written and otherwise, in contemporary social settings'. Secondly, 'text' describes the works discussed in this chapter and, more generally, the writings in the field of organization studies, which, it could be argued, in turn form a 'society as text', only that 'society' in this case is largely limited to the academic community. Whilst we can find several examples of academic articles which study organizational reality as text (Brown, 2000; Gephart, 1993; Ng and De Cock, 2002; Phillips and Brown, 1993), it is without doubt the field itself that has taken centre stage in the past decade and a half, with a focus not so much on the 'primary text', but instead on a 'second order' text where the field talks about itself (cf. Van Maanen, 1998 or Weick, 1999 for insightful commentary on this reflexive turn).

The use of Literary Theory in Organization Studies Texts: Three Close Readings

1. 'Management Research and Literary Criticism' (Easton and Araujo, 1997)

Geoff Easton and Luis Araujo explore directly the potential of literary theory for the field of organization studies:

> If a critical approach is required to examine a body of theory, if its quality is to be evaluated, if it is to be judged, then it seems sensible to borrow some of the ideas that already exist to help the process along... By literature we mean a written work of art which is intended not only to divert and entertain but to provide greater understanding of the world. (Easton and Araujo 1997: 100)

Here Easton and Araujo refer to Horace's famous definition of the purpose of poetry, namely that poetry should *aut prodesse aut delectare* (quoted after Zapf, 1991: 45), i.e. that it should either be useful/instructive or should delight/entertain, and at best combine the two by instructing through entertainment. Interestingly, the 'use' of literature, the *prodesse*, is already defined by Easton and Araujo as 'to provide a greater understanding of the world'. It seems that their stated goal of providing a 'somewhat radical alternative' in the 'debate around the issue of whether the field of management studies and its marketing subdiscipline are sciences' (Easton and Araujo, 1997: 99) might prove elusive. If literature has to 'provide a greater understanding of the world', then it is natural to conclude that some form of evaluation is required that would allow to indicate success or failure in providing this understanding of the world. In the case of literature, Easton and Araujo see 'literary criticism' – here used loosely in the context of theory-building – as the authority to pronounce on what is deemed to be good or bad literature and to do so in a well-defined system that it is possible for management research to emulate: 'Literary criticism […] has developed techniques, *modus operandi* [sic], theoretical underpinnings. Critics must have a basis upon which they can judge what is good literature, what is 'valid'. It would be helpful to novice critics such as ourselves if we had some sort of taxonomy of critical theories' (Easton and Araujo 1997: 101; original emphasis).

Easton and Araujo present the body of 'literary criticism' as a well-mapped foreign territory into which students of organization can 'foray' in order to bring back pearls of wisdom. Whilst it might be tempting to draw parallels with European colonialism and improvise around a theme from Joseph Conrad here, the straightforward point we want to make is that such 'uses' of literature tend to resemble the activities of a raiding party, plundering the wealth of the humanities in order to bring it back to the home discipline. The authors make this altogether plain when they continue: '[T]he schema developed by Abrams (1981) serves our purpose best since it is well articulated and *allows us to place within it the forms of criticism we had already identified a priori*' (Easton and Araujo, 1997: 101; our emphasis). Self-effacingly denying that what they propose is tantamount to a 'paradigm shift', Easton and Araujo's 'foray into literary criticism' leads them to five conclusions about how to do organization studies: to do more epistemology, to talk more with fellow academics, to read more sociology of knowledge, to read fewer papers more carefully, to be explicit about the criteria by which we critique and to be more reflexive about research and writing (1997: 105). Plus ça change then…

Using individual concepts such as Horacian literary theory, a specific definition of 'literary criticism', or a theoretical classification scheme by Abrams is in itself not necessarily problematic.[3] However, here these concepts are constructed in a way that suggests that – in contrast to organization studies – literary theory as a discipline has solved its epistemological and methodological problems, that it has, for example, achieved closure on whether or not literary theory is a science. This is not the place to discuss either the ongoing epistemological or methodological debates in literary theory or to explore the question whether or not to achieve 'science status' would indeed be desirable for any humanities discipline. What should have become clear, however, is that the absence or even denial of such issues from texts like the one by

Easton and Araujo poses problems for the way the field of organization studies sees itself. As much as the authors proclaim their desire to revolutionize their own discipline through an encounter with literary criticism, the ground of organization studies remains remarkably stable and the 'other' that they are importing is reified and fixed in a single identity.

2. 'Paradoxes of Participation: Textual Analysis and Organizational Change' (O'Connor, 1995)

Whereas Easton and Araujo refer to themselves as 'novice critics', O'Connor openly declares her credentials in connection with literary theory at the end of her article: 'This paper positions a literature Ph.D into the social science field [...] Here I had a work which I was confident would have earned me praise in my discipline of origin, but the reviewers of this journal challenged the validity and reliability of my interpretations' (1995: 792). At the outset, O'Connor makes plain her goal: 'This paper applies literary theory, concepts and methods to four accounts of organization [sic] change' (1995: 769). She also aims to 'demonstrate that attention to language, and specifically attention to it in the form of literary analytical methods, reveals the process of cultural production in organizations' (ibid.), whereby her case studies are considered as texts.[4] Somewhat incongruously, her introductory remarks are then followed by an overview of the literature covering the long tradition of the 'interpretive approach' in the social sciences, so that the three theoretical approaches that she chooses, namely theory of rhetoric, narrative, and metaphor, seem already well embedded into the social science literature and are no longer 'direct imports' from literary theory (O'Connor, 1995: 772-773). With this structured threefold approach, literary theory appears to form a solid foundation on which observations on organizational change can be based. This impression is confirmed when O'Connor later refers to a kind of checklist that 'literary criticism' purportedly provides: 'I meet the criteria that Bazerman articulates for literary criticism: my interpretations are consistent with (1)[...] (2)[...] (3)[...]' (O'Connor, 1995: 795). She also takes care to defend herself against the possible accusation of arbitrariness, revealing what almost looks like mistrust of the possibility of multiple interpretations: 'This paper is no accident; it is to some extent the story of my professional life, but neither is my reading of the texts a Rohrschach [sic]' (O'Connor, 1995: 795).

O'Connor's own references to literary theory seem rather less well structured. Our example is taken from the section on the 'Analysis of the Texts' (1995: 775 ff.). The context is the 'Theory of Metaphor'. No fewer than seven literary theorists, poets and philosophers are mentioned in the space of the two paragraphs opening the section:

> As Saint Augustine observed, language does not present – rather, it represents. [...] The very phenomenon of language itself is metaphor (Shelley [...]). Burke, citing Bentham, states that language follows from the concrete to the abstract [...]. Brodsky's observations about poetic language may be applied more universally to language as a whole [...] "Metaphor", says Aristotle, "is the application of the name of a thing to something else" [...] This movement in language, or turn, is described by de Man as error [...]. (1995: 787)

Here the general references to famous names open up scope for misunderstanding rather than clarify the concept of metaphor. For example, the reference to Shelley triggers a whole set of possible associations with Romanticism in general, or in particular Shelley's view of language and the nature and possible function of literature in his *Defence of Poetry* of 1821 (comp. Zapf, 1991: 110-115). For literary scholars these references encompass a vast area of study and very likely one of considerable debate, too. Quoting a string of famous names closes the concept of metaphor by referring it to 'authorities'. It also looks rather like short-hand or a code for 'those in the know', which – now again on the meta-level – says more about the textual strategies the author feels she needs to employ than about metaphor.

3. 'The Role of the Researcher: An Analysis of Narrative Position in Organization Theory' (Hatch, 1996)

Mary Jo Hatch's article draws on literary theory to address an epistemological problem, namely the 'crisis of representation [that] finally reached organization theory in the early 1990s' (Hatch, 1996: 359). It may seem odd for Hatch to 'consult' literary theory in this context because she sees it as having at least partly brought the crisis about, a crisis with 'roots that extend to philosophy and literary theory, the deepest of which run to linguistics' (1996: 359). And yet, she states emphatically: 'I believe [...] that *application of literary theory* to organizational text and issues opens organizational enquiry to new possibilities' (1996: 360; our emphasis). She then shifts her focus away from 'organizational text and issues' to the person of the researcher, thus moving to a different position in the imaginary triangle of *Author/Narrator–Text–Reader*. It is the narrative theory of the French literary scholar Gérard Genette that Hatch chooses as the central theoretical concept for her argument:

> This study continues exploration of narration in organization theory by focusing on the literary concept of narrative position as developed by Genette (1980, 1982, 1988, 1992) in his theory of narratology. [...] My thesis is that application of Genette's theory can help us to more clearly formulate the role of the researcher by identifying it with the positioning of the narrator of a literary text. (Hatch, 1996: 361)

This approach is very different to O'Connor's who had referred to a number of literary theory concepts in order to support her argument. We have criticised O'Connor's 'use' of literary theory as unhelpful, thereby perhaps inadvertently implying that the opposite, i.e. the reference to a specific model, would be more successful, and it is from this angle that we will now consider Mary Jo Hatch's approach. With 'Four Narrative Positions'[5] which she organizes into a matrix 'in Relation to Voice and Perspective', Hatch provides a considerable amount of detail in adapting, or in her words, 'applying' Genette's *narratology* (Hatch, 1996: 362, comp. Fig. 2). Given that the 'researcher as narrator' is the focus of Hatch's study, it strikes us as curious that in this matrix she twice conflates narrator and author ('Agatha Christie narrating Hercule Poirot' and 'Fielding in Tom Jones'; 1996: 362),[6] which is certainly unusual and which sits uneasily with Hatch's specialised exposition of narrative theory in connection with the 'role of the researcher'.

Genette's pioneering development of a terminology and of a structuralist taxonomy of narrative theory is generally seen as his main contribution to literary theory. Whilst his work is generally well-accepted amongst narrative theorists, it is nevertheless extremely complex and difficult to understand for non-experts and therefore a rather curious choice for 'application' to a different discipline. In his *Narrative Discourse* (1980), one of the titles Hatch refers to, Genette takes the narrative of Proust's *A la recherche du temps perdu* as the text basis for the explication of his narrative theory; certainly not an easy text, even for a reader well-versed in French literature. Moreover, the application here of theories of the fictional or literary text to texts in organization studies would, in our view, necessitate at least some theoretical consideration.

In view of the extensive use Hatch makes of the 'Four Narrative Positions', it is perhaps precisely the taxonomies and terminologies in Genette's theory that appeal to her as an organization theorist who has set out to 'prove' that the researcher is not (any longer) an objective observer. If this were the case, however, she would be reintroducing 'through the back door' the scientific objectivity she claims to refute. In this context, Deetz (1996) not only criticises Mary Jo Hatch's textual strategy, he also points out its implications for the field of organization studies:

> Hatch's own explicit rewriting of literary theory into the subjective/objective discourse happens throughout the article [...]. The interest in examining the Hatch piece is in seeing how she accomplishes translations, which reinstate older epistemological battles and remove the more radical impact of new conceptions. [...] Such translations isolate organizational theory from the deeper challenges of contemporary social theories [...]. (Deetz, 1996: 388)

Rather than opening 'new possibilities' for organization studies, Genette's narratology, in Hatch's case, provides the author with a textual-strategic tool for the support of her arguments, be they in the context of the subjectivity of the researcher, the 'editorial suppression of what are essentially subjectivist narrative styles' (Hatch, 1996: 368), or the possible 'direct benefit for managers' of her analysis (1996: 372). The strategy is likely to appear successful because Genette's model (although naturally not the only view of narrative theory) is well-accepted and sufficiently uncontroversial within literary theory to be rejected, a fact that may make it more 'applicable' to the field of organization studies. At the same time, however, this model is likely to be too complex and inaccessible for the fellow organizational researcher/reviewer/editor to raise questions about or to discuss in detail. In a later article on complexity theory and organizational complexity, Genette's theory resurfaces without adaptation or change (Tsoukas and Hatch, 2001: esp. 997, 1000). This rather confirms our suspicion that the literary theoretical concept is deployed as a textual device instead of being allowed to contribute to any theoretical debate in hand.[7]

Reflecting on the Reader with Wolfgang Iser

Thus far, we have explored three examples to illustrate how OMT texts make use of literary theory, either as a discipline in general (Easton and Araujo, 1997; O'Connor, 1995), or by referring to the work of an individual literary theorist (Genette's narratology in Hatch, 1996 and Tsoukas and Hatch, 2001). We will now extend our exploration to a concept that reoccurs in OMT texts and at the same time constitutes a major area of literary theory: the *reader*. Wolfgang Iser and *Reader Response Theory* (RRT) are likely to be the name/term most often associated with the concept of the *reader*.[8] 'Through the concentration on the role of the reader, [RRT] was mainly a counter-reaction to formalist and structuralist approaches [...] as well as to the representation aesthetics of the New Criticism' (Nünning, 2001: 549; our translation).

There seems to be a marked difference between the way in which RRT is treated in the OMT texts we consider here and the uses of literary theory we have discussed above. RRT and related concepts are not so much called upon explicitly but seem to permeate the texts in a curious way. For Karen Golden-Biddle and Karen Locke, for example, the reader is the 'researcher reader' mentioned above: 'Viewing the written work as 'text' highlights how rhetoric and the interactive researcher-text and reader-text relationships are inseparable from the discussion of convincing' (Golden-Biddle and Locke, 1993: 596). In this context, the authors also refer to Wolfgang Iser to support their argument regarding the 'interactive researcher-text and reader-text relationships': 'The discussion is informed by a long tradition of scholarship in the humanities, especially literature and the discipline of literary criticism (cf. Booth 1961, 1967; Iser 1989), which rhetorically analyzes written work as 'texts' to be constructed and interpreted' (1993: 596).

Barry and Elmes (1997: 438) also refer to 'the perspective of reader/response theory (cf. Iser 1989)' in their narrative analysis of strategic discourse. They state: 'The interplay of text, author, and reader suggests that the interpretation of a text is both pluralistic and dynamic, reflecting the author's intent and the reader's construction of meaning' (1997: 438). Note that 'a text' here is separated from the context of the literary and applied in the authors' exploration of 'strategic management as a form of fiction' (1997: 429). The references to Iser are not elaborated upon in either article, yet at the same time they open up a vast field of possible reference points, some of which we shall attempt to sketch out in this section.

Iser's 1989 book, *Prospecting: From Reader Response to Literary Anthropology*, which both articles refer to, develops Iser's ideas about the role of literature, the reader and the text. The term *literary anthropology* was first used by F. Poyatos in 1977, for whom 'literatures [are] archives of anthropologically relevant data' (Nünning, 2001: 374; our translation). Within literary theory, the concept is controversial because many theorists reject the idea of literary texts as a source of data. Wolfgang Iser discusses this theoretical approach from a different angle, exploring areas such as the 'Fiktionsfähigkeit' (*fiction-ability*) or the 'Fiktionsbedürftigkeit' (the *need for fiction*) in human beings. Theoretical considerations of this kind, although related, appear to be somewhat removed from the relatively simple statement in which they are referenced in the articles cited above.

Golden-Biddle and Locke also refer to one of Iser's by now 'classic' texts, namely *The Act of Reading. A Theory of Aesthetic Response* (1976/1978), again, as in the passage discussed above, without further explanation: 'Finally, the metaphor of the text suggests that because all texts are addressed to an audience, that is are intended to communicate, they are rhetorical (Burke 1950, Booth 1961, Iser 1978)' (Golden-Biddle and Locke, 1993: 597). At the beginning of the following paragraph they state: 'The above discussion emphasizes that reading is an interactive process in which readers not only receive the text and its appeals to engage it [sic] and find it convincing, but also act on the text to create interpretations' (1993: 597). Although Wolfgang Iser is not directly referenced here, elements of his theory are nevertheless recognisable, for example in the 'interactive process of reading' or the 'appeal of a text'.[9] 'Die Appellstruktur der Texte.' [The Appeal Structure of Texts.] was the title of Iser's 1967 inaugural lecture in Konstanz, and it was here that he formulated first what later became the central ideas of his theories. For Iser, the 'real' or historical reader is not identical with the *Implied Reader*, which is a theoretical construct designed to move away from the 'interferences of the socio-psychologically coded reality of the historic author and the (real) reader' (Nünning, 2001: 375; our translation). The reader is inscribed in the text as a *Leerstelle* (gap or indeterminacy): 'Unlike the real historical or contemporary reader, unlike the fictive reader whom the author addresses in a novel, the *implied reader* is a theoretical construct without empirical existence, for he represents the entire potential of a text that may unfold in the course of the reading process' (Zima, 1999: 74; original emphasis).

Barbara Czarniawska (1999) refers to Wolfgang Iser and Stanley Fish in a context similar to that of Golden-Biddle and Locke (1993). In her discussion of 'The Narrative in Social Sciences and Organization Studies' (Czarniawska, 1999: 14ff.), she critiques their view of how ethnographic texts convince their readers: 'Unfortunately, like the positivist criteria they criticize, these are again *ostensive* criteria of a text's success – that is, the attributes of a text can be demonstrated and therefore applied a priori to determine a text's success' (Czarniawska, 1999: 27; original emphasis). Interestingly, the only reference to Wolfgang Iser and RRT in her book follows immediately afterwards:

> Reader-response theory has counteracted such objectivist reading theories (Iser 1978),[10] but, in turn, it tries to subjectivize the act of reading and therefore neglects the institutional effect. [...] The pragmatist theory of reading to which I adhere, best known in the rendition of Stanley Fish but here represented by Rorty [...] gives preference to *performative* criteria. (1999: 27)[11]

Mentioning Iser's theory does not seem to serve any purpose in Czarniawska's book. Indeed, it is Rorty whom she continues to refer to.[12] Also, it is curious that the reference should occur in the passage critiquing Golden-Biddle and Locke's views who had themselves referred to Iser. In view of the complexities of Iser's theoretical edifice and its potential implications for OMT, it is somewhat puzzling to find it referenced more or less 'in passing'. The situation here is similar to that of Hatch's use of Genette's theory where the latter was a textual strategic device (as RRT seems to be for Czarniawska). In Golden-Biddle and Locke, the references are 'just there', permeating the text. In this form, literary theory is hard to engage with in terms of its relevance to OMT precisely because of the vagueness of the reference. The opportunity for theorising the *reader* in terms of RRT is hence largely lost.

In defence of Czarniawska, it has to be said that ten years on she offers a much more careful reading of Iser (Czarniawska, 2009). For example, she points out Iser's central concern with 'fictionalizing acts' (2009: 358) and emphasizes the crucial point that

> Iser would have liked the models to vanish altogether, as he clearly preferred "operational" to "architectural" theories. His aims were of course, connected to the aims of literary theory, and not organization theory; a literary anthropology would, among other things, answer the question of why literature exists. (Czarniawska, 2009: 360)

Whilst we are not necessarily convinced either by her defence of the realist novel or her argument that 'there is a strong similarity between a researcher reading an annual report and a literary critic reading a novel',[13] at the very least her engagement with Iser's work provides a basis that makes possible a critique of or disagreement with arguments put forward.

Iser developed his theories, first on the reader/RRT and later also on literary anthropology, over more than three decades, with his last theoretical contribution, *The Range of Interpretation*, published in 2000.[14] One particular theme permeates his work, indicating how broadly Iser conceives of the reader concept: 'Already motivating Iser's reader-response theory, the question of why we need fictions links the different phases and decades of Iser's work and continues to inform his recent turn to literary anthropology' (Schwab, 2000: 74).

Iser's work has also generated a substantial amount of discussion. For example, in 2000 *New Literary History* published a special issue on Iser. Thomas (2000) charts in detail the reception of Iser's earlier works in the United States and in Britain, with a particular focus on the attacks on Iser by Fish and Eagleton, which Thomas views as having contributed to a lack of reception of Iser's later works. Thomas points out that these often clarify 'some of the confusion that his earlier work on the act of reading generated' (Thomas, 2000: 14). What becomes very clear in this later work is Iser's 'resistance to manifestation' and his 'insistence on the irreducible openness of the aesthetic realm' (Schwab, 2000: 74, 78). This seems to suggest that in engaging with Iser's texts it is important to view them as dynamic structures rather than as a finished theoretical edifice from which individual aspects can be taken at will. Although it might mean stating the obvious, it is worthwhile pointing out in this context that Iser is concerned mainly with literature, with fiction, with the 'aesthetic object' and with the relation of these to human beings. Explanation, such a core concept in the social sciences, helps Iser to describe literature *ex negativo*: '[L]iterature is not an explanation of origins; it is a staging of the constant deferment of explanation' (Iser, 1989: 245), and the same goes for fiction, the theme so central to his work: 'The more fiction eludes an ontological definition, the more unmistakably it presents itself in terms of its use. If it is no longer confined to an explanatory function, its impact becomes its most prominent feature' (Iser, 1989: 267).

When organizational scholars simply ignore the rich texture of Iser's work, we encounter some perverse applications. One such unfortunate[15] example is Linstead's (2000) use of concepts from Iser's work on games/play in a text (agōn, alea, mimesis, ilinx) in his rhetorical analysis of a letter written to all staff of the *Asia Pacific Institute of Technology* by their President. It is worth quoting Linstead at some length:

> In texts, and I am arguing in human organization more generally, of which texts are a part and an exemplar, these prototypes combine, merge, and dominate each other in different ways. Iser (1993: 259-73) explores in some detail the ways in which the various games may combine, and particularly the effects of combination on the differences between results-oriented games (agon, alea) and process-oriented games (mimicry, ilinx). *For our purposes here it is not necessary to present his arguments in detail,* but we can return to our consideration of the President's letter to identify some of them in play. What dominant game was the President playing in writing what he did? I read it as primarily a combination of agon and mimicry [...] The fact that the rules are not well understood or obvious, and that there is an unvoiced opposition to which the President's letter is both anticipation and reply, lends the subversive shadow of ilinx to the piece [...] It is, however, most important for him to attempt to exclude wherever possible elements of alea (chance) and ilinx (anarchy) which would undermine his portrayal of a measurable world in which quality was unequivocal [...]. (Linstead, 2000: 76-77; our emphasis)

Here Linstead ignores Iser's explicitly stated objective that 'play' pertains particularly to the literary text, that it is precisely what distinguishes the literary text from other text forms: '[...] embodying different types of interaction between the fictive and the imaginary [...] independently of their practical functions in the worlds of discourse' (Iser, 1993: 271). Indeed, rhetorical analysis is precisely what Iser wants to get away from, as Thomas (2000: 25) argues: 'Specifically, Iser's theory challenged the tendency to treat literature as operating like all other forms of rhetoric, that is as a mode of persuasion [...] Literature in Iser's model is a rhetorical means to question the adequacy of present constructions of rhetoric'.

Iser's development of a heuristics for human self-interpretation through literature has the potential to make organizational scholars rethink fundamental concepts (such as, for example, 'explanation', 'representation', 'fact', 'fiction') and the relationships between them. Yet a direct projection of Iser's theory onto the texts of organization theory would pose considerable theoretical and practical/methodological difficulties. However *text* is defined in organization studies (either as in the academic community writing about organizations, or as text produced in organizations), it will not fall into the realm of literature or the aesthetic as Iser sees it. Organizational texts are always written for a particular purpose (this seems to be an institutionally defined requirement), and in order to be effective they have to deny their fictionality. The text we are dealing with in organization studies is what is external to the literary text; it is part of what the literary text is there to reflect on. Literature allows us to cope with the world, to 'gain shape', and it 'tends to be a kind of institution that undermines all institutionalizations by exhibiting what both institutionalizing acts and definitions have to exclude in view of the stability they are meant to provide' (Iser, 1993: 303). Armstrong (2009) encounters precisely such a practical difficulty in trying to use Iser's theory to question institutional reality. In his 'fictional encounter between Ian McEwan and Wolfgang Iser' he pays particular attention to the *Imaginary* dimension of the triadic relationship between the *Real*, the *Fictive* and the *Imaginary* which is so central to Iser's later work. Armstrong (2009: 189) explores the possibility that a radical imaginary could emerge from reading literary fiction – '[…] fiction of this kind works by inviting the reader to create an imaginary in which their taken-for-granted views of the world are called into question' – which in turn could interrogate institutional rationality. However, he has to acknowledge the limitations of marshalling Iser's theory for the construction of such a critical imaginary since 'Iser's reception theory guarantees nothing about how real readers respond to the literary text'. For Armstrong, Iser's *Imaginary* fails in the critique of institutional rationality, 'not because [it] is conservative in principle, but because it is too open to the possibility of turning out to be so […]' (ibid.: 198). Perhaps this is not so much a 'failing' on Iser's part (in fairness, Armstrong calls the failing 'generous') than an inevitable consequence of organizational (or political) scholars asking something from literature that it cannot deliver. We have tried to capture the tension between expectations and limitations of literature in the two contrasting epigraphs of our concluding section.

Final reflections

> Literature, against which a good many sociologists have [...] thought necessary to define themselves in order to assert the scientificity of their discipline [...], is on many points more advanced than social science, and contains a whole trove of fundamental problems [...] that sociologists should make their own and subject to critical examination instead of ostentatiously distancing themselves from forms of expression and thinking that they deem to be compromising. (Bourdieu and Wacquant, 1992: 208)

> [...] if literature is all that stands between us and suicide, then we might as well commit suicide. (Eagleton, 2003: 170)

For any interdisciplinary discussion to be significant, it must stand in a relationship with an entire body of discourse, a collective endeavour already in place. However, in its earliest encounters with literary theory, the field of organization studies has been most interested in what are particular constructs that emerged at a particular moment in time for a particular purpose but which were often mere punctuations in an ongoing dialogue, never meant to be 'endpoints' or 'frameworks' to be simply imposed like a grid. Of course, a discursive community can assign any meaning it wishes to particular concepts such as *fiction* or *Reader Response Theory* if the community thinks that such a meaning helps in addressing certain practical or theoretical problems. What we take issue with, however, is the ossification of literary concepts and theories, a process by which they become solid bricks in an ever expanding 'wall of knowledge' and where the context in which these concepts and theories have lived and continue to evolve is never explored in a serious fashion. Now that the field of organization studies is becoming increasingly interested in literature (cf. Elsbach et al., 1999; De Cock and Land, 2006; Land and Sliwa, 2009) it is important that early texts exploring the potential of literary theory do not stand unchallenged, lest they acquire some kind of canonical status and entice a new generation of researchers to adopt rather dubious practices.

In reading Iser's work it is inspiring to see him grapple with the dissolution and fluidity which is a consequence of his embrace of a post-foundational approach (thus dispensing with the need for ontological grounding of his key concepts), without facile recourse to any 'authorities' or intellectual trends. It is somewhat ironic that organizational scholars refer to literary theorists such as Iser in order to establish some 'solid ground' and thus artificially import closure from literary theory (as a kind of *deus-ex-machina*). When engaging truly with Iser's thinking, it is very much in his 'honest grappling' that the literary theorist acts as a source of inspiration. Fixed frameworks, lists, criteria and other such devices that refer difficult or contested issues to 'the authorities' and which have monopolised the strange encounter between organization theory and literary theory have ultimately little to contribute to the improvement of our intellectual practices.

References

Abrams, M. H. (1993) *A Glossary of Literary Terms*. 6th edition. n.p.: Holt, Rinehart and Winston.

Armstrong, P. (2009) 'Imagining institutional rationality? A fictional encounter between Ian McEwan and Wolfgang Iser', *Culture and Organization*, 15(2): 185-201.

Atkinson, P. and A. Coffey (1997) 'Analysing documentary realities', in D. Silverman (ed.) *Qualitative Research: Theory, Method & Practice*. London: Sage. 45-62.

Barry, D. and M. Elmes (1997) 'Strategy retold: Toward a narrative view of strategic discourse', *Academy of Management Review*, 22(2): 429-452.

Berger, J. (1972) *Ways of Seeing*. London: Penguin.

Bourdieu, P. and L. J. D. Wacquant (1992) *An Invitation to Reflexive Sociology*. Cambridge: Polity.

Brown, A. D. (2000) 'Making Sense of Inquiry Sensemaking', *Journal of Management Studies*, 37: 45-75.

Culler, J. (1981/2001) *The Pursuit of Signs*. London: Routledge.

Czarniawska, B. (1998) *A Narrative Approach to Organization Studies*. London: Sage.

Czarniawska, B. (1999) *Writing Management: Organization Theory as a Literary Genre*. Oxford: Oxford University Press.

Czarniawska, B. (2009) 'Distant readings: anthropology of organizations through novels', *Journal of Organizational Change Management*, 22(4): 357-372.

De Cock, C. and C. Land (2006) 'Organization/literature: Exploring the seam', *Organization Studies*, 27(4): 517-535.

Deetz, S. (1996) 'The positioning of the researcher in studies of organizations: De-Hatching literary theory', *Journal of Management Inquiry*, 5(4): 387-391.

DeVault, M. L. (1990) 'Novel readings: The social organization of interpretation', *American Journal of Sociology*, 95(4): 887-921.

Eagleton, T. (1996) *Literary Theory: An Introduction*. 2nd ed. Oxford: Blackwell.

Eagleton, T. (2003) *Figures of Dissent*. London: Verso.

Easton, G. and L. Araujo (1997) 'Management research and literary criticism', *British Journal of Management*, 8: 99-106.

Elsbach, K. D., R.I. Sutton and D.A. Whetten (1999) 'Perspectives on developing management theory, circa 1999: Moving from shrill monologues to (relatively) tame dialogues', *Journal of Management Inquiry*, 8: 627-633.

Genette, G. (1980) *Narrative Discourse: An Essay in Method*. Ithaca: Cornell University Press.

Gephart, R. P. (1993) 'The textual approach: Risk and blame in disaster sensemaking', *Academy of Management Journal*, 36: 1465-1514.

Golden-Biddle, K. and K. Locke (1993) 'Appealing work: An investigation of how ethnographic texts convince', *Organization Science*, 4(4): 595-616.

Hatch, M. J. (1996) 'The role of the researcher: An analysis of narrative position in organization theory', *Journal of Management Inquiry*, 5(4): 359-374.

Hatch, M. J. and D. Yanow (2008) 'Methodology by metaphor: Ways of seeing in painting and research', *Organization Studies*, 29(1): 23-44.

Iser, W. (1978) *The Act of Reading: A Theory of Aesthetic Response*. Baltimore and London: Johns Hopkins University Press.

Iser, W. (1989) *Prospecting: From Reader Response to Literary Anthropology.* Baltimore and London: Johns Hopkins University Press.

Iser, W. (1993) *The Fictive and the Imaginary. Charting Literary Anthropology.* Baltimore and London: Johns Hopkins University Press.

Iser, W. (2000) *The Range of Interpretation.* New York: Columbia University Press.

Iser, W. (2006) *How to Do Theory.* Oxford: Blackwell.

Land, C. and M. Sliwa (2009) 'The novel and organization: introduction from the editors', *Journal of Organizational Change Management,* 22(4): 349-356.

Linstead, S. (2000) 'Ashes and madness: The play of negativity and the poetics of organization', in S. Linstead and H. Höpfl (eds) *The Aesthetics of Organization.* London: Sage.

Linstead, S. (2003) 'Introduction: Text, organization and identity', in S. Linstead (ed.) *Text/Work: Representing organization and organizing representation.* London: Routledge.

Ng, W. and C. De Cock (2002) 'Battle in the boardroom: A discursive perspective', *Journal of Management Studies,* 39(1): 23-49.

Nünning, A. (ed.) (2001) *Metzler Lexikon der Literatur- und Kulturtheorie. Ansätze. Personen. Grundbegriffe.* 2nd revised and enlarged edition. Stuttgart and Weimar: Metzler.

O'Connor, E. S. (1995) 'Paradoxes of participation: Textual analysis and organizational change', *Organization Studies,* 16(5): 769-803.

Phillips, N. and J. L. Brown (1993) 'Analyzing communication in and around organizations: A critical hermeneutic approach', *Academy of Management Journal,* 36(6): 1547-1576.

Schwab, G. (2000) '"If only I were not obliged to manifest": Iser's aesthetics of negativity', *New Literary History,* 31(1): 73-90.

Thomas, B. (2000) 'Restaging the reception of Iser's early work, or sides not Taken in discussions of aesthetics', *New Literary History,* 31(1): 13-42.

Tsoukas, H. and M. J. Hatch (2001) 'Complex thinking, complex practice: A narrative approach to organizational complexity', *Human Relations,* 54: 979-1013.

Van Maanen, J. (1998) 'Different strokes: Qualitative research in the Administrative Science Quarterly from 1956 to 1996', in J. Van

Maanen (ed.) *Qualitative Studies of Organizations*. London: Sage. ix-xxxii.

Weick, K. E. (1999) 'Theory construction as disciplined reflexivity: Tradeoffs in the 90s', *Academy of Management Review*, 24(4): 797-806.

Zapf, H. (1991) *Kurze Geschichte der anglo-amerikanischen Literaturtheorie*. Munich: Fink.

Zima, P. (1999) *The Philosophy of Modern Literary Theory*. London: Athlone Press.

Notes

1 New Criticism describes the theoretical approach that dominated literary theory (especially in the USA) from ca. the 1920s to the 1960s. New Criticism was not a homogenous movement, but a similarity between the different directions is the focus on the text itself, without any reference to the historical circumstances of a literary work's creation and reception or to the biography of the author. In this theoretical view the meaning of a literary text can be revealed by solely studying the text itself (Comp. Abrams, 1993: 264ff.; Eagleton, 1996: 38-46).

2 Also compare Atkinson and Coffey (1997: 46): 'If we wish to understand how such organizations work and how people work in them, then we cannot afford to ignore their various activities as readers and writers.'

3 The main body of Easton and Araujo's text is based on a reading of Abrams's important but not uncontroversial book from 1953 *The Mirror and the Lamp* (for a critical review see Culler, 2001: Chapter 8).

4 Later, she proposes a broader concept of *text* that would have been closer to the organizational reality she was looking at: 'My analysis has been severely limited by its focus on language and text. Interviews and surveys would no doubt have illuminated other facets of change, particularly as regards the rhetorical functions of the texts, but this is not my expertise' (O'Connor, 1995: 795).

5 These are: 'The Narrator Tells the Story as an Objective Observer' (Hatch, 1996: 362f.), 'The Narrator as a Minor Character in the Story' (363f.), 'The Main Character Tells the Story' (364-366), and 'The Omniscient Viewpoint' (366f.).

6 An obvious example of why author and narrator are not the same is Anna Sewell's *Black Beauty* where the narrator is a horse. We admit that in the case of *Tom Jones* the narrative position is less obvious because of the frequent change of narrative perspective. Hatch also contradicts herself somewhat because she later states that '[i]n literature, the narrator is typically accepted as

fictional, whereas in social science the narrator is more likely to be confused with the author' (Hatch, 1996: 365).

7 We note that in a more recent article Hatch leaves literary theory behind and turns to painting for opening up organizational research to new possibilities, aligning Rembrandt and Pollock with 'realists' and 'interpretivists' respectively (Hatch and Yanow, 2008). The authors borrow their title from John Berger's famous book *Ways of Seeing* (1972) to highlight 'the importance of (re)presentation in research' (Hatch and Yanow, 2008: 24) without engaging at all with that book or Berger's broader body of work. Whilst it is beyond the scope of this chapter to examine the article in depth, it suffices to say that the critique put forward of the three examples – a colonial approach to the 'other' field, spurious referencing, and a predilection for neat categories – equally applies here.

8 Reader Response Theory is also referred to as "the Anglo-Saxon variation" of *Rezeptionsästhetik* [reception aesthetics] or *Reception Theory*. (Comp. Nünning, 2001: 549)

9 Also compare the title of the article: '*Appealing* Work: An Investigation of How Ethnographic Texts Convince' (our emphasis).

10 In what is probably an oversight, though in this context a curious one, Czarniawska (1999) references Iser's book as '*The Art* [sic] *of Reading: A Theory of Aesthetic Response.*' The actual title of Iser's book is *The Act of Reading* [German: *Der Akt des Lesens*].

11 This passage in its context also occurs verbatim in an earlier book (Czarniawska, 1998: 70).

12 Compare Index, s.v. "Rorty, Richard" (Czarniawska, 1999: 131).

13 Indeed, Czarniawska herself seems to highlight a certain tension when she ascribes a difference to the "function" of fiction in literature and organizational life but a similarity to the study of that "functioning": 'The fiction of accounting has a different function than does literary fiction, but their emergence and functioning can be studied in a similar way' (2009: 361).

14 *How to Do Theory* (2006) was his last published book (Iser died in 2007), but it is a sophisticated textbook rather than a research monograph, thus offering no new theoretical contributions.

15 Unfortunate because elsewhere Linstead is much more careful in his treatment of literature and literary concepts (e.g. Linstead, 2003).

9

From Bourgeois Sociology to Managerial Apologetics: A Tale of Existential Struggle

Peter Armstrong

Introduction

This chapter examines the 'reconstructed' labour process approach to the analysis of management proposed by Willmott (1997). Willmott argues that both the 'bourgeois' pluralist approach and that of 'orthodox labour process analysis' are deficient, the first because it neglects the primacy of the capitalist social relations of production and the second because it reduces the work of managers to an execution of the economic functions of capital. In their place he proposes a theorization in which the capitalist social relations of production are mediated by managerial subjectivities and in which those subjectivities, through a search for meaning and identity, react to the commodification of managerial labour in such a way as to incline managers against the prioritization of capital accumulation. The result, so he claims, is a theory which recognizes that the work of managers is conditioned by their position in the social relations of production but which avoids the tendency towards structural determinism which he finds in orthodox labour process analysis..

Despite his best efforts, Willmott's trawls through some of the major workplace ethnographies produced by 20th century social science reveal no evidence of the search for existential significance on which his theory hinges. Instead, and as if it were a substitute for such evidence, he repeatedly castigates the authors of these studies for their failure to produce any. Beyond that, his depiction of managerial subjectivities depends on an implausible and empirically unsupported assumption

165

that managers react to the surveillance and control of their work by rejecting the purpose behind those controls. He then misconceives the nature of the capitalist social relations of production to such an extent that these are seen as mutable by this non-compliance on the part of managers.

Many of the difficulties of Willmott's theory, and his persistent tendency to misread work of other authors, stem from the logical impossibility of the task which he sets himself: that of finding some way between a bourgeois pluralism which does not recognise the primacy of the capitalist social relations of production and a Marxist/ labour process approach which does. Faced with the obdurate fact that these alternatives exhaust the relevant field of possibilities, Willmott seeks to create space between them by constructing a parodied version of 'labour process orthodoxy' in which managers are depicted as doing *nothing but* perform the functions of capital. It is into this imagined space that he seeks to insert his own theory of a managerial contrariness driven by a proletarianisation of their conditions of employment. The ironic result is a labour process approach to management which neglects the role of managers in the labour process.

The chapter concludes with a brief suggestion that a better theory both of managerial practices and managerial subjectivities can be constructed by recognizing the contradiction between the roles which managers play within the labour process and the role which they play as the agents of capital in the extraction, realization and allocation of the surplus values created by that labour process. The one requires the establishment of co-operative relationships, in the ordinary way at least, whilst the other depends on the treatment of labour as a commodity. Many of the tensions and anxieties experienced by managers in the course of their work, it is suggested, can be traced to this contradiction between co-operation and exploitation (or complicity in exploitation) rather than some universalized search for existential significance. Although by no means original, such a theory has at least the merit of accommodating the surely undeniable fact that most managers accede to the controls to which their work is subjected rather than rebel against them.

Subjectivities and the 'Transformation' of Capitalist Social Relations

As set out in Willmott (1997), his theory of managerial subjectivities is fairly simple. The exposition, however, is complicated by his concern to distance himself from 'bourgeois forms of analysis' on the one hand (Willmott, 1997: 1340) and on the other from what he variously refers to as 'Marxian theory' (ibid.: 1333) or 'orthodox labour process analysis' (ibid.: 1351, footnote). Concerning bourgeois analysis, his objection is to an indiscriminate pluralism which fails to acknowledge the ultimate dominance of the capitalist social relations of production (ibid.: 1333) and to an assumption that the consciousness of individuals stands outside the historical conditions of its formation (ibid.: 1340). Concerning labour process orthodoxy, he seeks to avoid such theoretical misdemeanours as 'treating human agents as personifications of economic categories' (ibid.: 1333, 1341) 'reducing managerial work to the execution of capitalist functions' (ibid.: 1339) and a 'tendency toward determinism and reductionism' (ibid.: 1351 footnote).[1] How far these features are actually characteristic of the mainstream labour process tradition is a question which will be addressed later.

For reasons which will appear presently, Willmott's 1997 paper is additionally complicated by his need to argue an ontology which equates the capitalist social relations of production to their local enactment (Willmott, 1997: 1340) and by a tussle with ethnographic data which stubbornly resist the interpretations which he wishes to put upon them (ibid.: 1348-1353).

Willmott's wish to differentiate his approach from that of the conventional non-Marxist sociology of management is expressed at the level of rhetoric by his repeated reference to the latter as 'bourgeois' (e.g. Willmott, 1997: 1340, 1342), though whether the implied other of 'bourgeois'is to be taken as 'proletarian', 'radical' or merely 'critical' is a matter for conjecture. At the level of substance, the attempt at differentiation takes the form of a repeated insistence that a recognition of the primacy of 'capitalist social relations' (and similar) must lie at the heart of any adequate analysis of managerial work. On the face of it, this appears to be convincing. Testifying to the antipathy which such forms of words arouse in the hearts of bourgeois social scientists – and hence to his theoretical distance from their approach – he is able to quote Whittington's ringing denunciation of his own work, 'Managerial authority need not rely upon capitalist resources; managerial action need not be directed towards capitalist ends' (Whittington, 1992). The rhetorical effect is marred only slightly by the thought that these are sentiments which could have been expressed by any Marxist of a minimal sophistication.

It is only when one looks more closely at the meaning which Willmott attaches to such phrases as 'social relations of production' that doubts begin to creep in. In essence, he depicts those social relations as the moment-by-moment outcome of social action with the happy implication for his preoccupation with managerial subjectivities that these become consequential for the social structures within which they are produced (e.g. Willmott, 1997: 1340). For Willmott, it is important that 'relations of production are accomplished through the existential media of human conduct' and that they cannot, in consequence, be 'deemed to exist independently of the individuals or agents whose conduct is the medium of their reproduction (and transformation)' (ibid.: 1344). For this reason, 'It is necessary but insufficient' as he puts it, 'to focus on the "objective" conditions of action' – insufficient unless it is also recognised that 'the "micro" processes of enactment through which the "macro" structures of capitalism are *reproduced* (and transformed)' (ibid.: 1340, italics in original). But if the social structures of capitalism are so pliable that they can be *transformed* by the micro processes of interaction (my own italics this time – and the phrasing cannot be accidental because Willmott repeats it), one's first impulse is to question whether they are social structures at all, and to wonder of what they might consist. Certainly, Willmott cannot be referring to the ownership by capital of the means of production nor to the exchange of labour power against capital. Nor, by inference, can he be referring to the consequences which follow as a matter of logic from such bedrock features of the capitalist social formation, consequences both for the practice of management and for the labour process as it is managed.

The '"objective" conditions of action' mentioned by Willmott himself (the scare quotes are his own) are labour's real subordination to capital and the execution of capitalist functions by management. The first of these is not a definitive structural feature of capitalism because capitalist enterprises and indeed entire capitalist societies can exist perfectly well in the absence of detailed controls of the labour process. Concerning the second, it is certainly essential to the capitalist social formation that someone – either the owners of capital themselves or their agents – must attend to the economic functions of capital, most of the time at any rate. That does not mean, however, that those functions, either taken together or separately, have to be performed by managers, still less by particular managers and even when by particular managers, not all the time. In the particular locales wherein the micro processes of enactment are played out, both of Willmott's 'objective' conditions of action – the precise degree to which labour is 'really subsumed' and the extent to which managers are involved in the economic functions of capital – may well vary according to that enactment, but neither, by the same token, are they core structural features of capitalist society and nor, within wide limits, need they impact against those core structures. In Mouzelis' terms (1995: 19ff), what is lacking in Willmott's schema is any sense of how the micro and macro levels of analysis might articulate, in default of which he simply conceptualises the social relations of production in terms which *are* susceptible to the vagaries of local enactment.

Apart from a prioritization of those local social structures which he identifies as those of capitalism, in fact, Willmott's conception of the relationship between social action and social structure is remarkably similar to that of Giddens (1984). In one respect this comes as no surprise since he had earlier recommended the approach as 'a valuable alternative conceptual framework for advancing critical empirical research into managerial work' (Willmott, 1987: 265). If we go back a little further, however, it *is* a surprise since he was also party to the identification of an 'analytic void' at the heart of structuration theory which, so he and/or his co-author argued, renders it incapable of connecting concrete manifestations of social conflict with the structural contradiction between private appropriation and socialized production (Knights and Willmott, 1985: 31). Such a connection, the co-authors claimed at the time, could be achieved through a consideration of the *'strategies of securing self through social identity'* (ibid., italics in original). How these strategies or indeed the identities which they are intended to secure, might themselves connect with the structural contradiction in question remain matters for conjecture.

The real problem with Willmott's (and Giddens') duality of structure, is not so much its lack of a social psychology but that it ignores those macro structures which are not directly instantiated at the local level, but which nevertheless underlie the contingently derived substructures which *are* the subject of instantiation. The ownership by capital of the means of production is a case in point. This is not re-enacted as such in most workplaces, not even at the level of rhetoric. What *is* routinely re-enacted is a particular version of the managerial prerogatives deriving from, but not determined by, the delegated powers attaching to ownership. Though these are certainly aspects of local social structure in the sense that they constitute rules and resources available to those involved (Giddens, 1984: 19-25), they are also susceptible to change either through the creep of custom-and-practice (Brown, 1972) or as a result of direct challenge. *But* – they can change without touching the basic social structure which underlies them.

The point in the end is a simple one: that the social structures which make up a given social formation exist at different levels of embeddedness.[2] At the 'surface' level, there are those which exist through their enactment and can by the same token be changed through that enactment. It is structures of this kind which are recognised in the theory of structuration. Underlying these immediate and local structures, however, there are those which are more pervasive and persistent. These are missed by structuration theory because they are insulated from changes in any one of their particular manifestations, partly because they are anchored in so many others and partly because their articulation with their surface manifestations often allows for some degree of slack. Such is the case, to repeat the earlier example, with the ramified institution of private property as it exists in capitalist societies.

This means that Knights and Willmott (1985) are perfectly correct in their diagnosis of a void in structuration theory and, by implication, of a similar void in Willmott's (1997) partial replication of it. As it stands, both versions of the theory do indeed fail to connect the routines of structuration with the possible development of pressures for change in core social institutions. The nature of the void, however, points towards the need for a theory of how the structures at various levels might articulate, rather than the social psychology of identity envisaged by Knights and Willmott. Such a theory might begin in a rough way by visualising core structures as setting limits to the variability of those through which they are articulated at the surfaces of social interaction. Through some custom-and-practice drift of the processes of enactment, these limits might become more frequently and more widely encountered and thereby become the objects of conscious reflection. Demands for the democratization of the workplace, for example, might progress by degrees from those which can be accommodated within the core property relationships of capitalist society to those which cannot, with the result that these structural elements become the subjects of explicit critique and political action where they had once formed the taken-for-granted basis behind the rules and resources of Giddens' processes of structuration (c.f. Mouzelis, 1995: 119). This, of course, is just one possible mode of articulation between social structures at different levels of embedding, but to develop such conjectures further would take us too far from the matter in hand.

Willmott's ideas on the change-through-enactment of capitalist social relations, meanwhile, can only properly apply to those which exist at the level of surface manifestation. His repeated references to them, however, always in the abstract and always in general terms, have the effect of blurring the important distinction between surface and deeper structures and doing so in ways which favour his belief in the consequentiality of managerial subjectivities. For if what is true of the immediate employment relationship – that it is susceptible to the reworkings of structuration – is also true of the deeper structures which underlie it, he can argue a version of managerialism in which the greater part of the capitalist social order is subtended by nothing more than the play of subjectivities at the level of middle and junior management. Pushed this far, the argument self-evidently auto-destructs on the rampages of private equity and other predations of finance capital. Possibly, this is why Willmott, when he ceases his talk of the transformation of capitalist social relations, contents himself with the relatively modest claim that attention to the subjectivities of managers is necessary for a 'more adequate' understanding of the work which they perform.

Control and Resistance in Middle and Lower Management

But how far is he justified even in this? He obviously has right on his side to the extent that the states of mind of managers and everyone else involved in the capitalist social order are a legitimate object of interest in their own right. The more testing questions, however, concern the extent to which managerial subjectivities influence what managers actually do, and how far what managers actually do influences the lives and doings of the managed.

These are matters on which Willmott has opinions, if not always very decided ones. The subjectivities of most middle and lower managers, he maintains, do not just influence the manner in which they *interpret* their assigned roles in the processes of capital accumulation; they actually incline them against those aspects of their work. More, he also believes – most of the time at any rate – that these managers possess sufficient power and autonomy to act on these inclinations to the extent that their recalcitrance is a 'basic problem' for senior management (Willmott, 1997: 1348-9). Elsewhere he is not so sure. On the one hand, he points out that management control systems indicate the potential for 'misbehaviour' at the more junior levels (ibid.: 1338, 1348), though he does not make it clear whether or not he thinks this potential survives the imposition of the controls in question. On the other hand, he notes that the same controls leave managers with 'comparatively little "space" (or inclination it might be added) to pursue strategies which are overtly antagonistic to the "bottom line"' (ibid.: 1335). Even if the stress in this last quotation is on 'overt', with the implication that managerial resistance is mostly covert, there remain contradictions. How can there be even covert resistance to capital accumulation if managers are as enmeshed in performance controls, as Willmott says? And how, if their resistance is covert to the point that it is undetected by these controls, can it be a problem for senior management?

According to Willmott, it is only a small minority of the most senior managers, abetted by a few accomplices, who are wholeheartedly committed to the goal of profitability (Willmott, 1997: 1335, 1348). The rest, he tells us, are preoccupied with 'other concerns – such as career advancement and job security – which are not necessarily consonant with the reliable and effective stewardship of investors' interests'. (ibid.: 1338). In addition, they may play games of 'office politics' which have little to do with profitability (ibid.: 1339) or selfishly resist company policies which threaten to devalue their accumulated skills and knowledge (ibid.: 1348, footnote).

The first two arguments confuse the question of commitment to a goal with that of whether actors have a motive (i.e. any motive) for acting in furtherance of that goal. To most lay observers, a concern with career advancement and job security would seem to provide highly effective levers through which middle and lower managers might be induced to take a keen, albeit purely instrumental, interest in profitability, whilst 'office politics' might work either way. That leaves only resistance to changes which might devalue their personal capital as a genuine reason why managers might resist the prioritization of profit; not an uncommon situation, but not one which is universally applicable either.

To what does Willmott attribute this widespread disaffection? One observation that he offers is that only few managers own substantial portions of their companies or have a direct material interest in its profitability (1997: 1335). Theoretically speaking this is the good ol' Rock 'n Roll of 'sectional managerialism' (Nichols, 1969) – a long way from the close attention to subjectivities which he recommends elsewhere. Substantively speaking, moreover, they are reasons why managers might be indifferent to capital accumulation, rather than hostile to it. Nor are they even convincing as reasons for indifference. The proportion of a company's equity held by managers is no index of the proportion of their personal remuneration which is linked to its profitability, whilst the prevalence of indices of economic performance in the control systems of most modern companies, sometimes right down to the level of the business unit (Armstrong, Marginson, Edwards and Purcell, 1996), make it doubtful indeed that many managers have no direct interest in profitability, at least that of their own patch.

These attributions of interests aside, the main thrust of Willmott's argument concerns the employment relationship as it is now experienced by middle and lower managers. He quotes a number of authorities to the effect that middle and lower managers have experienced a proletarianisation of their conditions of employment. Although they remain economically privileged compared to the workers they manage, they have now come to 'share in the subjugation and oppression that characterises the lives of productive workers', a quotation from Braverman (1974: 418), which Willmott italicises as a key point in his argument (1997: 1334). What these various authorities do *not* go on to say, however, and what Willmott does, is that the density of performance controls, pervasive accountability and relative lack of autonomy typically mean that middle and lower managers now feel little or no allegiance to their companies or their profitability (ibid.: 1335).

This is a key point in Willmott's argument, and it hinges on a conceptual leap, and into the bargain an assumption about subjectivities, which is both logically unwarranted and, so far as the evidence goes, empirically falsified. It is unwarranted because a withdrawal of allegiance does not follow as a matter of logic from a loss of opportunities for self-expression. Elsewhere, in fact, Willmott has castigated other authors for the 'essentialism' of any assumption that the routinization of work even results in a sense of deprivation (Willmott, 1990). Even supposing that it does, Mills (1956: 243) has argued that the consequences may be the precise opposite of those claimed by Willmott: that routine white collar employees *compensate* for the fact that their work 'offers little chance for external prestige claims and internal self-esteem' by 'borrowing' prestige from the companies for which they work. Empirical evidence that routine work need not be associated with a lack of allegiance to the company was encountered during the ChemCo studies. There were, for example, the operatives who were described as 'like a stick of rock; break them in half and you'd find "ChemCo" stamped through the centre' (e.g. Harris, 1987: 93) and the cheers which rang out when one of the plants achieved a monthly production record, not in the plant itself, but amongst the clerks who had calculated the figures (not previously reported).

Willmott's thoughts on the proletarianising effects on middle and junior managers of organizational control systems are also at variance with a substantial literature on behavioural accounting. Most such systems nowadays take the form of targets against which performance is monitored, sometimes at intervals of as little as one week (Armstrong, Marginson, Edwards and Purcell, 1996). In the literature relating to such systems, the conventional wisdom is that, provided targets are set in consultation with those to whom they apply, and set at levels which are challenging yet attainable, far from provoking the resistance which Willmott assumes, they are actually internalised as personal goals (e.g. Caplan, 1971). To be fair, these are beliefs which are only patchily supported by empirical research. More persuasive is Hopwood's classic study (1973) which found that the *manner* in which senior managers used accounting information in the evaluation of their subordinates was the crucial variable. Hopwood distinguished between a non-accounting style of evaluation in which the accounting information was largely ignored, a budget-constrained style in which it was treated as the only relevant index of performance and a profit-conscious style in which it was melded with other relevant information to produce a rounded picture of the contribution of the manager to company profitability. If Willmott's picture of managerial reaction against organizational controls were correct, one would expect the non-accounting style to do the least damage to managerial motivation, the budget-constrained style to produce the antagonistic reaction of which he writes, with the profit-conscious style somewhere in between. In fact, Hopwood found the profit-conscious style of evaluation to be most effective – not an unexpected finding admittedly, but one which flatly contradicts Willmott's crudely determinist picture of dysfunctional management controls.

The weight of evidence, then, is against Willmott's supposition that the primary effect of organizational controls systems is to demotivate those managers to whom they are applied.

At points, Willmott argues that the potential for disarticulation between the requirements of capital accumulation and the practices of middle and junior managers arises not just from their conditions of employment but from influences external to the workplace altogether. In this vein, he argues that a reconstructed labour process theory *'must* incorporate an appreciation of how [managers'] work is coloured by diverse cultural and ideological influences in addition to being shaped by their career interests as sellers of valued skills' (Willmott, 1997: 1343, italics added). The mandatory incorporation of such extra-curricular influences might prove difficult, however, in view of the concurrent need to avoid the pitfalls of 'bourgeois' pluralism. As Willmott himself put it only ten pages earlier, 'It can readily be acknowledged that many influences (e.g. familial, religious, professional) do inform the practical accomplishment of managerial work. But in advanced capitalist societies, these influences are more-or-less directly conditioned – promoted or suppressed – by politico-economic pressures to sustain or revitalize processes of capital accumulation' (ibid.: 1333). Evidently, these are not easy waters to navigate.

It is on the basis of the foregoing arguments, fallible though they are, that Willmott feels able to sum up the case thus:

> In response [to 'various sticks and carrots'], managers may mobilize other values, agendas and concerns to *diffuse, resist, or circumvent* pressures that are intended to make their agency more predictable and profitable [reference omitted]. (1997: 1347, italics added)

Formally speaking, the logic of this is unassailable: it is indeed *possible* for managers to react in this way, although that requires an assumption that that those advisory staffs who design the relevant appraisal, reward and career progression schemes and those senior managers who operate them are 'judgmental dopes', a pejorative assumption which Willmott is quick to attack in connection with any suggestion that managers 'slavishly' (as he puts it) perform the functions of capital (1997: 1340). On that unlikely basis, nevertheless, he is still entitled to his claim that managers *may* resist the pressures on them. A page later, though, the 'may' has firmed up to the extent that it confronts senior management as an accomplished fact:

> For (senior) managers and other committed agents of capital who elevate "the business objective of making a profit" above all else, a *basic* problem is the *recalcitrance* of managers whose allegiance to this objective is partial, ambivalent and not infrequently dramaturgical. (Willmott, 1997: 1348, italics added)

In sum, Willmott believes that the subjectivities of middle and lower managers are influenced against the prioritization of capital accumulation by the very controls intended to procure their commitment. How far he also believes that they are able to act on these inclinations is less clear, but the balance of his statements on the matter, not to mention his insistence that managerial practices possess the capacity to influence 'capitalist social relations', certainly suggest some degree of autonomy.

A Preliminary Evaluation

The first thing to note about the vision of the capitalist corporation behind this characterization of managerial subjectivities is the sheer implausibility of the theory of power which informs it. How is it, the question poses itself, that a tiny oligarchy of zealots is so consistently able to squeeze profit out of a largely disaffected mass? In effect, we are asked to swallow what Foucault (1980, 78-108) called a 'juridical' theory of power: that it flows downwards from the persons of a ruling élite. Against this, one of Foucault's genuine insights was that overarching systems of power can only be constructed out of the raw material of lower-level networks through which power already 'circulates' (ibid.). In other words, all systems of power – even Willmott's imagined dictatorship of the boardroom – can only function through webs of complicity. But managerial complicity is precisely what he is concerned to deny.

Also implausible is the contention that the *primary* effect of managerial control systems is rebellion. In a number of the foregoing quotations, Willmott seems to imagine the corporation as controlled by a tightly-knit web of bureaucratic sanctions ('carrots and sticks'). Where this is the case, the response to the implicit low-trust employment relationship may well be *disaffection*, as Fox (1974) amongst others has argued, but disaffection can only become resistance in those interstices of the system which have not so far succumbed to advances in the techniques of monitoring. More usually, however, managerial control, especially at the more senior levels but to some degree at all levels, is achieved not through detailed performance controls but through the socio-cultural production of trust (Kanter, 1993), albeit backed up by procedures for the post-hoc evaluation of the discharge of fiduciary responsibilities. This means that a condition of access to those managerial positions characterised by high-trust employment relationships is an ongoing assurance to that the trust will not be abused, an assurance made and reaffirmed by a host of subtle signals given off in the course of daily practice and which are minutely scrutinised by colleagues and superiors in a normatively dense managerial culture (Whyte, 1960).

The fact that managers are already enmeshed in a culture with its ready-made significances and meanings also means that it is difficult to imagine that they routinely 'struggle with the existential significance of the purposive quality of human consciousness', as Willmott repeatedly contends (1997: 1354). In Knights and Willmott (1985), this personal quest for meaning and identity is argued from an individualized re-working of Berger and Luckman's concept of 'world-openness' (1967: 65ff). But world-openness in Berger and Luckman refers to the near-infinite possibilities for the *social* construction of meanings and practices, the aggregation of which comprises a culture. As Berger and Luckman themselves put it, 'Man's [sic] self-production is always and of necessity, a *social* enterprise', the consequence being that, 'world-openness, while intrinsic to man's biological make-up, is always prempted by social order' (ibid.: 69, italics added). In no way, therefore, does Berger and Luckman's concept of world-openness imply that individuals are routinely confronted with the 'existential anxiety of experiencing the natural and social world as separate and uncertain' (Knights and Willmott, 1985: 26-7), and none of the alleged shortcomings which Knights and Willmott believe themselves to have discovered in Berger and Luckman (and, inter alia, in Goffman) make it plausible that the concept should be so revised. It is true that there are occasions on which individuals may ask questions of their culture, for example when circumstances of personal calamity expose its taken-for-granted meanings, or in settings expressly designated for the purpose, such as a Kierkegaard reading-group or an MBA seminar on business ethics. Most of the time, though, as Mintzberg (1980) convincingly observed of managers, we don't have the time.

Finally, like many anti-structuralist thinkers (he would probably prefer 'post-structuralist'), Willmott seems insensitive to the emergent properties of co-ordinated action: that outcomes may be accomplished perfectly well without a commitment to those outcomes on the part of all concerned – as Lockwood (1964) long ago recognised in his distinction between system integration and social integration. As is realised by army commanders and was once realised by structural functionalists, a commitment to glory (or system goals) may be intensely gratifying to those whose business it is to personify these motivational abstractions, but it is normally enough that the division of labour is adequately designed and that 'the training kicks in'. In other words, there are many managers for whom a commitment to capital accumulation is no conscious part of their tacit notion of a job well done, a quasi-professional commitment to which may be sufficient to ensure their contribution to the extraction of surplus value. A 'well-engineered' production process, for example, would have the effect of reducing the porosity of the working day even if its designer thought of distributed profit as unmitigated parasitism.

In summary, Willmott's scenario of widespread disaffection within the managerial hierarchies of corporate capitalism is implausible and even if it were not, it would still not follow that it would make a difference to management practice.

Arguing the Case 1: Against 'Labour Process Orthodoxy'

It may be the very implausibility of this thesis of managerial contrariness which leads Willmott to concentrate so much of his fire on a stereotyped labour process orthodoxy which he describes as 'reducing managerial work to the execution of capitalist functions' (Willmott, 1997: 1333). Most often, as Edwards (2007) has pointed out of similar allegations in Ezzamel, Willmott and Worthington (2004), the practitioners of this reductionist creed are left anonymous. In Willmott

(1997), however, a substantial part of the argument is directed against three papers in which I develop a theory of intra-managerial competition within the capitalist agency relationship (Armstrong, 1989a; 1991a; 1991b), and on that basis I must assume that I am one of the culprits.[3] Since I now need to compare my theory with the one which Willmott criticises, it is necessary that I offer a brief exposition.

In general, managerial work consist of two parts: the intellectual labour of production and a contribution to the 'global function of capital', i.e. the extraction, realization and allocation of surplus value. The proportions vary with different managerial positions but generally speaking the capital functions dominate at the higher levels.

Insofar as they perform the functions of capital, managers act as agents of the principals who own the capital. That is, they are employed for the purpose of furthering the interests of capital through the management of their subordinates. This does not mean that managers carry out the instructions of the owners of capital, nor are they bureaucrats employed to follow rules laid down by those owners. Agency on behalf of a principle is not a matter of obeying instructions or of performing specified tasks in accordance with predetermined procedures. Instead, agents are expected to use their best abilities, their initiative and their judgment in the interests of the principle. When principals know less of the business in hand than the agents they employ (a condition which institutional economists call 'information asymmetry'), this means that all positions of agency are, in some degree, positions of trust.

Trust, however, is an expensive commodity. At its higher levels, it commands spectacular salaries and extensive benefits. It is also the subject of various forms of social production ranging from relatively formal schemes of appraisal and career progression to the clubhouse propinquity through which male managerial cultures achieve the feat of cloning, which Wilbert Moore memorably described as 'homosexual reproduction' (Moore, 1962: 109, quoted in Kanter, 1977: 48). These expenses mean that principals have an interest in economising on the extent to which trust is diffused downwards into hierarchically organized agency relationships. Crudely put, it may be cheaper to employ highly trusted managerial agents to control less trustworthy agents than to vest some intermediate level of trust all. So it comes about that the more junior positions, though still positions of agency, are also subject to supplementary controls by more trusted agents in positions of greater authority.

The disproportionate rewards attaching to positions of trusted agency sets up a competition in which the displacement of trust from one managerial position (or set of positions) to another is at stake. This competition exists at a number of levels, ranging from the individual, through the functional department, to the efforts of entire managerial professions to promote themselves as the proper custodians of some 'vital' aspect of company policy. Since the implementation of these policies (or decisions) necessarily involves authority over other professions (or individuals), trust, to a first approximation, can only be gained by one set of agents at the expense of others.

All of this means that the 'proletarianisation' of managers referred to by Willmott and other writers actually incorporates a number of potentially independent processes. There is, firstly, a proletarianisation of condition which refers to a deterioration of the conditions of employment. Secondly, a proletarianisation of function refers to a substitution of intellectual labour for some part in the global function of capital (Crompton, 1979). Thirdly, there can occur a withdrawal of trust within the global function of capital such that a particular position is subjected to additional performance controls and audits.

To go further is not possible within the confines of this chapter, but the interested reader is referred to Armstrong (1991b) for a fuller exposition. We are now in a position, though, to see what Willmott makes of this theory.

As Willmott presents the argument of my 1989a paper, I contend that 'managerial work forms no part of the labor process'. I am further accused of 'conceptualizing management *only* as "a means of degrading, controlling and driving manual labour" (Armstrong, 1989a: 309)'. 'This manager-as-an-agent-of-capital formulation,' Willmott continues, 'effectively denies, or at least views as insignificant, the *contradictory positioning* of many managers within capitalist work organizations' (1997: 1336, italics in original). This, of course, is exactly wrong: the contradiction between the employee status of managers and the expectation that they will act in the interests of their employers lies at the very heart of my approach. As for Willmott's quotation from my 1989a paper, that is lifted from a sentence, the first half of which explicitly points out that the productive contribution of intellectual labour remains productive (i.e. a labour process) even when it is co-opted as 'a means of degrading, controlling and driving manual labour', as it is in Scientific Management. Thus Willmott's truncation of the quotation and his addition of a gratuitous and italicised 'only' is a gross distortion of its actual meaning. Far from contending that managerial work forms no part of the labour process, both the sentence in question and the preceding paragraph make it perfectly clear that the intellectual components of productive work, whether performed by specialized advisory staffs or incorporated into the work of managers are indeed to be regarded as labour processes. In the light of this, it is more than a little galling to read Willmott's comment that, in making precisely the same point in a later paper of 1991a, 'Armstrong (1991a) appears to acknowledge his mistake' (Willmott, 1997: 1336).

It is those parts of managerial work which are devoted to the extraction, realization and allocation of surplus value which should not be considered as labour processes, for the simple reason that work of this kind produces and reproduces nothing but the capitalist social relations of production. It is hard to see what Willmott finds to disagree with in this restriction of the term 'labour process'. In Willmott (1990) we read that a 'more adequate appreciation of subjectivity *must be* founded upon the materialist premise that the labour process "is, first of all, a process between man and nature, a process by which man, through his own actions, mediates, regulates and controls the metabolism between himself and nature" (Marx 1976: 283)' (italics added). It is not immediately apparent, to say the least, how such a definition might be stretched so as to include the extraction, realization and allocation of surplus value. Willmott and I are also as one, or so it appears, in objecting to the promiscuous use of the term to describe any and all occupations within the capitalist social order because doing so ignores the social relations of production (Willmott, 1997: 1336). It is only when the question moves on to specifics, to the matter of which managerial work, if any, Willmott would exclude from his definition, that matters become more imprecise. Quite soon in his 1997 paper, in fact, all mention of any such restriction disappears and a labour process approach *to* management surreptitiously morphs into an unproblematic treatment of everything managers do *as* a labour process. In the course of this conceptual slippage, the deficiency which Willmott earlier condemned in 'bourgeois sociology' – namely, its denial that management occupies a particular position within the social relations of production (1997: 1333) – creeps into his own analysis. This denial then becomes overt when he recommends an 'analytic move' in which the 'capital-privileging exploitative organization of labor processes' are considered to be undertaken by at different times by 'different elements within the *collective worker*' (ibid.: 1337, italics added). This bizarre redefinition of Carchedi's (1977) collective worker, with its correlative erasure of the distinction between managers and workers in respect of their placement in the capitalist social relations of production is achieved by arguing that autonomous groups of workers are, in the very fact of their self-organization, acting as agents of capital. Directly counter to Willmott's own strictures against 'bourgeois analysis', it is also an insight from academia, which will come as a retrospective clarification to the former colliers of the National Union of Mineworkers. It is, of course, the product of mistaking organization *within* the labour process for the organization *of* the labour process for the purpose of extracting surplus value. Self-organizing groups of workers do not control the whole of the wage-effort bargain, and it is on this that the rate of exploitation depends.

Part of Willmott's objection to the idea that management involves agency on behalf of capital, or that they perform the functions of capital, may lie in an overly-mechanical view of what this entails. Burawoy's surely uncontentious observation that management 'is concerned with securing co-operation and surplus' (Burawoy, 1985: 39),[4] for example, is castigated for '*reducing* managerial work to the execution of capitalist functions' (Willmott, 1997: 1339, italics added), as if the performance of capital functions were a programmable task. It is not of course. As I have already explained, it is characteristic of principal-agent relationships that the actions of the agent are *not* wholly specified, that they are expected to use their best judgment and creative capacities in the furtherance of the principals' interests, with all the misperceptions of those interests, failures of judgment and infirmities of capacity which decision-making autonomy entails. Further, that same autonomy exposes agents – and through them, principals – to whatever 'moral hazards' have survived the systems of incentivization and monitoring on the one hand, and the social production of trust of the other. Provided such defalcations remain the exception, there is no incompatibility between an agency theorization of management and such instances of misplaced trust. As for Burawoy's so-called 'reduction' of managerial work to capital functions, it needs to be remembered that these are economic categories, not concrete forms of managerial action. Once it has been recognised – as it is in Burawoy's treatment – that some of management consist of the intellectual labour of production, there is no *reduction* involved in speaking of the rest of it as the execution of capitalist functions.

An Unproductive Encounter with Unproductive Labour

Willmott also objects to my use of the term 'unproductive labour' in Armstrong (1991a) to describe that part of managerial work which consists of agency on behalf of capital,[5] though it is a little difficult to see why this is so, since he also allows that the distinction is 'heuristically and politically useful insofar as it recollects how, within capitalist labor processes, managers are hired to perform the "unproductive" task of ensuring that surplus value is pumped out of the collective laborer' (Willmott, 1997: 1336). As I have already pointed out, I do not myself think of management in such infantile leftist terms, though I sympathise at this point with what I take to be Willmott's general drift. For a theorist who insists that managerial work is not reducible to a function of capital, however (ibid.: 1339, 1343), this still does not seem a very intelligent thing to say.

'Mistakes' apart, Willmott's makes two objections to my identification of capital functions with unproductive labour (and by the same token, presumably, to Braverman's also, 1974: Ch. 19). The first is his claim (already discussed and dismissed) that elements of unproductive management are actually dispersed throughout the 'collective worker'. The second is that it is difficult to separate the productive and unproductive elements in any given act of management. This is admitted in the general case, although there are aspects of managerial work which fall clearly into one category or the other. Attempts to unpick the weave of managerial work in this mechanical fashion, however, are largely beside the point. What matters about the work of managers is not so much the elements of which it is made up but the outcomes which it achieves, and these are comparatively easy to separate into productive and unproductive aspects. Performance monitoring systems, for example, can easily distinguish between the volume and quality of production on the one hand, and measures of financial performance on the other.

In an attempt to further explicate and justify the distinction between the productive and unproductive aspects of management, I also sought to show that the distinction between management as intellectual labour and management as an agency of capital is one which is recognised – roughly speaking – in the practitioner tendency to restrict the term 'management' to the capital functions (Armstrong, 1989a: 310), and that this usage is an historical product of the capture of 'management' from industrial engineering by educational and consultancy interests (Armstrong, 1991a). On the first point, and as a proxy for many similar discussions I cited Koontz and O'Donnell's (then) widely used textbook, thus:

> Failure to distinguish executive functions from nonmanagerial technical skills is another source of confusion . . The manager . . may or may not possess such technical skills. In his managerial capacity he is certainly not utilising such operating expertness [sic] . . if he [sic] can rely on upon and successfully use the technical skills of others, he need not possess a nonmanagerial skill at all. (Koontz and O'Donnell, 1968: 55)

To this, I might have added:

> In a very real sense, the goal of every manager must be surplus . .the goal of managers as managers is fundamentally the same in business and non-business enterprises. It is also the same at every level. (ibid.: 7)

And similar pronouncements can be found in other influential writers, ranging from Henri Fayol to Drucker. From these I drew the inference that talk of 'management', at least within the culture of Anglo-Saxon capitalism, refers not to the entirety of what managers do, but to the generalised task of producing, realizing and allocating surplus values through the control of people as distinct from any technical expertise and ability to organize which managers contribute to the productive process itself. It is in that sense, not the crude generalisation about the work of actual managers implicit in Willmott's critique, that I identify 'management' with unproductive labour.

Having criticized my work for views it does not express, and for views which it does express but are shared by himself, Willmott feels able to sum up and dismiss its overall conclusion thus, '[a]sserting that managerial work forms no part of the labor process is no way to defend the distinctiveness of labor process theory' (1997: 1336). Though he refers to my paper of 1991b, the one in which my theorization of the dynamics of trust within the capitalist agency relationship is set out in its most developed form, he does so only to remark that, 'Management hierarchies, as *even Armstrong* (1991b: 18) allows are "battlegrounds of mutual obstruction and ideological warfare, in which as much effort goes into subverting opponents as into constructive efforts on behalf of the principal"' (Willmott, 1997: 1348, italics added). From Willmott's form of words, the uninformed reader would assume that 'even Armstrong' referred to some leftwing bigot for whom the monolithic nature of capitalist management was an article of faith, albeit one reluctantly abandoned in the face of evidence to the contrary. In fact, even the title of the paper in question, 'Contradiction and Social Dynamics in the Capitalist Agency Relationship', makes it clear that the view of management as a conflictual plurality lies at the core of my theorization of the agency relationship. The quotation which Willmott presents as an untypical gleam of illumination actually refers to my summary of a spectacular illustration of intra-managerial conflict in a fascinating – and decidedly non-Marxist – case study of product championship and organizational politics by Wilson (1982).

Arguing the Case 2: In Search of Recalcitrance

For Willmott, it is important that 'relations of production are practically accomplished through the existential media of human conduct' (1997: 1344). That they allow for a good deal of variation in their enactment is common ground. The capitalist agency relationship, as I describe it in Armstrong (1991b), is built on trust as well as on incentives and monitoring, and this implies precisely that managers bring their personal capabilities, perceptions and values to the business of capital accumulation. This, however, is not enough for Willmott, since, as we have seen, he objects to any suggestion that managers can be adequately understood as agents of capital:

> managers do not "just" operate or supervise the physical and organizational means of production in ways dictated by the imperatives of capitalism. Their materiality as human subjects also obliges them to struggle with the existential significance of the purposive quality of human consciousness and not just with its contribution to productive activity. (Willmott, 1997: 1354)

In more accessible language, Willmott believes that the attitudes of many (most?) managers are inimical to the prioritization of capital accumulation, and that these attitudes (sometimes?) influence what they actually do.

Since the quotation is taken from his conclusion, it is not unreasonable to expect the body of his paper to marshal some supporting evidence. Recognising this, Willmott devotes two pages to a discussion of 'Managers as (Misbehaving) agents' (1997: 1338-1340). In fact, these two pages contain little evidence of managerial recalcitrance of any kind and none at all of refusals to act in the interests of capital accumulation. He quotes Braverman (1974: 151) on the existence of 'unbounded cynicism and revulsion', but neglects to inform his readers that Braverman was speaking of workers in the cited passage, not managers. He castigates Burawoy (1985: 10) for his portrayal of managers as 'compliant functionaries who unproblematically perform the task of securing and obscuring surplus value'. He argues that games of office politics 'cannot be assumed to be consistent with, or fully functional for, the extraction of surplus'. He tells us of Hyman's (1987) opinion that managers have more opportunities for misbehaviour than other employees. And apart from more exhortation to take note of existential subjectivities and so forth, that, believe it or not, is all.

In a later section entitled 'On the Materiality of Managerial Subjects' we learn more of the managerial recalcitrance which figures so prominently in Willmott's analysis. A Manufacturing Director 'at one of our case study companies' bemoans the difficulty of getting his middle managers to use computers (Willmott, 1997: 1347). Sir John Harvey-Jones has a grumble about obstructive bureaucrats at ICI (ibid.: 1348), and in a footnote to the same page, Goffee and Scase (1986) discover that managers often resist changes which devalue their accumulated skills and knowledge. In fact, this last is highly believable, but is also explicable as resistance to a degradation of their positions within the capitalist agency relationship, as I point out in Armstrong (1991b).

None of it, either separately or cumulatively, holds up as evidence for the case Willmott is trying to make.

The strange thing is that such evidence should have been easy to find. Though the capitalist enterprise depends on the extraction of surplus value, competitive conditions permitting, it is not essential that the maximum amount of it should be extracted the entire time. This being the case, it should have been possible to find examples of small acts of managerial kindness performed at the expense of capital accumulation. Part of the problem may be that managerial ameliorations of the conditions of employment at the expense of profitability have typically been interpreted as 'indulgency patterns' of the kind first described by Gouldner (1955). That is, they have been viewed as a control strategy rather than a principled protection of the workforce from the full impact of capital accumulation. Whether through ignorance, complacency or lack of competition, there are circumstances in which senior managers and shareholders can be placated with sub-maximum levels of output. It then becomes possible for junior managers to reach an accommodation with the workforce in which informal concessions are traded for co-operation in achieving the required levels of performance. As an account of managerial motives, it is possible that this reading is overly cynical: whatever their efficacy in achieving a smoothly running workplace, it is entirely possible that some managers may enter these arrangements out of a genuine desire to treat their fellow human beings decently.

If and where this is the case, two things need to be borne in mind. The first is that is that the managers who enter such arrangements with their workforces are not really resisting the demands of capital accumulation; rather they are making use of a temporary and local slacking of that demand in a particular way – choosing the 'welfare goods' of a pleasant working relationship over the possible career advantages of maximising output. The second is that 'indulgency patterns' are extremely vulnerable to changes in personnel or policies. This, in fact, was demonstrated in Gouldner's own study when a new manager took over, determined to make his name by boosting the financial performance of the plant (ibid.). The implicit analogy with the takeover bidder suggests that this kind of erasure of indulgency patterns is a process general to the capitalist economy as a whole, but more particularly to the newly 'impatient capitalism' described by Sennet (2006).

All this said, it is still striking that it is so difficult to find instances in which managers have sheltered their workers from the demands of profit. The reasonable conclusion, surely, is that such instances are thin on the ground and that Willmott's depiction of managerial subjectivities and the way they act on them is broadly incorrect.

Arguing the Case 3: Re-Reading ChemCo

Having made so much of the divergences between managers' private values and motivations on the one hand, and the demands imposed upon them in the name of profitability on the other, there is something distinctly odd about Willmott's violent reaction to Nichols and Beynon's exploration of exactly the same moral problem in their 'ChemCo' studies (Nichols and Beynon, 1977). Willmott (1997: 1349) picks up Nichols and Beynon's story at the point where a plant manager has come across a left-wing leaflet which described managers like himself as 'pigs'. The manager's outraged reaction was, 'I'm not a pig. I bloody well care about what I'm doing' (Nichols and Beynon, 1977: 39).

Willmott objects, first of all, to Nichols and Beynon's interpretation of this outrage as a conflict between 'personal morality and economics' (ibid.: 40). 'Keeping faith with the precepts of orthodox Marxist analysis', as Willmott puts it, Nichols and Beynon have failed to consider the possible agency of this manager in 'shaping and reforming the social relations of production'. As we have already seen, phrases of this kind in Willmott's lexicon, mean something like the face-to-face styles of social interaction between managers and workers – habits rather than structures and, as such, most definitely susceptible to managerial agency since they are its proximate expressions. Even in this sense any meaningful revision of the terms on which managers and workers interact might prove difficult, since Willmott himself has previously pointed out just how limited is the scope for managers to neglect the priorities of capital accumulation (1997: 1333, 1335). And having himself commended 'Marxian theory' as offering a 'penetrating analytical framework' (ibid.: 1333), it is hard to understand what he finds objectionable in the 'precepts of orthodox Marxian analysis' when he believes himself to have encountered them in Nichols and Beynon (ibid.: 1349). Undeterred by these contradictions, Willmott proceeds to accuse Nichols and Beynon of assuming that managerial work is 'wholly "structured by the needs of capital" (Nichols and Beynon, 1977, p. v)'.

Before considering the accusation itself, notice the forty-or-so pages which separate the quotation taken from Nichols and Beynon's preface and the passage which Willmott is currently considering (Nichols and Beynon, 1977: 39). Such a gap suggests that there is a cut-and-paste job going on. Sure enough, on Nichols and Beynon's page xv (not v) we find that it is the future of both managers and workers which will be 'structured by the needs of capital', *not* managerial work as such. Naughty!

On the next page of their book (ibid.: 40), Nichols and Beynon report a conversation between the same manager – the one who objected to the 'pigs' leaflet – and his engineer-in-charge. In it, the manager expressed concern that the seemingly interminable experiments in human relations which were going on in ChemCo at the time tended to deflect attention from the fact that 'we are in business to make money'. For Nichols and Beynon, this is further evidence of the same conflict between personal morality and the treatment of labour as a commodity. They describe the manager as 'one of those who hesitatingly inspect themselves for cynicism', and provide an extended quotation in which he does just that, reflecting on his experiences of selecting people for redundancy. Despite his misgivings, the manager also recognises that he had 'a job to do' (ibid.: 40-41).

Willmott's reading of this passage is tortuous indeed. He first tells us that Nichols and Beynon interpret the exchange as 'unambiguous confirmation of the plant manager's identification of managerial work with making profits', where, in fact, they have just told us that he also identifies it with making distasteful moral choices. Having chosen his ground, Willmott then takes Nichols and Beynon to task for their supposed failure to realise that the manager's 'rationalisation of his position' is context-dependent – when Nichols and Beynon themselves have just made exactly the same point: that there is a 'task-specification' view of management in tendential conflict with a moral one. For Willmott, however, context-dependence does not refer to the differing frames of reference within which the repercussions of one's work may be considered, that of personal morality and that of the 'realities' of business. For him, it is a more superficial and calculative matter of talking about money in the presence of one's superior (remember that the manager was in conversation with his engineer-in-charge) and about personal morality for the benefit of 'lefty researchers' (Willmott, 1997: 1350, footnote). If this last contemptible insinuation were true, we could indeed expect this manager, and most others for that matter, to act as the unproblematic agents of capital, since 'lefty researchers' are thin on the ground in most companies whereas the presence of one's superiors, both in person and in the implicit form of performance monitoring and appraisal schemes, is more-or-less continuous. Perhaps realising that what he has just said conflicts with his conviction that there exists the possibility of a disarticulation of managerial action from the dictates of capital accumulation, Willmott immediately qualifies it with the observation that there may not be a *complete* break between personal morality and the performance of a role.

Having made this point – and then having unmade it too – Willmott kicks off in a big way. Nichols and Beynon, he thunders, are 'blinkered by the framework of orthodox Marxism' in that they 'assume the existence of a stable managerial identity' (1997: 1349).[6] This, one observes *sotto voce*, is a feature of orthodox Marxism which seems to have escaped the notice of previous scholars. The assumption, continues Willmott *fortissimo* – wherever it comes from – leads Nichols and Beynon to assume the plant manager must be dissembling when he insist that "I bloody well care about what I'm doing"'.

No they don't. They say the exact opposite. It is *Willmott* who assumes that the manager must be dissembling – and then does not assume it (Willmott, 1997: 1350, footnote). What Nichols and Beynon actually say is that the manager is 'doubtful and a little confused, even about what his own motives are' (Nichols and Beynon, 1977: 40).

Now, Willmott is a major figure in, and on some accounts, the co-founder of, Critical Management Studies, a sub-discipline not noted for the clarity of its expositions. How is it that he is unable to grasp the literal meaning of some of the most accessible prose in the entire field of industrial sociology? And why, having commended a Marxian approach for its 'penetrating analytic framework' (supra) does he become so incensed when he believes himself to have encountered it in Nichols and Beynon?

Recognising that we are in the realms of conjecture, it appears that Willmott needs data from ethnographic fieldwork to lend substance to an otherwise unconvincing argument but also needs to take issue with Nichols and Beynon because their findings contradict the manner in which he wishes to portray middle management. Elsewhere, as we have seen, he writes as if profitability in capitalist economies is a minority preoccupation, largely confined to senior executives plus a few hangers-on, and that it is imposed by these on a largely apathetic or disaffected majority of managers through the machinery of performance monitoring, appraisal schemes and incentives (Willmott, 1997: 1348-9). From this point of view it was remiss of Nichols and Beynon to discover that Chemo's plant managers accepted both the legitimacy of profit *and* a personal morality which sometimes conflicts with it, and downright inconsiderate of them to report that on these occasions, it was profit which won out. These are findings which cast doubt on Willmott's whole thesis – that the personal and moral commitments of managers may bring them into significant conflict with the demand for profitably. This might explain why he constructs Nichols and Beynon as straw men who believe that the ChemCo managers are *unproblematically* committed to profit since it enables him to disregard the (for him) damaging finding that the managers' moral misgivings were practically inconsequential.

Over two pages of convoluted argument, in fact, Willmott manages to convince himself that these managers' declared opposition to human relations experimentation in the name of profit 'may be conjectured' (1997: 1351) to have been a contextually acceptable means of articulating a defence of their preferred way of doing things. By thus constructing an interpretation of the managers words in diametric opposition to their literal meaning, Willmott is able to pull an interpretive victory from the jaws of empirical defeat. As Thompson (2005: 372) has remarked of similar acrobatics of interpretation by others of the Critical Management Studies school, it is an impressive demonstration of the theory-dependence of data.

Willmott's masterful way with empirical work is again in evidence in his discussion of Harris' (1987) putative replication of the 'ChemCo' studies. His first move is to select a passage from Harris in which senior managers express doubts about their subordinates' commitment to the efficiency and profitability of their plants, claiming that it provides 'further evidence of managers' "identity work"' (Willmott, 1997: 1351). Not in itself it doesn't. Willmott's interpretation depends on two assumptions of his own: firstly that the senior managers concerned were by implication emphasising the indispensability of their own supervision and secondly that this was a means of reinforcing their own view of themselves. These things may have been so, of course, but equally they may not. It is just as likely that the senior managers concerned were expressing their exasperation at what they saw as an unnecessary distraction from all the other important things which senior managers have to do.

Willmott then uses Harris' material to mount yet another attack on 'orthodox labour process analysis'. The problem is that Harris' book is *already* written as an attack on labour process orthodoxy – at least as that is represented in the work of Nichols and Beynon (1977)[7] – but it is an attack from a unitarist position which would reject a labour process approach even as Willmott seeks to 'reconstruct' it. Objecting to a view of the employment relationship as the site of conflicting interests, Harris prefers, as she puts it, to see the employer as the *Arbeitgeber* – the 'giver of work'. Willmott's solution to this problem – incredibly – is to use Harris' data to concoct 'orthodox labour process' interpretations all of his own and then to demonstrate their inadequacy. The material he chooses is Harris' account of the junior managers' resistance to an 'industrial relations strategy' (probably the 'New Working Arrangement' described by Nichols and Beynon (1977: Ch. 7). The first of Willmott's analyses makes the 'Panglossian assumption' that whatever managers do will turn out to be to the ultimate benefit of capital. The second assumes that it would have done so had the design of the scheme taken into account the reactions of workers and junior managers. Having himself set up both of these feeble efforts, Willmott has no difficulty in knocking them down again.

Arguing Against the Case

Whereas Willmott cannot discover, or cannot convincingly re-work, evidence which will support of his imputations of managerial resistance, I can produce some which shows managers reacting to proletarianisation, both of position and function, by *intensifying* the exploitative pressures on their workers. The case material comes from four months' full-time observational fieldwork which I performed in a medium-sized shoe factory in 1978. It has been previously reported in Armstrong, Goodman and Hyman (1981) and Armstrong (1983, 1989b).

The managers concerned were the first-line supervisors, badly paid and routinely abused by the production manager whenever the operatives which they supervised were discovered to be waiting for work or otherwise idle. Added to this proletarianisation of condition (cf. Crompton, 1979), they had also suffered a proletarianisation of function in that they could only discharge their responsibility for maintaining the flow of production by searching for the materials which would keep their operatives occupied and personally hauling these materials into position. Far from reacting to this 'double proletarianisation' (ibid.) by resisting the pressure to make profits or by making common cause with their operatives, however, these supervisors repeatedly clashed with them over the rates to be paid in the event of work stoppages.

According to the national agreement between the trade union and the employers' association, various standby hourly rates were supposed to be paid in the event of stoppages. Wages thus paid out, for which there was no corresponding production, were counted as departmental 'losses' for which the supervisors were held responsible. In extreme cases, the supervisors concerned would have to account for these losses in an inquisition chaired by the universally-feared production manager. In order to avoid this, they would go to extraordinary lengths to avoid paying the standby rates. The favoured tactic was to assign responsibility for the stoppage to the operatives themselves, since the agreement stipulated that the standby rate applied only to stoppages outside the operatives' control. Since this tended to provoke confrontation, the less assertive of the supervisors would do this surreptitiously in the hope that the discrepancy in the operatives' pay packets in a fortnight's time would go unnoticed. The female supervisors (of female workers) were more confrontational. One of them went so far as to thrust a brush into the hands of any stopped pieceworker, refusing to authorise a standby payment on the grounds that 'you can't be stopped because there's always work to do in a factory'. This author of this particular syllogism was said to 'pay you as if it was her own money'.

In summary – and there was much more – the rancour which existed between the supervisors and their operatives was palpable, bitter and clearly related to the functions which the supervisors were supposed to perform for capital. Spoken of by senior management as an 'unproductive' cost, their situation was precarious. They could only justify their position, and so hang onto the little they had, by demonstrably playing what part they could in maximising the ratio of output to wage costs – the rate of exploitation in Marxist terms. In other words, they reacted to the degradation of their position in the capitalist agency relationship – and the immiseration of condition which went with it – by hanging onto that position as best they could.

This, it will doubtless be objected, was just one factory, was a factory observed thirty years ago, and observed into the bargain by the labour process fundamentalist 'even Armstrong'. It is, on the other hand, *evidence*, and it is evidence against a belief in favour of which

Willmott is able to produce none: the belief that managers react to a degradation of their position by resisting the demands of capital.

It is also arguable that similar processes have occurred at the collective level. During the decline of collective bargaining which took place in the early 1980s, personnel managers, as many of them still styled themselves, did not react to the threat to their livelihoods with a collective disaffection which expressed itself in an attempt to shield workers from the pressures of capital accumulation. Re-branded as human resource managers and their professional organization as the Institute of Personnel and Development, they sought instead to restore their position within the global function of capital by finding new ways of contributing to profitability, achieving this principally by annexing and extending the training functions previously carried out by line managers.

Concerning subjectivities, there may also be lessons to be learnt from the conduct of the production manager who featured in the foregoing account. Notorious as a bully, his most recollected exploit was to terrorise the workers in the factory's largest department by smashing up the chairs which they had installed in their toilet for the purpose of enjoying a quiet smoke. More routinely encountered during this period of fieldwork was the managerial saying 'In this job you can be a bastard or a bloody bastard' – a bloody bastard being one who is in the habit of adding gratuitously inflicted deprivations and humiliation to the routine pressures of capital accumulation (see also Nichols and Beynon, 1977: 34). That 'bloody bastards' are quite commonly the product of the search for meaning and identity in managerial work is suggested by the substantial literature on bullying in the workplace (e.g. Einarsen, Hoel, Zapf and Cooper, 2002), a literature which includes surveys which indicate that it is widespread (I.P.D., 1996). Insofar as this is the case, the hidden injuries of capitalist management may lie not only in the habitual suppression of the decent impulse in the furtherance of capital accumulation but also in the seepage of the delegated power attached to the ownership of the means of production into the psychology of the procedural sadist and the petty tyrant (Ashforth, 1994).[8]

Concluding Remarks

First, the procedural issues. Reading Willmott on the sources from which he constructs his theories, one is struck by the virtual absence of unqualified approval.[9] There are always 'failures' to report, always the 'unfortunately' or 'however' which prefaces the 'deeper reflections', 'more adequate appreciations' or 'fuller theorizations' which are required, almost invariably on the topic of subjectivities or identities. Reading these disquisitions as closely as has been required for the production of this critique, one is also struck by how often Willmott's own readings turn out to be at best careless and at worst unscrupulous, with most of them somewhere in between. As Friedman (2004) has pointed out, positions from which Willmott, and sometimes his co-authors, wish to express their differences are subject to various forms of 'strawmanning', the most blatant of which involves the appropriation of an author's core ideas and their representation as the critics' own corrections of that author. Such is the case with my own thinking on intra-management competition within the global function of capital. Quotations are lifted out of context, truncated so as to distort their meaning and sometimes juxtaposed with others so as to suggest a continuous flow of thought when they actually occur in remote and quite different contexts – all of this in a manner which recalls nothing so much as the black arts of the blurb-writer. Casual forms of words which are quite peripheral to the main thrust of an author's argument are exhibited as if they were major position statements, the failings of which then testify to the importance of the critic's work of intellectual purgation. Such is the case with Burawoy's summation of management as concerned with 'co-operation and surplus' in a participant observation study which was contextually limited to the shopfloor of a machine shop.

The empirical evidence mustered by Willmott in support of his belief in the ubiquity of middle management resistance and the centrality of a search for existential significance is treated no better. Classic ethnographies of the workplace and elsewhere are subjected to a series of 'reinterpretations', in every one of which Willmott accuses the authors of misreading their own data and into which he projects his own preoccupations with subjectivity and identity by way of correction.

Much of Willmott's manner – the misreadings, the opacity of expression and the pile-up of qualifications which teeter on the edge of self-contradiction and sometimes topple into it – stems from the logical impossibility of the position which he is trying to take up. He objects to bourgeois pluralism because it does not recognise the primacy of the capitalist social relations of production, but also to what he calls 'orthodox labour process analysis' which does. As far as one can tell, since he does not name any of its practitioners, this orthodoxy appears to be his own invention. This being the case, one can only reconstruct it from the authors criticised (say) in Willmott (1990; 1997) and on that basis deduce that that its only common features are a disregard of existential subjectivities and a belief that managerial capitalism is still a form of capitalism. Since bourgeois pluralism is simply the negation of this latter position – coinciding in that respect with what Nichols (1969) called 'non-sectional' managerialism, there is simply no space between the two positions. Either the capitalist social relations of production are the primary context of managerial behaviour or they are not.

Willmott's response to this logical impasse is to try to create such a space by constructing a 'labour process orthodoxy' which asserts that managers do *nothing but* instantiate and maintain the capitalist social relations of production. This probably explains why he represents a few chance remarks by Burawoy and more extended passages from my own work as arguing just that. Thus hamstrung, 'labour process orthodoxy' can indeed offer no explanation of the very obvious fact that (most) managerial work involves more than a performance of the functions of capital, a deficiency which leaves the theory thus disabled unable to compete with the satisficing of stakeholder interests posited by bourgeois pluralism. It is into that manufactured aporia that Willmott inserts his theory of managerial subjectivities. By positing that these incline managers to react against the prioritization of capital accumulation he can simultaneously claim to recognise the primacy of the capitalist social relations of production and account for the fact that managers do other things besides execute the functions of capital. The problem, of course, is that such a theory relies on the improbable assumption (and Willmott presents no evidence that it is anything more) that most managers (and Willmott always writes of them in general terms) react to organizational controls by rejecting the purpose behind them.

Given that Willmott presents this theory of managerial contrariness as a reconstructed labour process approach, one of its extraordinary features is precisely its neglect of the labour process. Managers do other things besides execute the functions of capital not because their subjectivities so incline them – or not in the first instance – but because they must first ensure that use-values are produced. Without these there can be no exchange values, no surplus of those exchange values over the values of the inputs which went into them and hence nothing for capital to appropriate realise and allocate. The problem for (many) managers is that they must contribute to the co-operative division of labour required in the production of use-values and simultaneously ensure that the surplus value thus created goes to capital. The moral dilemmas described by Nichols and Beynon (1977) amongst others stem from the resulting conflict between the psychological conditions of co-operation and the pressures upon managers 'at the end of the day' to treat labour as a commodity. As compared to the theorization of subjectivities offered by Willmott, a very traditional theory of this kind – which would be my own view of what an labour process orthodoxy would look like – has the merit of locating the existential anxieties experienced by (some) managers in the fact of their general conformity to the pressures upon them rather than in a general – and empirically elusive – rebellion.

Finally, a comment may be in order on the quasi-existentialist[10] preoccupations which run through the entire Knights-Willmott corpus of writings on the labour process: the unwavering assumption that managers, workers and everyone else for that matter, are engaged in projects of self-exploration variously described as 'a struggle with the existential significance of the purposive quality of human consciousness' (Willmott, 1997: 1354), the pursuit of 'elevated identity' (Knights, 1990: 312) or a search for a 'sense of order in which identity is "secure"' (Knights and Willmott, 1985: 33). Since this process (these processes?) seem to have been missed in every one of the ethnographic studies reviewed by Willmott and his co-authors, the weight of evidence, surely, is that they are either insignificant in most cases, or even non-existent.

It is not hard to see why this might be the case. From Dubin's (1956) discovery that work, for most workers, is not a 'central life interest' to Goldthorpe, Lockwood, Bechhofer and Platt's (1968) identification of 'instrumental privatization' to Gouldner's (1969) reflections on the 'unemployed self', alienated labour was a major theme of industrial sociology from the 1950s to the late 1970s, meaning that work for most people is precisely *not* an expression of the 'purposive quality of human consciousness'. As C. Wright Mills memorably put it, 'Each day men [sic] sell little pieces of themselves in order to buy them back each night and weekend with the coin of fun' (Mills, 1956: 237). Mills' observation has since been expanded into a major theme of the sociology of the 1980s onwards: that identities in late capitalism are mostly constructed not through work but in the sphere of consumption and constructed there through a bricolage of commercially available significations. du Gay (1996) has even re-imported this theme back into the workplace, arguing that identities are formed therein, not by reflection on the involvement of the individual in the labour process but by the consumption of a discourse of enterprise which bears only the most tenuous connection with it. Though du Gay's particular argument and evidence are ultimately unconvincing (Armstrong, 2001), they do suggest that the experience of the labour process for many is so void of content that almost any script can be written onto it.

One of the odd things about the Knights-Willmott treatment of identity is that they both recognise the prevalence of alienated labour – en passant at least – yet still expect it to be the subject of existential ratiocination. For example, Knights (1990: 312) observes that the raw materials of 'elevated identity' are not commonly available to shopfloor workers whilst Willmott argues that the primary orientation of most managers 'is likely to be to their careers, their families and perhaps to their "profession"' (1997: 1335, 1338), a fairly clear statement of instrumental privatization as it relates to managers, albeit one which is largely untested.

Obviously, the prevalence of alienated labour does not mean that there is no fulfilling work to be found in capitalist societies. Reality is always messier than theory and capitalist societies are never capitalist in every nook and cranny. Notwithstanding Willmott's conjectures on the effects of organizational control systems, there may be many middle and junior managers for whom work is a major means of self-expression, and we know for a fact that there are a few for whom that involves the bullying of subordinates. In such cases we could indeed expect work to figure prominently in the process of identity formation, though not in the contrarian manner envisaged by Willmott. Where alienation prevails, on the other hand, we would not.

It is as well to remember, perhaps, that academia – for some at least – is one of the enclaves of expressive possibility which have so far resisted the alienating tendencies of capitalist rationalisation. It is from academia that researchers such as Willmott and I observe the work of those who are not so privileged, sometimes at first hand but often through the reports of other fieldworkers, and it is back to academia that we render our accounts. As with any translation between two forms of life there are pitfalls, one of which is that the method of *verstehen* as applied to the social sciences can so easily morph into a projection of one's own preoccupations into the interpretation of social action. Specifically, the self-absorption of reflective intellectuals, whose preoccupation with their own identities depends on a degree of insulation from the urgencies of 'impatient capitalism' (Sennett, 2006), cannot be assumed to be shared by managers and workers who are not. To proceed otherwise, surely, is to slip back into a 'bourgeois sociology', the pole of repulsion from which Willmott began.

References

Armstrong, P., J. F. B. Goodman, and J. D. Hyman (1981) *Ideology and Shopfloor Industrial Relations*. London: Croom Helm.

Armstrong, P. (1983) 'Class relationships at the point of production', *Sociology*, 17(3): 339-358.

Armstrong, P. (1989a) 'Management, labour process and agency', *Work Employment and Society*, 3(3): 307-322.

Armstrong, P. (1989b) 'Variance reporting and the delegation of blame: a case study', *Accounting, Auditing and Accountability Journal*, 2(22): 29-46.

Armstrong, P. (1991a) 'The divorce of productive and unproductive management' in C. Smith, D. Knights and H. Willmott (eds) *White Collar Work: the Non-Manual Labour Process*. London: MacMillan.

Armstrong, P. (1991b) 'Contradictions and social dynamics in the capitalist agency relationship', *Accounting Organization and Society*, 16(1): 1-25.

Armstrong, P. (2001) 'Styles of illusion', *Sociological Review*, 49(2): 155-173.

Armstrong, P., P. Marginson, P. Edwards and J. Purcell (1996) 'Budgetary control And the labour force: Findings from a survey of large British companies', *Management Accounting Research*, 7(1): 1-23.

Ashforth, B. (1994) 'Petty tyranny in organizations', *Human Relations*, 47(7): 755-778.

Ashforth, B. (2007) 'Petty tyranny in organizations: A preliminary examination of antecedents and consequences', *Canadian Journal of Administrative Science*, 14(2): 126-140.

Berger, P. L. and T. Luckman (1967) *The Social Construction of Reality*. Harmondsworth: Penguin.

Braverman, H. (1974) *Labor and Monopoly Capital: the Degradation of Work in the Twentieth Century*. New York: Monthly Review Press.

Brown, W. R. (1972) 'A consideration of custom-and-practice', *British Journal of Industrial Relations*, 10(1): 42-61.

Burawoy, M. (1985) *The Politics of Production: Factory Regimes Under Capitalism and Socialism*. London: Verso.

Caplan, E. H. (1971) *Management Accounting and Behavioural Science*. Reading, MA: Addison-Wesley.

Carchedi, G. (1977) *On the Economic Identification of Social Classes*. London: Routledge and Kegan Paul.

Crompton, R. (1979) 'Trade unionism and the insurance clerk', *Sociology*, 13: 403-426.

Du Gay, P. (1996) *Consumption and Identity at Work*, London: Sage.

Dubin, R. (1956) 'Industrial workers' worlds: A study of the "central life interests" of industrial workers', *Social Problems*, 3: 131-142.

Edwards, P. (2007) The state of the labour process debate after 25 years: Some reflections from industrial relations and industrial sociology', Notes for remarks to plenary panel at the 25th International Labour Process Conference, Amsterdam, April. Available at: http://www2.warwick.ac.uk/fac/soc/wbs/research/irru/publications/recentconf/pe_lpc07.pdf (accessed 9 September 2007).

Einarsen, S., H. Hoel, D. Zapf and C. L. Cooper (2002) *Bullying and Emotional Abuse in the Workplace: International Perspectives in Research and Practice*. London. Taylor and Francis.

Ezzamel, M., H. Willmott and F. Worthington (2004) 'Accounting and management-labour relations', *Accounting, Organizations and Society*, 29(3-4): 269-302.

Foucault, M. (1980) *Power/Knowledge: Selected Interviews and Other Writings, 1972-77*. Brighton: Harvester Wheatsheaf.

Friedman, A. L. (2004) 'Strawmanning and labour process analysis', *Sociology*, 38(3): 573-591.

Fox, A. (1974) *Beyond Contract: Work, Power and Trust Relations.* London: Faber.

Giddens, A. (1984) *The Constitution of Society: Outline of the Theory of Structuration.* Oxford: Polity Press.

Giddens, A. (1989) 'A reply to my critics' in D. Held and J. B. Thompson (eds) *Social Theory and Modern Societies: Anthony Giddens and his Critics.* Cambridge: Cambridge University Press.

Goffee, R. and R. Scase (1986) 'Are the rewards worth the effort? Changing managerial values in the 1980s', *Personnel Review*, 15: 3-6.

Goldthorpe, J. H., D. Lockwood, F. Bechhofer and J. Platt (1968) *The Affluent Worker: Industrial Attitudes and Behaviour,* Cambridge: Cambridge University Press.

Gouldner, A. W. (1955) *Wildcat Strike, a Study of an Unofficial Strike,* London: Routledge and Kegan Paul.

Gouldner, A. W. (1969) 'The unemployed self' in R. Fraser (ed.) *Work: Twenty Personal Accounts: Vol. 2.* Harmondsworth: Penguin.

Harris, R. (1987) *Power and Powerlessness in Industry: an Analysis of the Social Relations of Production.* London: Tavistock.

Hopwood, A. (1973) *An Accounting System and Managerial Behaviour.* Farnborough: Saxon House

Hyman, R. (1987) 'Strategy or structure: Capital, labour and control', *Work, Employment and Society*, 1(1): 25-56.

I.P.D. (Institute of Personnel and Development) (1996). Available at: http://www.bullyonline.org/media/nr2.htm (accessed 3 March 2007).

Kanter, R. M. (1977) *Men and Women of the Corporation.* New York: Basic Books.

Knights, D. (1990) Subjectivity, power and the labour process' in D. Knights and H. Willmott (eds) *Labour Process Theory.* Basingstoke: MacMillan.

Knights, D. and H. Willmott (1985) 'Power and identity in theory and practice', *Sociological Review*, 33(1): 22-46.

Koontz, H. and C. O'Donnell (1968) *Principles of Management: an Analysis of Managerial Functions*. 4th ed. New York: McGraw-Hill.

Layder, D. (1994) *Understanding Social Theory*. London: Sage.

Lockwood, D (1964) 'Social integration and system integration' in G. K, Zollscahn and W. Hirsch (eds) *Explorations in Social Change*. London: Routledge and Kegan Paul.

Marx, K. (1976) *Capital Vol. 1*. Harmondsworth: Penguin.

Mills, C. W. (1956) *White Collar: the American Middle Classes*, Oxford: Oxford University Press.

Mintzberg, H. (1980) *The Nature of Managerial Work*. New York: Prentice-Hall.

Moore, W. (1962) *The Conduct of the Corporation*. New York: Random House.

Mouzelis, N. (1995) *Sociological Theory: What Went Wrong? Diagnosis and Remedies*. London: Routledge and Kegan Paul.

Nichols, T. (1969) *Ownership Control and Ideology: an Enquiry into Certain Aspects of Modern Business Ideology*. London: Allen & Unwin.

Nichols, T. and H. Beynon (1977) *Living with Capitalism: Class relations and the Modern Factory*. London: Routledge and Kegan Paul.

Sennett, R. (2006) *The Culture of the New Capitalism*. London: Yale University Press.

Thompson, J. B. (1989) 'The theory of structuration', in D. Held and J. B. Thompson (eds) *Social Theory and Modern Societies: Anthony Giddens and his critics*, Cambridge: Cambridge University Press.

Thompson, P. and C. Smith (2000) 'Follow the redbrick road: Reflections on pathways in and out of the labour process debate', *International Studies in Management and Organization*, 30(4): 40-67.

Whittington, R. (1992) 'Putting Giddens into action: Social systems and managerial agency', *Journal of Management Studies*, 29(6): 693-712.

Whyte, W. H. (1960) *The Organization Man*. Harmondsworth: Penguin.

Willmott, H. (1987) 'Studying managerial work: A critique and a proposal', *Journal of Management Studies*, 24(3): 249-270.

Willmott, H. (1990) 'Subjectivity and the dialectics of praxis: Opening up the core of labour process theory' in D. Knights and H. Willmott (eds) *Labour Process Theory*. Basingstoke: MacMillan.

Willmott, H. (1997) 'Rethinking management and managerial work: Capitalism, control and subjectivity', *Human Relations*, 50(11): 1329-1359.

Wilson, D. C. (1982) 'Electricity and resistance: A case study of innovation and politics', *Organization Studies*, 3(2): 119-140.

Notes

[1] Willmott repeatedly refers to these methodological devices as 'stratagems', a word which carries overtones of trickery or deception, as compared to 'strategy' (e.g. Willmott, 1997: 1340-2).

[2] As Thompson (1989) points out, Giddens himself has recognised something of this, albeit as a difference in the levels of *abstraction* rather than embeddedness. Whilst the two certainly connect in that more deeply embedded structures are also more abstract in the sense that they are capable of articulation in many surface forms, the term abstraction, suggesting as it does, a difference only in the way these structures must be apprehended, fails to capture the idea that the more 'abstract' are also less susceptible to change. Layder (1994: 138-9) has made substantially the same point, noting that Giddens' conception of social structure as 'rules and resources' simply omits all those features of a social formation which are not articulated as vocabularies of motive.

Thompson also argues that Giddens has not so far explained how his theory of structuration might apply to the instantiation and reproduction of the more 'abstract' structures, a point not adequately dealt with in Giddens' (1989) reply to his critics. Whether something like the process described in the main text might do the trick is as yet an open question of course.

[3] Readers are entitled to a frank account of a writer's motives. Writers, though, are entitled to offer one only to those readers who are conscientious enough to truffle through the footnotes. It is here, therefore, that I confess that an irritation at Wilmott's treatment of my work is a supplementary motive for the production of this chapter.

[4] In its context, this summary form of words is Burawoy's description of the particular management interest in the game of 'making out' (the workers' practice of making the maximum possible bonus allowed by the incentive payment system). Whatever else managers may do, it is reasonable to suppose that their *particular* interest in a payment system is to do with its efficacy as a means of extracting surplus value. That Burawoy points this out tells us nothing about his view of other aspects of management work and Willmott is out of order in suggesting that it does. Even reading Burawoy as referring to

the generality of managerial work, his 'co-operation and surplus' need not refer to capital functions at all. Work in *any* social formation must yield a surplus and if management exists at all, it must be its primary task to see that it does so. Capitalism is not distinguished by the production of surplus value but by the fact that the surplus goes to capital.

5 On this there is a tale to tell, and it is one which says as much about the quality of the editing which has gone into the successive volumes from the Labour Process Conferences as it does about my own failings as a theorist. On being told by one of the editors of the 1991 volume that they wished to include my paper, I intimated that I wished to reconsider my remarks on unproductive labour in the light of comments made at the conference. The reply was as illuminating as it was succinct, 'Too late mate'. Since the work was published under my name, nevertheless, I make what defence I can in the main text.

6 So intent is Willmott on taking a swipe at Nichols and Beynon that he fails to notice that his backswing takes an inadvertent hack at his own theory. If, as he maintains, 'identity' is context-dependent, it is difficult to see how it differs from 'rôle' and also hard to see how it might have any explanatory value independent of the expectations which attach to a rôle.

7 Since Willmott sees fit to recall my 'unequivocally hostile critique' of Harris' work at the 1988 Labour Process Conference (Willmott, 1997: 1351, footnote) it is as well to set the record straight. Harris' work was presented as a replication and refutation of Nichols and Beynon (1977). It was based on an ethnographic study of some of the same plants studied by Nichols and Beynon and is addressed throughout to the interpretations made in that study. In fact Nichols and Beynon (1977) is by far the most frequently cited work of industrial sociology referred to in Harris' book, being mentioned on almost half of Harris' pages and always in unequivocally hostile terms. Since I was one of the research assistants employed on Nichols and Beynon's research, the 'critique' to which Willmott refers was actually a reply to Harris' own criticisms and should have been evaluated as such.

8 Blake Ashforth is an honest man. Having produced a widely-quoted paper on the subject of petty tyranny he subjected the syndrome to empirical investigation thirteen years later. Much less widely quoted, this second paper reported that the construct was actually quite rare, at least as he operationalised it (Ashforth, 2007).

9 Thompson and Smith (2000) have commented on this aspect of Willmott's writing, albeit from a slightly different point of view: 'All contributors are picked over to see whether they matched the appropriate analytical criteria or demonstrated the favourite sins of post-structuralism: determinism, essentialism and dualism.'

10 Willmott (1990: 372) has commented on the 'baggage' carried by the terminology of existentialism. If this is a complaint, it is a disingenuous one coming from an author who has used it with such consistency. Words are the medium of academic production and it is a basic competence that they should be handled with an adequate grasp of their connotations.

www.ingramcontent.com/pod-product-compliance
Lightning Source LLC
Chambersburg PA
CBHW051511030726
47592CB00006B/2205